Grassroots Global Governance

Grassroots Global Governance

Local Watershed Management Experiments and the Evolution of Sustainable Development

CRAIG M. KAUFFMAN

OXFORD
UNIVERSITY PRESS

OXFORD
UNIVERSITY PRESS

Oxford University Press is a department of the University of Oxford. It furthers
the University's objective of excellence in research, scholarship, and education
by publishing worldwide. Oxford is a registered trade mark of Oxford University
Press in the UK and certain other countries.

Published in the United States of America by Oxford University Press
198 Madison Avenue, New York, NY 10016, United States of America.

© Oxford University Press 2017

Library of Congress Cataloging-in-Publication Data
Names: Kauffman, Craig M., author.
Title: Grassroots global governance : local watershed management experiments
and the evolution of sustainable development / Craig M. Kauffman.
Description: New York, NY : Oxford University Press, 2016. |
Includes bibliographical references and index.
Identifiers: LCCN 2016020387 (print) | LCCN 2016032703 (ebook) |
ISBN 9780190625733 (hardcover : alk. paper) | ISBN 9780190625740 (Updf)
Subjects: LCSH: Watershed management—Political aspects—Ecuador. |
Integrated water development—Political aspects—Ecuador. |
Sustainable development—Political aspects—Ecuador. | Local government—Ecuador. |
Globalization—Political aspects—Ecuador. |
Watershed management—International cooperation. |
Integrated water development—International cooperation. |
Sustainable development—International cooperation. | Globalization— Political aspects.
Classification: LCC TC447 .K38 2016 (print) | LCC TC447 (ebook) |
DDC 333.7309866—dc23
LC record available at https://lccn.loc.gov/2016020387

1 3 5 7 9 8 6 4 2

Printed by Sheridan Books, Inc., United States of America

To my parents, Ralph and Laurel, who taught and inspired me.

To my wife, Keerti, who supported and believed in me.

To my daughter, Kaavya, who will inherit the Earth we leave behind.

CONTENTS

LIST OF FIGURES

LIST OF TABLES

ACKNOWLEDGMENTS

Climate change, driven by unsustainable development, is the biggest global problem we face. While governments fail to muster the political will to take meaningful action, ordinary people in the Global South are experimenting with new solutions. They do so because they are paying the price of unsustainable development degrading the ecosystems on which they depend. They cannot displace the negative consequences to another community. For nearly 10 years I have watched and learned from Ecuadorians working to improve the quality of life in the biotic and social communities of which they are a part. Their vision and dedication to overcoming seemingly insurmountable challenges are humbling and inspiring. I pray their efforts pay off.

The ideas in this book began to germinate in 2006 when I went to Ecuador to study local governance reforms. I am eternally grateful to all the Ecuadorian activists, scholars, professionals, bureaucrats, and community members who generously provided their time, wisdom, and knowledge during my many visits over the last 10 years. Too many people contributed to this effort to name them all individually. However, several people went above and beyond the standard call of duty. First and foremost I want to acknowledge Santiago Medina and Carlos Racines, who literally opened their homes to me and without whom this book would not have been possible. Others deserving special mention include Marta Echavarría, Andrea Garzón, Alberto Acosta, Rodrigo Chontasi, Francisco Musabalím, Miguel Tisalema, Paulo Bustamante, Jimmy Cuenca, Trotsky Riera, Esteban Zarria, Bolivar Freire, and Natalia Greene. These individuals generously shared information and used their social capital to open doors and bring me into their networks. I could not have conducted the research for this book without their help. I also thank Antonio and Susi Grijalva and the professors at the Academia de Español Quito for being my family in Ecuador.

My thinking about the issues discussed in this book evolved significantly over time due to the wise council and mentorship of several scholars who read multiple drafts of the entire manuscript and provided invaluable feedback. I am especially grateful to Cynthia McClintock, Susan Sell, Margaret Keck, Ken Conca, Katherine Hochstetler, Matt Hoffman, and Henry Hale for honing my thinking and inspiring new (I hope better) ideas. Many other scholars also provided detailed, constructive comments on elements of the book presented at conferences and meetings. While I cannot list them all, I particularly want to acknowledge Marty Finnemore, Ron Mitchell, Virginia Haufler, Gerry Berk, Dennis Galvan, Pam Martin, Michele Betsill, Kent Eaton, Jennifer Brinkerhoff, Burke Hendrix, Tyler Dickovick, Tulia Falleti, Stephanie McNulty, and several anonymous reviewers. I am indebted to these scholars, and many others, for their thoughtful comments, which undoubtedly improved the book.

The research for this book was made possible by the generous financial support of the Inter-American Foundation Grassroots Development Fellowship and the Rotary Foundation Ambassadorial Scholarship. These awards allowed me to study local governance reforms in Ecuador for 31 months between 2006 and 2011. Funding from the University of Oregon allowed another three-month trip in 2015. Institutional and research support was provided by the Facultad Latinoamericana de Ciencias Sociales-Sede Ecuador (FLACSO-Ecuador; Latin American School of Social Sciences-Ecuador Branch), where I was a visiting researcher during 2009 and 2010. I thank Simón Pachano and Carlos de la Torre for making this possible.

I also thank Sneha Pai for using her impressive graphic design skills to help me create the book's illustrations. To the degree the illustrations clarify the ideas presented in this book, the credit goes to Sneha, who converted my primitive drawings into elegant digital images. Keerti Hasija Kauffman also contributed her artistic skills. Any blame for conceptual problems with the illustrations is mine alone. I thank Rodrigo Chontasi of IEDECA and Sufiet Erlita of CIFOR for granting permission to reproduce images used in some illustrations.

Finally, I could not have completed this project without the love and support of my parents, Ralph and Laurel Kauffman, who for better or worse raised me to believe I could do anything. Thanks also go to my sister Janelle Moore and her family, who provided moral and financial support to begin the fieldwork. Most important, I thank my wife Keerti, who was literally at my side every step of the way and who carried me through the most difficult periods.

LIST OF ACRONYMS

AGRECO Fundación de Agroecología y Agroturismo (Foundation for Agroecology and Agrotourism)

AIET Asociación de Indígenas Evangélicos de Tungurahua (Association of Evangelical Indigenous Peoples of Tungurahua)

AME Asociación de Municipalidades Ecuatorianas (Association of Ecuadorian Municipalities)

CAMAREN Consorcio Capacitación en Manejo de Recursos Naturales Renovables (Consortium Training in Management of Renewable Natural Resources)

CEDERENA Corporación para el Desarrollo de los Recursos Naturales (Corporation for the Development of Natural Resources)

CESA Central Ecuatoriana de Servicios Agrícolas (Ecuadorian Center for Agricultural Services)

CNRH Consejo Nacional de Recursos Hídricos (National Council for Water Resources)

CODEAMA Fundación por la Conservación y el Desarrollo Sostenible de la Región Amazónica (Foundation for Conservation and Development in the Ecuadorian Amazon)

CONAM Consejo Nacional de Modernización del Estado (National Council for State Modernization)

CONCOPE Consorcio de Consejos Provinciales del Ecuador (Consortium of Provincial Councils of Ecuador)

CORICAM Conservación de los Recursos Naturales y Riego Campesino de la Cuenca Alta del Río Ambato (Conservation of Natural Resources and Rural Irrigation of the Upper Ambato River Watershed)

DFC	Desarrollo Forestal Comunitario (FAO's Community Forestry Development Program)
ECLAC	UN Economic Commission for Latin America and the Caribbean (Comisión Económica para América Latina de las Naciones Unidas)
EMAPA-I	Empresa Municipal de Agua Potable y Alcantarillado de Ibarra (Municipal Potable Water and Sewer Company of Ibarra)
ESPEA	Escuela Superior Politécnica Ecológica Amazónica (Ecological Polytechnic School of the Amazon)
FAO	UN Food and Agriculture Organization (Organización de las Naciones Unidas para la Alimentación y la Agricultura)
FEPP	Fondo Ecuatoriano Populorum Progressio (Ecuadorian Populorum Progressio Fund)
FONAG	Fondo para la Protección del Agua (Water Protection Fund)
FPLPT	Fondo de Páramos de Tungurahua y Lucha contra la Pobreza (Fund for Tungurahua's Páramos and Fight Against Poverty)
FUNDIAT	Fundación para el Desarrollo Integral de los Agricultores de Tungurahua (Foundation for the Holistic Development of Tungurahuan Farmers)
GTZ	Deutsche Gesellschaft fuer Technische Zusammenarbeit (German Organization for Technical Cooperation)
GWP	Global Water Partnership (Asociación Mundial para el Agua)
IDB	Inter-American Development Bank (Banco Interamericano de Desarrollo)
IEDECA	Instituto de Ecología y Desarrollo de las Comunidades Andinas (Institute of Ecology and Development of Andean Communities)
INEFAN	Instituto Ecuatoriano Forestal y de Areas Naturales y Vida Silvestre (Ecuadorian Institute for Forestry, Natural Areas and Wildlife)
IWM	Integrated Watershed Management (Gestión Integral de Cuencas Hidrográficas)
MACRENA	Corporación para el Manejo Comunitario de los Recursos Naturales (Corporation for the Community Management of Natural Resources)
MAE	Ministerio del Ambiente (Ministry of Environment)
MAGAP	Ministerio de Agricultura, Ganadería, Acuacultura y Pesca (Ministry of Agriculture, Livestock, Aquaculture and Fisheries)

MIT	Movimiento Indígena de Tungurahua (Indigenous Movement of Tungurahua)
MITA	Movimiento Indígena de Tungurahua-Atocha (Indigenous Movement of Tungurahua-Atocha)
NCI	Naturaleza y Cultura Internacional (Nature and Culture International)
PES	Payment for Ecosystem Services (Pago por Servicios Ecosistémicos)
PROCOSA	Programa Conservación de Suelos y Agroforestería en la Región Andina (Soil Conservation and Agroforestry in the Andean Region Program)
PRODERENA	Programa de Gestión Descentralizada de Recursos Naturales (Program for the Decentralized Management of Natural Resources)
PROFAFOR	Programa FACE de Forestación del Ecuador (FACE Forestry Program of Ecuador)
PROMACH	Proyecto Manejo de Cuencas Hidrográficas (GTZ's Watershed Management Project)
PROMUSTA	Proyecto Manejo del Uso Sostenible de Tierras Andinas (CARE's Project for the Sustainable Use of Andean Lands)
REDLACH	Red Latinoamericana de Cooperación Técnica en Manejo de Cuencas Hidrográficas (Latin American Technical Cooperation Network on Watershed Management)
SAMTAC	GWP's South American Technical Advisory Committee
SENAGUA	Secretaría Nacional del Agua (National Water Secretariat)
SENPLADES	Secretaría Nacional de Planificación y Desarrollo (National Secretariat for Planning and Development)
SFA	Servicio Forestal Amazónica (Amazon Forestry Service)
SNV	Netherlands Development Organization
UCPACE	Unidad Cantonal de Productores Agropecuarios de Celica (Cantonal Union of Agricultural Producers of Celica)
UDMIT	Unidad y Desarrollo de los Movimientos Indígenas de Tungurahua (Unity and Development of the Indigenous Movements of Tungurahua)
UNDP	United Nations Development Programme (Programa de las Naciones Unidas para el Desarrollo)

Grassroots Global Governance

The Nexus between Global
and Local Governance

In March 2012, Ecuador's national indigenous movement CONAIE led a two-week, 350-mile March for Water, Life, and Dignity from the southern province of Zamora-Chinchipe to the capital city, Quito. Indigenous marchers were joined by members of other social movements and by rural farmers who shared their concerns about access to water. The protesters' main demand was that the government approve a new water law that would respect and guarantee peoples' right to water in accordance with the Ecuadorian concept *buen vivir*, roughly translated as "good living." Buen vivir, or *sumak kawsay* in Kichwa, is a normative framework held by Ecuador's Andean indigenous groups regarding development and humans' relationship to nature. It stresses balance rather than growth and refers to living in harmony with nature, as opposed to either dominating nature or solely conserving it like a museum to watch, but not live within. To this end, the marchers asserted local communities' right to participate in managing water-related natural resources to ensure equitable access and sustainable use. They also demanded that large-scale mining and oil extraction be restricted, particularly in fragile watershed ecosystems.[1]

The protesters delivered their demands to Ecuador's government on March 22, 2012—World Water Day. Their choice to use this global symbol reflects the connection between local Ecuadorian efforts to improve water-related resource management and a global movement with the same goal. World Water Day was formally proposed in Agenda 21, the global plan for promoting sustainable development produced at the 1992 United Nations Conference on Environment and Development (UNCED) in Rio de Janeiro, Brazil. The idea was to raise popular awareness and support for a set of principles and best practices for managing the world's water-related resources. These principles and practices—known as

---

[1] "Pedidos de organizaciónes," *El Universo*, March 22, 2012, www.eluniverso.com/2012/03/22/1/1355/pedidos-organizaciones.html (accessed February 3, 2015).

Integrated Watershed Management (IWM)—were also included in Agenda 21 as a sustainable development strategy.[2] In 2000, a global network of states, intergovernmental organizations (IGOs), nongovernmental organizations (NGOs), experts, and others set the goal of implementing IWM plans and strategies in all countries by 2015 (Global Water Partnership 2000, 12). These "global governors" worked to achieve this goal by incorporating IWM promotion into their development projects in Ecuador and elsewhere.[3]

The connection between Ecuadorian demands for a new development approach rooted in buen vivir and global efforts to promote sustainable development through IWM reform is not merely symbolic. Events related to the 2012 Rio+20 Conference on Sustainable Development illustrate a more tangible and interesting connection. As Ecuadorian protesters negotiated their demands with the Ecuadorian state, the organization UN Water sponsored a Water Day celebration in conjunction with the Rio+20 conference. It presented its report on the status of IWM around the world. The report showed that of the 130 countries surveyed, 82% had changed their laws to incorporate IWM principles. Yet despite these laws, IWM programs were only implemented in some 40% of less-developed countries (UNEP 2012, viii, 17), and implementation was uneven within these countries.

These statistics show that national policy is no predictor of changes on the ground. This finding is not unique to IWM. Sociological institutionalists have long observed that when states create institutions reflecting global norms, these are often hollow institutions that produce little actual change in behaviors on the ground (Finnemore 1996; Meyer et al. 1997). It has become a cliché to note that laws often remain unimplemented in lower-income countries. The challenges to implementing global principles and policies in lower-income countries are many, and range from weak state institutions, corruption, and political instability to poverty and inequality.

The disappointing results of transnational IWM promotion were illustrative of the general failure to reach the sustainable development goals first outlined in Agenda 21. States meeting at the Rio+20 conference agreed to launch a process to create a new set of sustainable development goals. At the conference, a block of 33 Latin American and Caribbean countries, led by Ecuador's government,

[2] Chapter 18 of Agenda 21 addresses the "Application of Integrated Approaches to the Development, Management, and Use of Water Resources." As I discuss in chapter 3, the term Integrated Water Resources Management (IWRM) is more commonly used than IWM. Since IWM refers to the application of IWRM at the watershed level (Dourojeanni 2001), and most descriptions of IWRM include management at the watershed level, I use the term IWM throughout the book.

[3] Following Avant et al. (2010, 2), I define global governors as actors that "exercise power across borders for purposes of affecting policy."

advocated a new approach to sustainable development rooted in the concept buen vivir. They, along with a newly formed Global Alliance for the Rights of Nature, pressed UN members to adopt a Universal Declaration of the Rights of Nature as an instrument for achieving buen vivir (CELEC 2012). While a universal declaration was not adopted, buen vivir advocates did incorporate the language of buen vivir into the conference's final document.[4] Such language now permeates the UN system. Calls for "living in harmony with nature" and references to the rights of nature appear in everything from annual reports of the Secretary General and the UN General Assembly's annual Dialogues on Harmony with Nature, to convention documents on climate change and biodiversity. The new discourse shows how a transnational network advocating an alternative approach to sustainable development rooted in buen vivir and the rights of nature is altering the global debate over how to conceptualize and implement sustainable development.

The above anecdotes illustrate two puzzles regarding global governance, by which I mean "collective efforts to identify, understand, or address worldwide problems" that go beyond individual states (Weiss and Wilkinson 2014, 2). First, when states fail to address a global problem, either through multilateral agreements or national laws, why and how do you nonetheless get things done on the ground? Second, how do ideas regarding the best way to tackle global problems evolve? What drives the evolution of global ideas like sustainable development and the emergence of new global ideas like buen vivir and rights of nature?

This book shows that these two questions are linked. The experience of getting things done locally has global reverberations, driving the evolution of global ideas. When states fail to solve global problems through multilateral treaties, transnational networks form to address these problems through the application of "best practices," like IWM, at the local level around the world. These efforts are full of political struggle. Often, local actors neither accept nor reject these best practices as initially presented by outsiders. Rather, they negotiate with outsiders on whether and how to adapt them to fit local realities. Sometimes, this contestation results in experimentation, learning, and the creation of innovative local governance arrangements—unique institutional applications of this global idea. Local experiments that endure come to be perceived as successful and can have global reverberations. International actors learn from their interactions with locals and consequently change their discourse and strategies for tackling global problems. Those involved work to scale up and diffuse innovative local governance models nationally and globally. Sometimes these models carry local

---

[4] See in particular Article 39 (United Nations 2012). More details on buen vivir and its adoption in international forums are given in chapter 8 of this book.

norms and practices to the international level and provide viable alternatives that challenge traditional global approaches.

To show how this works, the book ventures inside rural, Ecuadorian communities similar to those found throughout the developing world. It explores the interactions among municipal officials, farmers, indigenous and other community organizations, businesses, and the myriad national and international organizations seeking to create new, local watershed management systems in accordance with IWM principles and practices. I compare attempts to implement IWM reforms in five cantons (Zamora, El Chaco, Celica, Pastaza, and Ibarra) and one province (Tungurahua).[5] The cases show how reform attempts both succeeded and failed under diverse political, economic, social, demographic, and ecological conditions described in chapter 3.

One purpose of the case comparisons is to explain why some attempts to institutionalize global ideas—in this case IWM—at the local level succeeded while others failed. The answer lies in the ability of transnational governance networks to expand by constructing and mobilizing networks of grassroots actors influential in local policy arenas. Their ability to do so depends on the combination of strategies used to: (1) *motivate* influential local organizations to join the governance network and contribute their resources, time, and energy to the cause; and (2) enhance the network's *capacity* to combine the resources accessible to each network member and convert these into action. For reasons discussed in chapter 2, I call this *network activation*.

Policy advocates employ various network activation strategies to create the requisite motivation and capacity. These include: (1) strategic framing; (2) providing knowledge, technology, and resources; (3) building local "knowledge communities" of like-minded experts and activists; (4) creating "linking institutions" that connect various stakeholders, concentrate the distinct resources available to each through their network ties, and provide a focal point for converting these into action; and (5) creating new governing institutions to steer society toward new policy goals. Chapter 2 explains why the combination of network activation strategies employed by transnational governance networks

---

[5] A canton is a political territory analogous to a U.S. county. The corresponding governing unit is a municipality. The watersheds involved in each case are as follows: In Tungurahua, the upper Ambato River sub-watershed; in Celica, the Quilluzara and Matalanga micro-watersheds; in El Chaco, the San Marcos, Santa Rosa, Linares, Sardinas, and Rumipamba micro-watersheds; in Zamora, the Limón micro-watershed; in Pastaza, the Pambay and Puyo River watersheds; and in Ibarra, the Tahuando River watershed. Although watersheds frequently cross political boundaries, the watersheds analyzed here lie predominantly within one canton, and reform attempts involved one local government and the communities living within that watershed. In Tungurahua, the one case involving the provincial rather than municipal government, the targeted watershed and reform activity fell largely within a single canton, Ambato, making the case comparable.

determines whether efforts to implement global ideas locally succeed or fail, as well as the stage in the process where failed efforts break down.

The Ecuadorian cases show that global governance is not just about foreign experts from the World Bank or international NGOs parachuting in to tell locals what to do. While outside policy advocates used the above strategies to catalyze local IWM reform processes, local actors had the real power when it came to implementing IWM reform. They alone had the power to determine whether reform processes endured or broke down. They also determined the institutional outcomes, using their power to adapt global ideas by infusing them with local norms and practices. The cases therefore call for an expanded understanding of how global governance is constructed and who is involved. This book shows that, for many important global problems, global governance happens because local people make it happen.

The book's second purpose is to trace the processes by which local experiments with watershed management influenced the global discourse regarding sustainable development. Chapters 7 and 8 show, for example, how grassroots farmers and indigenous activists experimented with an innovative IWM governance arrangement that combined global IWM principles with local norms and practices associated with buen vivir. Organizations involved in this local experiment used the network activation strategies described earlier to scale up the model nationally, resulting in Ecuador's National Plan for Buen Vivir. Similar network activation strategies were used to catalyze an international movement to promote buen vivir and the rights of nature globally. This and similar cases show how local experimentation with global ideas can alter global discourse and organizing around global problems, as well as the policies and practices promoted by international actors.

The book's case studies reveal an important lesson regarding multilevel governance, a topic of current interest among global and environmental governance scholars (Andonova and Mitchell 2010; Bulkeley and Betsill 2013; Corfee-Morlot et al. 2009; Hooghe and Marks 2001; Williams 2013). Multilevel governance does not simply mean that actors at all levels—local, national, and international—are involved in managing global environmental problems. It also means there are complex interactions among these actors and that influence is multidirectional in these exchanges. Research on norm diffusion reveals a complex network of pathways that combines top-down and bottom-up processes (Bob 2005; Brysk 1996; Risse et al. 1999; Sikkink 2011; Tarrow 2005). At the intersection of these processes lie local political struggles and learning processes that are rarely analyzed, but which fuel a dynamic process of normative and institutional development at both the local and global levels. This book examines the intersection of top-down and bottom-up processes to show how global and local governance arrangements are co-constituted at the grassroots level.

A main lesson is that one cannot fully understand how global governance works by looking only at UN conferences and other interactions that occur in the international arena. One must also examine the grassroots level as a distinct, but no less important, terrain where global governance is constructed. It is at the grassroots level that concepts like sustainable development, climate smart agriculture, participatory budgeting, and community policing—global ideas meant to tackle global problems—get worked out in practice. This is particularly true for low-income countries. Organizations commonly thought of as "global governors"—IGOs, bilateral development agencies, and international NGOs—focus their programming and resources on grassroots communities in low-income countries since this is where they perceive the need to be greatest. These countries possess high poverty rates, heightened vulnerability to disease, and most of the world's biological diversity (Steinberg 2001, 4). Consequently, global strategies for tackling problems like poverty, tuberculosis, and deforestation get "road tested" in local communities in such countries. The test results reverberate back to the global level and influence the evolution of global ideas.

I argue that the grassroots level should not be viewed merely as the object of global governance, but rather a terrain (hidden in most analysis) where global governance is constructed. Viewing global governance from this perspective reveals the importance of various grassroots actors—municipal bureaucrats, smallholder farmers, indigenous activists, rural community organizers, and others—who are normally left out of global governance analysis. They contest, translate, and adapt global ideas to fit local realities; they mobilize pressure to overcome local apathy and opposition; they experiment with new local governance arrangements; and they engage international actors in negotiation and learning processes. By guiding the way global ideas are applied at the local level and consequently evolve, and by reshaping the thinking and strategies of international actors, these grassroots actors participate in the global governance process.

A second lesson of the book is that a variety of grassroots actors often considered marginalized and powerless are actually important agents of global governance. These are not highly educated, urban globetrotters like Tarrow's (2005) "rooted cosmopolitans" or Steinberg's (2001) "bilateral activists." They are normal people living in rural communities and small towns—smallholder farmers, small business owners, teachers, neighborhood association leaders, community organizers, municipal bureaucrats, and others. Most have never left their country; many rarely leave their province. Their influence comes not from some cosmopolitan worldview, but from their ability to leverage their community ties to pressure fellow community members. By designing new ways of addressing global problems locally and steering fellow community members toward them, these grassroots actors help forge new global frameworks. This makes them *grassroots global governors.*

Watershed Management and Global Governance Problems

The two research questions motivating this book—(1) absent formal global agreements, why and how do things nonetheless get done locally; and (2) how do ideas regarding the best way to tackle global problems evolve?—are not only relevant to the issue of watershed management. These questions are central to understanding how global governance works for many of the world's greatest problems—from poverty, hunger, and disease to deforestation and climate change. Often described as "local-cumulative problems" (e.g., Conca 2006; O'Neill 2009), they are construed as global problems not because they transcend national borders, but because they exist everywhere, and their cumulative effect causes global concern.

While their ubiquitousness makes local-cumulative problems global, their effects are felt most directly at the local level. Moreover, their proximate causes are individual behaviors at the local level. For example, deforestation worldwide is primarily driven by local actors who cut down trees to make fuel, paper, and wood products; expand cattle ranching; and plant crops like soy and palm oil (Bradford 2015). While globalization influences these behaviors, so too do local political, institutional, socioeconomic, and demographic conditions. Therefore, local-cumulative problems ultimately must be addressed in the different local contexts in which they occur. The problem of watershed degradation illustrates why this is the case.

Watershed Management

Like a bathtub collecting and then directing the water that falls within its sides, a watershed includes the physical area involved in capturing precipitation, filtering and storing water, and determining the amount of water released into stream and river systems at lower levels. Watersheds may be large or small, and smaller watersheds (sub- or micro-watersheds) join to become larger watersheds. Figure 1.1 illustrates the inverse pyramid shape of a typical Andean watershed and shows how watersheds connect catchment areas in upper elevations with different kinds of water users below. Since human survival and economic development depend on water and other natural resources located in watersheds, they are not simply geographic territories. Watersheds have economic and social aspects that are intertwined with the environment. For thousands

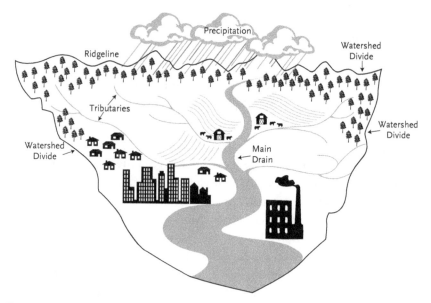

Figure 1.1 Typical Andean Micro-Watershed.

of years, people have manipulated watershed resources—including water, soil, vegetation, and wildlife—to spur political and socioeconomic development. Watershed management is about this strategic use of watershed resources.

Watershed management strategies are shaped by local political, socioeconomic, and cultural conditions. People and organizations representing a wide array of interests live and work in watersheds. Farmers use the land to raise crops and livestock and may rely on water for irrigation. Businesses may extract a watershed's natural resources, such as timber or minerals, or simply help tourists enjoy the natural beauty. Hydroelectric companies rely on water flow to produce electricity. In fact, all businesses and households consume water in their daily activities. They also rely on the watershed ecosystem to absorb their waste, whether it is dumped in rivers or landfills. NGOs may have other interests, such as protecting the watershed's biodiversity and integrity as a functioning ecosystem. For some communities, watersheds may have spiritual or cultural significance. Local governments are often responsible for managing the natural resources in their jurisdiction and must navigate these competing interests. Throughout the book, I refer to these interest groups collectively as "local stakeholders."

Watersheds connect people through their ability to affect each other by impacting the watershed ecosystem on which they all depend. For example, watersheds link higher catchment areas, where water collects, with lower areas where people use water for various purposes. People in upper catchment areas often engage in economic activities such as agriculture, logging, and mining that pollute the soil and water and damage the vegetation maintaining the natural water cycle. This can decrease the quantity and quality of water available to communities downstream.

Without some system for reconciling the competing interests of people who depend on watershed resources, conflicts inevitably arise. All too often, these conflicts lead stakeholders to consume watershed resources (e.g., forests, soil, water, biodiversity, etc.) at an unsustainable rate, threatening the integrity of watershed ecosystems and making everyone worse off. While people living in watersheds feel the effects of watershed degradation most directly, it is construed as a global problem because it threatens an estimated two billion people worldwide (Millennium Ecosystem Assessment 2005b, 3). Damage to watershed ecosystems limits peoples' access to food and water and exacerbates problems of poverty, disease, and climate change. During the 1990s and 2000s, transnational networks of IGOs, state development agencies, NGOs and experts promoted local IWM programs around the world as the best strategy for tackling this problem.

Integrated Watershed Management Principles, Institutions, and Practices

IWM is the process of coordinating the conservation, management, and development of water, land, and related natural resources across sectors (e.g., agriculture, hydropower, water supply, mining, tourism, as well as conservation of forests, soil, and biodiversity) within a given watershed in order to maximize the resultant economic and social benefits in an equitable manner while ensuring the sustainability of related ecosystems.[6] IWM is an "integrated" approach in that it recognizes the interaction between water and other components of watershed ecosystems, including soil, vegetation, biodiversity, and humans. It therefore requires a holistic approach that manages these resources in an integrated fashion. This marks one of the main differences with how watershed resources are traditionally managed in most countries.

Within this ecosystem approach, IWM frames water in terms of "ecosystem services," or benefits that people receive from watershed ecosystems (Kareiva and Wiens 2005; Millennium Ecosystem Assessment 2005a). Watershed ecosystem services include various natural processes that affect the quantity and quality of water, as well as recreational and cultural benefits.[7] In Ecuador, for

---

[6] This definition is adapted from definitions provided by Jones et al. (2003) and the Technical Advisory Committee of the Global Water Partnership (Rahaman and Varis 2005).

[7] Examples of watershed-related ecosystem services include "flood prevention, control and mitigation; regulating runoff and water supply; improving the quality of surface waters and groundwaters; withholding sediments, reducing erosion, stabilizing river banks and shorelines and lowering the potential of landslides; improving water infiltration and supporting water storage in the soil;

example, forests and *páramos* (high Andean grasslands) serve as collectors and regulators of water flow and prevent soil erosion that damages water quality (Célleri 2009). These ecosystem services link the conservation and sustainable use of forests and *páramos* upstream with the quantity and quality of water available to communities downstream. Therefore, IWM often frames watershed management activities in terms of protecting and restoring these ecosystem services (Cordero 2008; Garzón 2009; Ravnborg et al. 2007).

The need for watershed stakeholders to coordinate management activities makes IWM not just a technical challenge but also a sociopolitical challenge. To equitably balance competing interests and facilitate collaboration, IWM calls for all stakeholders to be included in decision making through a participatory process (Gleick 1998; Jaspers 2003). Moreover, decision making should be decentralized to the "lowest appropriate level" (Turton et al. 2007b, xxii, 45) to allow meaningful participation by local stakeholders and a flexible approach tailored to the unique needs of each watershed ecosystem.

Implementing IWM locally involves creating new institutions, policies, and practices to achieve these goals. In this book I focus on the creation of two institutions. The first is a local, participatory, decision-making structure in which multiple stakeholders jointly identify needs, develop integrated watershed management plans, and oversee management activities. The second institution is a financing mechanism that raises local revenue to provide stable funding for watershed management activities. Due to concerns about the sustainability of IWM programs, advocates increasingly call for stable, local financing mechanisms that can sustain watershed management activities "beyond the exodus of [national] or foreign financing, technical assistance, and the repayment of loans" (Heathcote 2009, 389). The principle underlying these financing mechanisms is that those who benefit from ecosystem services pay to fund activities that ensure these services continue. It is worth stressing that this does not necessarily involve privatization. Nor does it mean that price is the only, or even best, way to value watershed services. IWM allows flexibility in how to design economic instruments, but argues that some instrument is needed to provide "incentives to change behavior [and raise] revenue to help finance necessary investments" (International Conference on Water and Environment 1992, xi).

Along with these institutions, new administrative systems must be created to support changes in watershed management. These include systems for gathering information, creating and implementing plans, monitoring the restoration of watershed resources, monitoring stakeholder compliance, and sanctioning

and facilitating groundwater recharge. Water-related ecosystem services also include cultural services, such as recreational, aesthetic and spiritual benefits of forests and wetlands" (United Nations Economic Commission for Europe 2007, 2).

violators. These systems are typically supported by local government ordinances; voluntary, written community agreements; and/or legal contracts among stakeholders, all of which must be negotiated.

Arguably the biggest changes that come with IWM reform, however, are the changes to land-use practices and economic activities. Projects to conserve and restore water catchment areas often require smallholder farmers to remove crops and animals from significant portions of their land and switch to more ecologically friendly economic activities. In some cases, whole households and farms relocate to less fragile areas. Restrictions are placed on logging, the burning of vegetation, and various forms of pollution. Areas along the banks of rivers and streams are fenced off to prevent pollution from animals, households, and industry, as well as to allow vegetation to regenerate in order to reduce sediment runoff. Education campaigns are launched to encourage and teach people how to use water more efficiently and reduce pollution. Ideally, this is combined with projects to improve the efficiency of water delivery systems. All this costs money. Where local financing mechanisms are created, water users and other beneficiaries of watershed ecosystem services pay more to finance all these activities.

Global Governance of Local-Cumulative Problems

Efforts to make these changes globally must contend with the political, socioeconomic, and cultural conditions shaping behaviors in each watershed. This is why global efforts to solve local-cumulative problems like watershed degradation are so challenging; ultimately, they must be addressed in the local contexts in which they occur. This makes them difficult to address through formal treaty arrangements—the main mechanism of global governance (Conca 2006).

The failure of states to negotiate formal agreements capable of addressing many of the world's most pressing local-cumulative problems is leading scholars and policymakers alike to search for alternatives (e.g., Biermann et al. 2010; Hoffmann 2011; Okereke et al. 2009). Unwilling to wait further, many NGOs and governmental organizations (international, national, and subnational) are working across borders to experiment with new, collective efforts to address such problems in the local contexts where they originate. In these circumstances, global governance often involves efforts by transnational networks of IGOs, state agencies, NGOs, and experts to change local governance arrangements around the world to conform with principles and "best practices" developed at the global level. Hereafter, I refer to these networks as *transnational governance networks*, and I call these collections of principles and practices *global ideas*. IWM is one such global idea, but there are many more. Transnational governance networks promote various global ideas to address a host of global problems, including poverty (sustainable development), poor governance (participatory budgeting), climate change (climate smart agriculture), and inse-curity (community policing).

We know relatively little about how these new structures for organizing and exercising global authority operate. As Weiss and Wilkinson (2014, 207) ob-serve, we do not fully understand how national and local systems intersect with these structures of global authority and push back against them; how power is exercised; how interests are articulated and pursued; what ideas and discourses give substance to power and interests and perpetuate the system; and what drives change in the system. The theoretical framework presented in chapter 2, and which is applied to the case of global watershed governance in subsequent chapters, begins to fill this gap. It illuminates the relationship between global, national, and local governance by explaining how, why, and when global princi-ples and policies are implemented at the local level—or not—and how the in-teraction between local and outside actors determines policy responses to global challenges, not only locally, but also globally.

Grassroots Global Governance

The book's analytical framework is a process model that explains how global and local governance arrangements are co-constituted through a dynamic process of interaction among foreign, national, and local actors at the grassroots level. I call this process *grassroots global governance*. The model, detailed in chapter 2, conceptualizes grassroots global governance as occurring in three phases. In phase 1, transnational governance networks *diffuse* global ideas to the local level and form coalitions to institutionalize related policies and practices in par-ticular localities. In phase 2, members of these local coalitions *experiment* with unique institutional arrangements that combine elements of the original global idea with new features influenced by local norms, institutions, and practices. Contestation, negotiation, experimentation, and learning among local and out-side actors produce innovative local governance arrangements that adapt global ideas to fit local contexts. In this way, global ideas begin to evolve at the local level. In phase 3, these local experiences prompt international actors to change their discourse and strategies for tackling global problems. Through evolution-ary learning and the scaling up of local experiments, new global ideas emerge and existing ones *evolve* internationally.

Grassroots global governance theory explains why this process continues to advance through these phases in some cases while in others the process breaks down at various points, in the sense that transnational governance networks either fail to form local coalitions or disband before new local governance sys-tems are put into practice. The theory argues that whether the process endures or breaks down depends on the ability of transnational governance networks to incorporate actors that are influential in various policy arenas relevant to each stage of the process. As mentioned above, their ability to do so depends on the combination of network activation strategies they employ. Chapter 2 details these strategies and describes why various combinations explain not only whether the process endures (success) or breaks down (failure), but also the point where failed cases break down.

This book focuses especially on the under-studied importance of contestation over global ideas at the local level, and calls attention to two important features that become visible at this level: pressure from "beside" and local experimentation. Frequently, policy changes coming from the global level face widespread apathy and resistance at the local level. This was the case for IWM advocates in Ecuador. Local farmers, loggers, miners, and businesses resisted changing land-use practices to conserve and restore vegetation in key areas, like water catchment areas and riverbanks. Accustomed to water subsidies, households and businesses opposed paying more to finance the protection of watershed ecosystem services. Initial proposals for local financing mechanisms invariably involved assigning an economic value for ecosystem services and creating markets to "sell" them. This clashed with indigenous norms against commodifying nature. For these and other reasons, local politicians often viewed IWM as politically risky.

Local Pressure from Beside

The global governance literature typically assumes that foreign IWM advocates—representatives of IGOs, bilateral development agencies, and international NGOs—will be the main ones exerting the pressure needed to overcome this apathy and resistance. Wealthy international organizations make access to resources conditional on adopting certain policies. On issues like human rights or democracy promotion, powerful states have even threatened economic sanctions and military action. The transnational advocacy networks literature refers to this international pressure by foreign actors as coming from "above" (Brysk 2009; 1996; Franklin 2009; Risse et al. 1999; Sikkink 2011).

My research finds, however, that it was local stakeholders themselves who provided the requisite pressure. Local IWM advocates had far more power than their foreign counterparts to influence local behaviors; they alone could exploit the vulnerabilities of resistant stakeholders. One reason was the interdependence of local actors when it came to the health of watershed ecosystems. For better or worse, the actions of one stakeholder group affected all other groups in the watershed (a common scenario with local-cumulative problems). This interdependence empowered stakeholders lacking more traditional forms of power. Poor, indigenous, smallholder farmers effectively pressured local government officials, wealthy ranchers, urban businesses, and others by altering land-use practices in ways that affected the flow of water downstream. Of course, local officials still had political power and the wealthy had economic power.

The point is that when all forms of power were recognized (in part through the actions of IWM advocates), members of each group effectively pressured members of other groups, and all groups were vulnerable to pressure from at least one other group. Overcoming resistance and apathy therefore involved creating a complex system of mutual, multidirectional, self-reinforcing pressure involving members of all major stakeholder groups. Rather than pressure from "above," successful policy reform was associated with horizontal pressures better characterized as coming from "beside"—that is, from other local stakeholders. For this reason, successful IWM coalitions were those able to recruit representatives of all major stakeholder groups. Some coalitions, by contrast, focused on mobilizing support among one or two groups seen as particularly important, such as local government officials or landowners in water catchment areas. Those cases fared much worse; IWM reforms were never implemented.

The need to exert pressure from beside meant that, as transnational governance networks switched from diffusing global ideas (phase 1) to implementing them locally (phase 2), local IWM advocates increasingly replaced their foreign counterparts as coalition leaders—the organizations at the center of the governance network. This matters because when grassroots IWM advocates took the lead, they rarely followed the standard, international script.

Local Experimentation and Innovation

Program documents show that the IWM reforms originally proposed in each Ecuadorian case were virtually identical. They used the same language and advocated extremely similar institutional reforms, policies, and practices. Yet, Ecuador's local watershed governance arrangements resemble neither the standard international template nor other systems created under similar political, socioeconomic, demographic, and ecological conditions. This is because each was forged through negotiation among foreign advocates and local stakeholders, including locals who both advocated and resisted reform.

The experience in Ecuador's Tungurahua province is illustrative. As in Ecuador's other cases, international advocates initially proposed creating a local financing mechanism based on a "payment for ecosystem services" program. Tungurahua's indigenous movements fiercely rejected the plan. They argued that the market transaction and payments to individual landowners constituted the commodification and privatization of nature, both of which violated indigenous principles. Despite their opposition to specific policy proposals, some indigenous leaders accepted basic IWM principles, including the need to locally finance a sustainable watershed management system. They negotiated with outside advocates and other local stakeholders to design an innovative financing mechanism based on voluntary contributions to a trust fund directed collectively by local stakeholders. Instead of individual payments, this money was used to finance projects at the watershed and/or community level. These two institutional features—voluntary contributions and no individual payments—were crucial for overcoming local concerns about privatization and the commodification of nature. But they were quite different from the global conception of what IWM should look like.

Ecuador's local watershed management reforms are curious because they contradict two conventional stories regarding the relationship between the local and international levels. The traditional understanding in international relations is the "cascade" model, in which policies reflected in international agreements flow down to states, which either implement them through national policies or ignore them. The effects of this decision then flow down to the subnational level (Bulkeley and Betsill 2003, 15–17). Local governments are assumed to act under the direction of national governments. The second story is rooted in the research on common pool resources pioneered by Elinor Ostrom and her colleagues.[8] Here, the story is about local actors generating self-governing institutions for managing natural resources on their own. Whether or not local actors have the incentive to do so is determined primarily by local environmental, demographic, and social conditions. National actors and conditions are important mainly in terms of whether they restrict the autonomy of local actors to develop and follow their own rules. International actors, and the international level in general, are typically absent from this story.

If either of these classic stories were true—that international actors and forces either dictate policies to the local level, or are largely irrelevant to the local level—then the outcomes of local IWM reform attempts should be similar, at least among cases with similar conditions. But this is not the case. Some reform attempts produced new institutions and practices; some did not. Moreover, reform processes produced unexpected outcomes that cannot be predicted from either international proposals or local conditions alone. Rather, the Ecuadorian cases show that local watershed governance systems resulted from the dynamic interaction among international, national, and local actors at the grassroots level. This interaction fueled a creative process of experimentation producing unique institutional adaptations of global IWM principles.

---

[8] For summaries of this vast literature, see Ostrom (1990; 2002) and Agrawal (2002).

From Grassroots to Global

Just as transnational actors activate local networks to change local governance arrangements, coalitions formed at the grassroots level can similarly activate networks of organizations operating at national and global levels to scale up local adaptations of global ideas and convert these into action globally. As grassroots governance networks expand internationally, local norms and practices diffuse to the global level, where network members advocate them as viable alternatives to preexisting strategies for tackling global problems.

The Tungurahua case is again illustrative. Tungurahua's new governance arrangement for watershed management reflected both global IWM principles and local indigenous norms and practices associated with the indigenous concept sumak kawsay, or buen vivir (discussed earlier). Tungurahua's experimentation with IWM reform produced an innovative local governance system that provided one of the first concrete examples of what buen vivir might look like when operationalized through local government and society. This "proof of concept" resonated with other Ecuadorian communities and organizations, particularly Ecuador's national indigenous movements, who had long advocated an alternative to neoliberal notions of sustainable development. They mobilized to make buen vivir the cornerstone of Ecuador's new constitution and national development plan. National government planners modeled Ecuador's National Plan for Buen Vivir in large part on the Tungurahuan system. This plan has become part of a greater international campaign for buen vivir and alternative approaches to sustainable development.

Internationally, Ecuador's experience is altering the global debate over how to conceptualize sustainable development by providing a concrete example of an alternative to the dominant approach pursued through the Rio+20 UN Conference on Sustainable Development. It is also stimulating new international governance structures for promoting this new approach. In 2010, environmental, development, and indigenous organizations from around the world met in Ecuador to found the Global Alliance for the Rights of Nature. Ecuador's constitution presents buen vivir as a set of rights for both humans and nature. Seeking to build on the momentum provided by Ecuador's constitutional rights of nature, the network mobilized at the June 2012 Rio+20 Summit to advocate the global application of buen vivir. Efforts led by the Ecuadorian and Bolivian governments also led the UN General Assembly to establish annual dialogues dedicated to "living in harmony with nature" (as buen vivir is now translated in international forums). Among the resolutions passed was one requiring the UN Secretary General to issue annual reports on how to achieve a sustainable development rooted in "living in harmony with nature." In these and similar discussions, Ecuador's National Plan for Buen Vivir is held up as a roadmap.

Studying Grassroots Global Governance

To analyze the grassroots global governance process I compared six efforts by transnational networks to implement local IWM programs in Ecuador beginning in the late 1990s. By 2009, IWM reforms had been attempted in 26 localities. I selected six cases that varied greatly in terms of ecosystem, demographic, social, economic, and political conditions commonly thought to shape natural resource management. Much of the literature focuses on identifying propitious conditions that make collaboration among watershed stakeholders more likely. Scholars have identified dozens of social, institutional, and environmental conditions that shape actors' incentives to collaborate.[9] The problem, as Abers (2007) points out, is that in many watersheds, particularly in the developing world, these propitious conditions rarely exist and must be constructed. This highlights the need to explore the role of agency, which I do by analyzing the strategies used by networks of IWM advocates.

To better analyze strategy in relation to local conditions, I included cases that were both "typical" and "deviant" (Seawright and Gerring 2008) from the perspective of common explanations of watershed management reform. I compiled a dataset of indicators of these common explanations for Ecuador's 221 municipalities and used this to calculate the predicted probabilities that each IWM reform attempt would succeed.[10] I then used the predicted probabilities to select cases that spanned four categories: typical-success, typical-failure, deviant-success, and deviant-failure. Two cases, Tungurahua and Celica, were predicted to successfully reform and did. Zamora's efforts were predicted not to succeed, and they were less successful. Such "typical" cases are useful for identifying the micro-causal processes leading to successful reform (George and Bennett 2005). By contrast, two cases, Pastaza and Ibarra, were strongly predicted to reform, but their attempts were unsuccessful. The sixth case, El Chaco, was predicted not to succeed, but it did. These "deviant" cases are useful for uncovering new explanations and causal mechanisms (Seawright and Gerring 2008).

Comparing these four case types permitted several forms of analysis. The typical cases allowed me to analyze the importance of transnational networks' strategies vis-à-vis common explanations rooted in structural conditions. The

---

[9] For summaries, see Agrawal (2002); Dinar et al. (2005); Leach and Pelkey (2001); Ostrom (1990); Sabatier et al. (2005); Wade (1988). Propitious conditions include institutional arrangements (e.g., clear rules and ability to sanction violators); characteristics of local social groups (e.g., group size, mobility, interdependence among group members); characteristics of the natural resource system (e.g., size, definition of boundaries); and external structural conditions (e.g., state of technology; relationships with the state).

[10] See Kauffman and Terry (2016) for details of the dataset.

deviant cases allowed me to test whether these strategies facilitated reform even where propitious conditions did not exist (deviant-success), and whether their absence explained failure to reform even where propitious conditions did exist (deviant-failure). Together, these case comparisons constituted a harder test to provide more confidence in the generalizability of grassroots global governance theory.

I used three main methods to document and analyze grassroots global governance in these cases. These include: (1) frame analysis to compare the framing strategies used and their ability to motivate action; (2) social network analysis to compare networks' expansion and their capacity to mobilize necessary resources; and (3) process tracing to analyze the evolution of strategies over time and link these to outcomes. Much of the information for this analysis was collected during nearly three years of fieldwork in Ecuador, conducted between 2006 and 2015. I spent an average of four months in each of the six cantons and a year in Quito, interviewing key stakeholders; observing meetings, watershed conditions, and watershed management activities; and collecting primary documents. I invite readers to consult the Methodological Appendix for more information on the data collected and its use in the three methodological techniques.

Outline of the Book

The book is organized as follows. Chapter 2 presents the process model of grassroots global governance, discusses the dynamics of each phase, and identifies key points where the process breaks down. It then details grassroots global governance theory, describing key network activation strategies and explaining how various combinations of these strategies determine whether the process endures or breaks down, and where failed cases break down.

The remaining chapters examine grassroots global governance through the lens of Ecuador's IWM reform attempts. Chapter 3 sets the stage by contrasting IWM with preexisting watershed management practices in Ecuador and describing the degree to which IWM reforms were implemented in the six cases. One purpose is to introduce the different local contexts where IWM reforms were pursued and local actors involved. In doing so, the chapter shows how success and failure does not correlate with local political, socioeconomic, cultural, demographic, or ecological conditions. The chapter's second purpose is to clarify what successful IWM reform looks like and to describe the various outcomes in the six cases.

Chapters 4 and 5 analyze phase 1 of grassroots global governance by examining the diffusion of IWM to particular Ecuadorian localities through the expansion of transnational IWM networks. Chapter 4 shows how Ecuador's national context acted as a filter, empowering some transnational networks and disempowering others, thereby influencing how IWM was defined and operationalized domestically. The chapter also analyzes the network activation strategies IWM advocates used to navigate Ecuador's national context and shift contestation to local arenas. Chapter 5 examines national network activation from the grassroots perspective and shows how the level of network activation experienced in a locality during phase 1 determines the prospects for success during phase 2. To illustrate this, the chapter traces the transition from phase 1 to phase 2 in two similar Andean cases: one where local IWM reform efforts succeeded (Celica) and one where they failed (Ibarra).

Chapters 6 and 7 examine phase 2 of grassroots global governance. Chapter 6 presents the results of frame analysis and social network analysis for all six cases. The results show how various combinations of network activation strategies explain why some local IWM reform attempts broke down while others led to experimentation with innovative institutional arrangements. The chapter highlights the strategies used in El Chaco to show how the right combination produces the pressure from beside needed for experimentation to endure. Other cases illustrate the strategies that cause phase 2 to break down during agenda setting, rule-making, or implementation efforts. Chapter 7 traces the entire IWM reform process in Tungurahua to show how changes in strategy produce different outcomes. The case illuminates how network activation strategies interact and reveals grassroots actors' power to contest, translate, and adapt IWM principles to fit local realities. By showing how ordinary farmers, community organizers, and indigenous activists guided the way global IWM principles were applied locally and consequently evolved, the chapter demonstrates how grassroots actors become global governors.

Chapter 8 examines phase 3 of grassroots global governance. It shows how Tungurahua's experimental IWM system institutionalized indigenous norms, associated with the concept buen vivir, which challenged the dominant international model of sustainable development. The chapter then explains how Tungurahua's experiment was scaled up nationally through network activation, resulting in Ecuador's National Plan for Buen Vivir. Ecuador's experience catalyzed international organizing and action around a new global idea—the rights of nature—as a means for "living in harmony with nature" (buen vivir). Consequently, the Tungurahua case illuminates how local populations working with competing interpretations from international agendas experiment with innovative local governance regimes and how the scaling up of these regimes carries local norms, principles, and practices to the global level, where they challenge traditional thinking.

The concluding chapter reflects on some broader implications for understanding global governance structures that commonly form around local-cumulative problems like poverty, disease, deforestation, and climate change. In addition, the chapter offers several policy lessons with the hope that future reformers can learn from the Ecuadorian experience, and that Ecuadorians can use this research to improve their own efforts to solve local environmental programs and sustainably manage their natural resources for the benefit of local communities.

2

Grassroots Global Governance

Theory and Process

This chapter presents a theory of grassroots global governance. The theory explains: (1) how "global ideas"—policies and best practices for solving global problems negotiated at the global level—get implemented at the local level; and (2) how the experience of implementing global ideas locally contributes to the evolution of these global ideas. The theory's overarching framework is a process model that views grassroots global governance as a cyclical process of contestation, experimentation, and learning that occurs among international, national, and local actors. The model identifies three main phases as well as multiple points where this process breaks down. Grassroots global governance theory explains why this process endures or breaks down at different points.

Phase 1 begins when transnational governance networks form to promote a global idea around the world. Often, rival policy networks advocate competing policies and practices associated with a global idea. Grassroots global governance theory explains why some versions of global ideas diffuse to particular localities while others do not. I discuss later in this chapter how a country's national context acts as a filter, affecting the influence of rival global policy networks and their ability to expand domestically. Navigating the national context constitutes the first challenge for transnational governance networks and constitutes the process's first breakdown point. The first phase ends (and the second begins) when transnational governance networks expand to the local level by incorporating grassroots actors, who help form coalitions dedicated to institutionalizing global ideas in particular localities.

The model's second phase explains why global ideas that diffuse to the local level get institutionalized and applied in practice in some cases and not others. To examine this question, I subdivide the second phase into sections modeled on the stages of the policy cycle.[1] While the policy cycle oversimplifies the policy process, it provides a useful analytical tool for studying distinct tasks all transnational governance networks must carry out. Problems must be identified and placed on a politically consequential agenda. New rules and institutions must be designed. Support among politicians and private stakeholders must be mobilized. Ultimately, new institutions, policies, and practices must be created and put into practice. Each task presents unique challenges and constitutes a point where the process may break down.

Figure 2.1 depicts these tasks in a circle to emphasize that they are not independent and do not proceed in a linear fashion; rather, there is a dynamic interaction among them. The circle also reflects the fact that new institutions, policies, and practices must constantly be reconstituted and renegotiated. As a result, they evolve and are adapted due to evolutionary learning and changing local conditions. This leads to experimentation with unique institutional applications of global ideas. In some cases, phase 2 endures long enough to produce innovative applications of global ideas. Other attempts "fail" in that coalition members abandon their efforts and disband before new governance systems are put into practice. In this way, the process breaks down.

When local experiments endure long enough to produce innovative governance arrangements perceived as successful, transnational governance networks diffuse lessons learned from the experience. They may also scale up local policies and practices nationally and internationally. As local experiments diffuse internationally, they not only carry local norms and practices to the international level, but also provide concrete, viable alternatives to traditional approaches promoted internationally. This can prompt a change in international discourse as well as the policies and strategies pursued by international actors. In this way, local experiments shape the evolution of global ideas. This constitutes phase 3.

Grassroots global governance theory argues that whether the process endures or breaks down depends on the ability of transnational governance networks to expand to include actors that are influential in the policy arenas relevant to each phase of the process. This in turn depends on the strategies they employ. Therefore, variation in outcomes—that is, whether the process endures (success) or breaks down (failure) and the point where failed cases break down—is explained by the combination of network activation strategies used to expand transnational governance networks (described in subsequent sections and identified in the circles of Fig. 2.1).

---

[1] The policy cycle is a tool used to analyze the development of policy. It is commonly described as having five stages: agenda setting, policy formulation, decision making, implementation, and evaluation (Sabatier 2007).

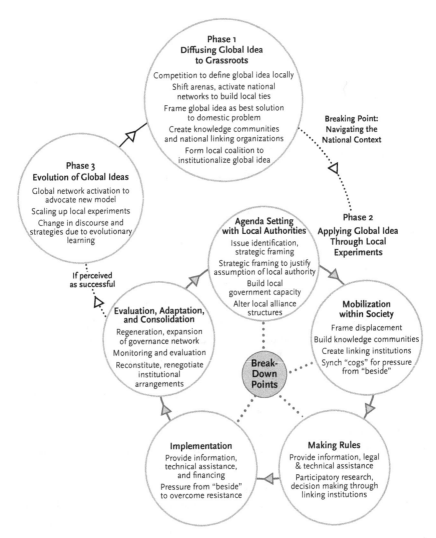

Figure 2.1 The Grassroots Global Governance Process.

This chapter explains grassroots global governance theory in two parts. The first half of the chapter presents a general framework for understanding how governance works in an age of globalization. Globalization has expanded the diversity of actors involved and the number of ways authority is organized and expressed. Given the complex relationships among actors and the problems they seek to solve, I describe global governance in network terms.[2] I explain how various actors govern through network activation and describe the strategies used.

[2] On networked governance, see Dedeurwaerdere (2005); Newig et al. (2010); Wallerstein and Duran (2003).

The chapter's second half applies this general framework to the grassroots global governance process, examining the three phases in sequence. I highlight the unique dynamics of each phase and explain how variation in the network activation strategies employed by members of transnational governance networks influences their ability to progress through each phase of the process.

Governing through Network Activation: Strategies and Arenas

Following Burris (2004, 336), I define governance as "the management of the course of events in a social system." Societies at all levels of analysis are the objects of governance, from the international society of states to a country's national political elites to the collection of stakeholders in a micro-watershed. This definition highlights that governance is not merely a process resulting from structure; it contains agency. It involves the purposive efforts by both state and nonstate actors to "steer" society toward the pursuit of particular goals (Andonova et al. 2009; Brand 2005; Kjaer 2004). "Governors" use a wide variety of mechanisms—force, persuasion, economic pressure, and norm creation—to steer society and affect policy.

Inevitably, some people resist efforts to change policies and practices. Governance is therefore marked by contestation. To analyze this contestation, I draw on two insights from the social movement literature. First, analyzing actors' strategies is a useful way to study the role of agency in relation to structure, which is necessary to capture the open-ended nature of contestation involved with sociopolitical change (Jasper 2004; 1997; Ganz 2000; 2003). Agency is fundamentally about choice, and strategies offer a concrete way to analyze choice. The second insight is that actors' strategies, and thus contestation, are shaped by context.

I borrow Jasper's (2004; 2006) concept of "arena" to conceptualize the context in which contestation over policy occurs. An arena "is a loosely delimited setting where the same open-ended bundle of rules and resources guide all social interactions" (Viterna 2013, 47). Societies at all levels—global, national, and local—contain multiple arenas in which policy can be contested. These include legal-political arenas, like national legislatures, courts, government bureaucracies, and the UN treaty system. But they also include social and economic arenas, including the media, the marketplace, and the streets.

Each arena has a unique set of rules and resources. Organizations are therefore better equipped to contest policy in some arenas than in others, and each arena privileges different organizations. For example, institutional power makes government officials and IGO representatives better equipped than local social movements to contest policy in national and international legal-political arenas like government bureaucracies and UN conventions. However, social movements and civic associations often have more power than national politicians or IGO representatives to influence events in the social arenas of rural communities.

Grassroots global governance involves the shifting of contestation over policy both within and across levels of analysis, first from global arenas to national and local arenas, and then from local arenas back to national and global arenas. The need to shift arenas—and the fact that rules, resources, and power relationships vary across arenas—means that transnational governance networks must incorporate a diverse array of actors able to exercise multiple forms of power in multiple arenas. Networks that do so can exploit more pathways of influence; when blocked in one arena they can shift to another. Network expansion is thus key to governance.

Because different arenas privilege different actors, the organization at the center of a transnational governance network—the one with the most power—shifts depending on the arena where global ideas are being contested. Since arenas of contestation vary across the three phases of grassroots global governance, so too do the organizations leading governance networks. As discussed below, grassroots actors become influential during phase 2 because they have the most power in the local arenas where global ideas are contested at that point. This insight, along with the fact that phase 2 is when global ideas get adapted through experimentation, partially explains how grassroots actors become influential global governors.

To analyze the relationship between arenas (structure), strategy (agency), and network expansion, I draw on nodal governance theory.[3] Nodal governance theory builds on network theory by looking not only at how ideas and resources transfer across network structures, but also the agency involved in converting these into action. Nodal governance theorists focus on the formal and informal organizations that constitute nodes in governance networks. As Burris et al. (2005) note, these organizations constitute the site of governance—the space where knowledge and resources are mobilized to exert influence on society.

In contrast to conventional ways of analyzing global governance arrangements, nodal governance theory does not distinguish organizations by type (e.g., government, corporation, or NGO) or scale (e.g., international, national, or local). Nor is any organizational type given analytical priority. Rather, what matter are organizations' views on the issues they seek to govern, who they are

---

[3] On nodal governance theory see Boutellier and van Steden (2011); Burris (2004); Burris et al. (2005); Drahos (2004); Hein et al. (2009); Shearing and Wood (2003); Wood et al. (2011).

connected to, and the resources and technologies they can wield to exert influence on other organizations through the network. This framework is useful since relationships in global governance networks often go far beyond the NGÓ activists and experts commonly associated with transnational advocacy networks. Moreover, as the following chapters illustrate, network members' identities and relationships crosscut the categories used by conventional frameworks in ways that make differentiating among these categories problematic. Nodal governance theory provides a way out of this problem.

Organizations govern by projecting power across network ties to steer societies toward particular policy objectives. They use the resources and technologies at their disposal to pressure and persuade others to support their policy objectives. A main insight of nodal governance theory is that policy advocates may expand the range of their influence and govern indirectly by influencing the individuals and organizations accessible to them through networks, and who in turn have the power to govern others. They do this by: (1) constructing network ties with organizations and actors that have the potential to influence targeted populations; (2) working to change these actors' way of thinking about the issues they seek to govern; and (3) persuading them to use their own resources (and those available to them through their network ties) to take action. Governance is therefore a process of network expansion and resource mobilization. I call this process "network activation."[4]

By governing indirectly, a relatively small number of organizations can spur a process of policy change. A metaphor from the game of pool illustrates the point. If the cue ball hits just one or two other balls, and those are in a position to impact several more, the act of hitting the cue ball can set in motion a chain reaction that fundamentally reshapes the game. Similarly, a small number of organizations can indirectly govern areas where they have little direct influence by influencing organizations accessible to them through their networks, and who in turn have the power to exert influence in those areas (or at least have the power to activate networks of actors that can exert influence in those areas). This insight has important implications for understanding how influence flows across arenas at different scales, whether from global to local or from local to global, and for understanding how grassroots actors become global governors.

There are two key elements to expanding governance networks through network activation. One is *motivating* organizations to join the governance network and contribute their resources, time, and energy to the cause. The second is enhancing the network's *capacity* to combine the resources accessible

---

[4] Nodal governance theorists typically refer to this as "nodal activation" (e.g., Burris et al. 2005). I use "network activation" for the sake of simplicity and clarity.

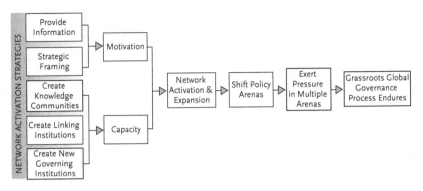

Figure 2.2 Structure of the Argument.

to each network member and apply them to a particular purpose. Grassroots global governance theory argues that network members create the requisite motivation and capacity by employing various network activation strategies. These include: (1) strategic framing; (2) providing knowledge, technology, and resources; (3) building "knowledge communities" of like-minded experts and activists; (4) creating "linking institutions" that connect various stakeholders, concentrate the distinct resources available to each through their network ties, and provide a focal point for converting these into action; and (5) creating new governing institutions to steer society toward new policy goals.

Figure 2.2 illustrates the structure of my argument for how network activation strategies determine whether or not the grassroots global governance process endures or breaks down. These strategies allow transnational governance networks to expand by incorporating a diverse array of organizations able to influence contestation in different policy arenas at different levels of analysis. This, in turn, allows transnational governance networks to exert the pressure needed to overcome resistance at each phase of the grassroots global governance process, allowing the process to endure. The remainder of the chapter explains this argument in detail. I first discuss each network activation strategy in turn and then explain how different combinations determine whether the process endures or breaks down at various points.

Information and Framing
(Strategies for Creating Motivation)

Some organizations share very similar viewpoints on an issue, making collaboration relatively easy to motivate. Forest conservation NGOs in the United States and Ecuador, for example, are natural allies. More often, however, individuals targeted by policy advocates are apathetic. Many local actors do not have clear preferences regarding global ideas like integrated watershed management, and they lack the information necessary to determine whether or not they have an interest in collaborating to implement them (Abers 2007). Local farmers, for example, are often unsure whether particular policies for managing forests and other watershed resources will be good or bad for them, or even what criteria to use to judge those policies.

Members of transnational governance networks motivate individuals by strategically using ideas and knowledge to shape their perceptions of what kinds of policies and practices are possible, appropriate, and necessary. New information can motivate action by changing people's awareness of a problem and how they perceive their interests. People also need knowledge to make decisions and take action. Those with the most knowledge have an advantage when it comes to shaping the debate: they define problems and the range of possible solutions. This is particularly true for highly technical and complex issues, such as most global problems. Transnational networks govern in part by providing information and technical expertise.

For example, transnational networks promoting local IWM reform wield influence by: (1) providing information on the functioning of ecosystem services and their impacts on local stakeholders; (2) supplying various technologies, such as techniques for valuing ecosystem services; (3) providing legal advice; and (4) offering models for designing IWM institutions. These activities are partly about building capacity. But they are also a way for network members to shape the perceptions of local stakeholders regarding appropriate methods of watershed management. Through these mechanisms, IWM advocates influence how local governments understand their environmental management obligations and options. They alter local perceptions of the political climate and actors' room to maneuver within it. They shape local perceptions regarding the state of ecosystems and the value of ecosystem services for socioeconomic development. They persuade local actors that creating IWM programs is important.

Of course, new information alone does not necessarily motivate people to take action. Meaning must be assigned to this information. This is where strategic framing comes in. Strategic framing is a well-established mechanism for motivating collective action by altering peoples' beliefs, understandings, and the discourse surrounding an issue (Snow 2007; Tarrow 2005). The verb "framing" is used to conceptualize the way advocates of a particular policy "assign meaning to and interpret relevant events and conditions in ways that are intended to mobilize potential adherents and constituents, to garner bystander support, and to demobilize antagonists" (Snow and Benford 1988, 198). The resulting "frames" are shared understandings of reality that structure how people perceive themselves, their relationship to one another and the world around them, and what constitutes legitimate action (McAdam et al. 1996). Advocates of policy change manipulate social frames to identify an important problem and assign blame (diagnostic framing); to specify what can and must be done to solve the problem (prognostic framing); and to provide a "call to arms" for addressing the problem, usually by stressing the urgency of the issue (motivational framing) (Snow and Benford 1988).

To mobilize local support for social change, transnational advocates must construct a coherent master frame that has the potential to integrate a diverse set of actors (Gerhards and Rucht 1992; Snow and Benford 1992). To be successful, frames must resonate with the personal experiences, beliefs, and values of targeted audiences (Snow and Benford 1988; Tarrow 2005). This presents a challenge since enacting social change requires activists to propose frames that challenge the status quo, but that still resonate with traditional cultural understandings, which tend to buttress the status quo (Tarrow 2005). David Snow and his colleagues (1986) call this activity "frame alignment." Frame alignment is typically a contested process. When policy advocates challenge an issue's existing master frame there are those who resist and defend the status quo. This leads to "framing contests" in which rival groups compete to make their frame dominant (Ryan 1991). Despite extensive research, little is known about why some frames resonate more than others and thus why some framing attempts succeed while others fail.

One argument is that the intrinsic characteristics of an issue or frame may determine its influence (Bob 2002; Carpenter 2011; Finnemore and Sikkink 1998; Nadelman 1990). However, efforts to identify beneficial frame attributes are complicated by research showing many contradictions. Master frames that succeed in one scenario fail in another (McCarthy 1996; Payne 2001). Multiple frames can produce a desired outcome, and multiple outcomes are possible with any frame (Rein and Schön 1993). We therefore need to look beyond attributes.

A second argument is that new frames will be more successful when they are "grafted" on to existing frames that are already influential (Price 2003). The idea that new issues must "resonate" with existing frames is widely recognized (Florini 2000; Kjellman 2007; Price and Tannenwald 1996). This is undoubtedly an important part of issue identification and agenda setting. But implementing a new policy involves frame contests precisely because the policy conflicts with the dominant master frame for the relevant issue. Also, each of the competing frames may be rooted in existing values and norms; by definition, an existing master frame is resonant with local culture. The ability to graft a new master frame onto existing ones says nothing about whether the new master frame will be more or less resonant than the frame it seeks to replace.

A third argument is that the relative power of opponents will influence the results of a frame contest (Marullo et al. 1996). Yet, Sell's (2003) research on the struggle to establish global intellectual property laws shows that the outcome of frame contests cannot be explained merely in terms of power dynamics. Sell's is but one of a growing number of studies seeking to explain how actors construct a convincing counter-frame strong enough to replace an alternative interpretive frame (Hein 2007; Hein and Kohlmorgen 2008; Johnston and Noakes 2005).

Grassroots governance theory argues that the resonance of a new master frame, and thus the success of policy advocates, is a function of the framing strategy used rather than frame attributes or power relationships. In their comparison of conflicts in the European Union over intellectual property policies, Haunss and Kohlmorgen (2009, 109) find evidence suggesting that "displacement strategies, which attempt to reframe an already existing hegemonic frame and give it new meaning," may be more fruitful than counter-framing strategies.

Drawing on Haunss and Kohlmorgen's insight, I group framing strategies into two categories: counter-framing and frame-displacement. This grouping captures a fundamental difference in strategy. A counter-framing strategy tries to undermine and replace an existing master frame while a frame-displacement strategy co-opts and transforms the existing master frame to incorporate the new policy agenda. The core of the latter strategy is to keep the original master frame, but to displace its original meaning, for example by "bundling it with other frames that change the content of the whole package" (Haunss and Kohlmorgen 2009, 124). This redefinition of the master frame is what distinguishes frame-displacement from counter-framing, which seeks to replace one master frame with another. Grassroots global governance theory argues that local experiments with institutionalizing global ideas (i.e., phase 2 of the process model) are more likely to endure when policy advocates employ a frame-displacement strategy. Doing so is more effective at creating the requisite motivation among local stakeholders to join the transnational governance network and contribute to its mission.

Creating Local Knowledge Communities (Strategies for Building Network Capacity)

Transnational coalitions also differ in the degree to which they employ strategies that enhance governance networks' capacity to take action. When it comes to applying global ideas at the grassroots level, an important capacity-building strategy is to create local "knowledge" communities of like-minded experts and activists. A knowledge (or "epistemic") community is a "network of professionals with recognized expertise and competence in a particular domain and an authoritative claim to policy-relevant knowledge within that domain or issue area" (Haas 1992, 3). Members come from different backgrounds, but are united by a shared "set of norms that motivate their common action, a set of beliefs about central problems in their area of expertise, shared criteria for evaluating knowledge, and a common policy enterprise" (Clunan 2013, 1).

The importance of knowledge communities for coordinating international policy is well-documented. They interpret complex problems and promote particular responses to decision makers within national governments and international organizations. I argue that local knowledge communities (comprised of local residents rather than outside experts) are equally important for institutionalizing global ideas at the local level. When global ideas first emerge, however, local knowledge communities often do not exist, particularly in rural areas of developing countries. Creating them becomes an important mechanism of network activation.

Transnational networks create local knowledge communities through both direct and indirect strategies. The experience of transnational IWM networks is illustrative. Some members work directly in communities for years to recruit and train community organizers, who in turn organize and sustain IWM programs in their communities. Another, less direct, strategy is to create environmental management programs espousing IWM principles in local universities. These two strategies, employed across the developing world in the 1990s, produced a new generation of local experts working to improve watershed management in their communities.

Local experts and activists enhance transnational networks' capacity to govern locally by serving as important brokers between transnational networks and local stakeholder groups. They bridge the cultural divide between foreign advocates and local farmers, loggers, miners, social movements, politicians, businesses, and others. They translate global ideas, both in a linguistic and conceptual sense, and use their own social and cultural capital to build trust between community members and transnational coalitions advocating local governance reforms (Fox 2009). In this way, they facilitate the network activation process at the local level.

In some respects, members of local knowledge communities resemble Steinberg's (2001, 10) "bilateral activists"—cosmopolitan elites from developing countries who "encounter foreign ideas by virtue of their travels, . . . embrace them as a function of their worldly outlook," and then use their knowledge of national policy culture and access to political resources to design national environmental policies. Members of local knowledge communities are similar in that they serve as bridges between the international and domestic realms and they become activists for policy change in their communities. Yet, many look very different from Steinberg's description of bilateral activists. They are not "rooted cosmopolitans" in the usual sense (Tarrow 2005). Most are not highly educated, urban professionals accustomed to circulating in international (or even national) policy circles. Rather, they are ordinary people—smallholder farmers, craftspeople, small business owners, municipal bureaucrats, and the like. Many have never traveled to the capital city, much less gone abroad. Their exposure to global ideas comes instead from programs established in their communities by transnational networks. For reasons described later, it is precisely their rootedness in their local communities, and not a cosmopolitan outlook or experience, that makes them effective "global governors."

In one sense, creating knowledge communities is a motivation strategy. Through repeated attendance in meetings, seminars, and training events, local organizers are socialized to view IWM principles and practices as the best solution to locally identified problems (Checkel 2005). However, these local organizers also enhance a governance network's capacity in several respects. First, they provide a reservoir of local expertise that gives continuity and a sense of embeddedness to local governance efforts. Second, their status as local community members makes them better situated than their foreign counterparts to facilitate the dissemination of global ideas, adapt them to fit local contexts, and recruit additional local support. For reasons discussed later, their ability to exploit local vulnerabilities also makes them better equipped than their foreign allies to pressure resistant stakeholders. Finally, local knowledge communities build capacity by providing transnational governance networks with access to local resources, including information, social capital, and access to local social networks, as well as to key decision makers in local government and community organizations. For these reasons, grassroots global governance theory argues that the grassroots global governance process is more likely to endure when and where transnational governance networks train local knowledge communities.

Community-Based Participatory Research

Grassroots global governance theory argues that community-based participatory research is an important tool for enhancing local knowledge communities' capacity to implement policy change. Grassroots global governance requires activating a broad, diverse array of community members, for reasons discussed earlier. Academics and practitioners alike widely acknowledge that active community involvement and dialogue among diverse constituencies are critical for effecting local policy change (Atwood et al. 1997; Freudenberg et al. 2005; Gauvin and Abelson 2006). Yet, most policy advocacy models inadequately specify how to enhance the capacity of community members to engage in the policy change process (Freudenberg 2004; Israel et al. 2010; Minkler et al. 2003; Nelson et al. 2008).

The literature on community-based participatory research suggests this is an effective strategy for building the capacity of community members to effectively promote policy change (Israel et al. 2010; Minkler et al. 2003; Minkler et al. 2006; Petersen et al. 2007). In community-based participatory research, community members partner with outside practitioners and technical experts in all aspects of research, from needs analysis and information gathering to data analysis and decision making. This approach empowers community members to contribute their expertise and share decision-making responsibility and ownership. This has a number of benefits for network activation (Wallerstein and Duran 2003). The community-based, participatory approach increases the transparency of the process, which facilitates local buy-in and participation. It improves the quality of information collected, due to local knowledge, and increases local actors' understanding of problems and their technical capacity to address them. It also provides a mechanism for incorporating new stakeholders into the governance network, embedding it locally. For these reasons, grassroots global governance theory argues that phase 2 of the grassroots global governance process is more likely to endure when transnational governance networks use community-based participatory research, rather than a purely technical approach to information gathering and needs analysis.

Creating Linking and Governing Institutions (Strategies for Building Network Capacity)

An equally important network activation strategy is to create "linking institutions." These are formal or informal structures that bring together actors representing different networks in order to concentrate the resources and technologies available to each and to use these to achieve a common goal.[5] In nodal governance theory, these linking institutions are the "command centers of networked governance." As Burris et al. (2005, 38) explain, "tying together networks is one very important way in which nodes [i.e., network members] gain the capacity to govern a course of events. This tying together creates a node with increased resources at the same time as it creates a structure that enables the mobilization of those resources to produce action by other nodes in the network."

Health GAP is an example of a linking institution in a transnational health governance network.[6] Health GAP links AIDS and human rights activists, public

---

[5] Nodal governance scholars refer to these institutions as "superstructural nodes." For the sake of simplicity and clarity, I use the more descriptive term "linking institution." For the role of superstructural nodes in nodal governance theory, see Burris (2004); Burris et al. (2005); Drahos (2004); Hein et al. (2009).

[6] "GAP" stands for "Global Access Project." See www.healthgap.org (accessed January 28, 2016).

health experts, fair trade advocates, and concerned individuals, allowing them to concentrate their diverse resources for the purpose of increasing poor people's access to essential medicines around the world. Burris (2004, 343–344) notes that despite its limited economic resources and lack of formal authority, Health GAP governs by using "information gathered by its constituent members, demonstrations, and its access to media networks to influence governments, drug companies and other powerful [organizations] influencing pharmaceutical access."

National and local linking institutions play important roles in phases 1 and 2, respectively. In phase 2, for example, local linking institutions connect organizations operating at multiple scales for the purpose of steering local communities toward particular policy goals. Local watershed management committees, for example, connect local groups like farmers, water utilities, local governments, hydroelectric companies, and others, as well as foreign donor agencies, international NGOs, IGOs, and outside experts. These linking institutions provide a space for identifying and framing problems, sharing experiences for tackling these problems, learning, and planning projects. They also provide a focal point for mobilizing the material, informational, technical, and social resources available to watershed stakeholders through their respective networks. Most important, they provide a structure for directing these resources toward the implementation of local IWM programs. In this way, linking institutions build the capacity of transnational governance networks to apply global ideas like IWM locally.

Finally, governance networks build capacity by creating new governing institutions (i.e., new nodes in the governance network) at the local, national, and international levels. These organizations focus the resources, knowledge, and capacities available to network members and direct them toward pressuring and persuading individuals and organizations "to act or refrain from action" (Burris 2004, 344). A good example is the environmental management units IWM advocates helped create within local governments across the developing world during the 1990s. These environmental management units provide an institutional platform for newly trained, local IWM experts (members of local knowledge communities) to pursue their policy agenda full-time. Some become municipal bureaucrats, giving IWM networks access to local government resources and the ability to influence policies and procedures from within local governments.

Explaining Grassroots Global Governance

The Ecuadorian cases of IWM reform detailed in subsequent chapters show that members of different transnational governance networks employ the above network activation strategies to different degrees and in different ways. To motivate new actors to join the network, some members employ counter-framing strategies while others use frame-displacement strategies. Network members also differ in the degree to which they engage in the network capacity-building strategies described earlier. Some spend years training knowledge communities and creating new linking and governing institutions, while others do not. Some design new institutions through community-based participatory research programs, while others rely on small groups of experts.

Grassroots global governance theory argues that these differences in strategy explain variation in transnational governance networks' ability to expand to include the influential actors needed to propel the grassroots global governance process forward at each phase. Specifically, I argue that the grassroots global governance process is more likely to endure when members of governance networks: (1) provide information and employ frame-displacement strategies to motivate influential actors to join the network; and (2) engage in high-level network-capacity-building activities, particularly training knowledge communities and creating new linking and governing institutions. When network members do not employ these strategies, or employ some but not others, the process breaks down at different points, as described later.

Of course, governance networks do not operate in a vacuum. The national and local arenas in which network members operate shape their ability to pursue their policy objectives. To explain how strategy and context interact, and how variation in strategy leads to variation in outcomes, the following sections discuss the role of network activation at each phase of the grassroots global governance process. I examine the phases sequentially. The dynamics of each phase are unique, and present different puzzles regarding grassroots global governance:

- Why do some global ideas and not others diffuse to particular localities (phase 1)?
- Why do some attempts to institutionalize and apply global ideas locally succeed while others do not (phase 2)?
- Why and how do local institutional experiments reverberate back to the global level and contribute to the evolution of global ideas (phase 3)?

The following sections show how the answer to each question lies with the strategies used to expand transnational governance networks and project power across network ties. They explain why power within networks shifts as contestation over global ideas shifts arenas in each phase. They also explain why grassroots actors become particularly important when contestation shifts to local arenas in phase 2, when grassroots actors use their power to adapt global ideas to fit local conditions. In phase 3, grassroots actors govern indirectly by activating networks to scale up local adaptations nationally and globally. In this way, grass-roots actors become global governors, influencing the evolution of global ideas.

Phase 1: Diffusing Global Ideas to the Grassroots

In phase 1, grassroots global governance theory explains why some versions of global ideas diffuse to particular localities and others do not. To answer this question, it is useful to first think about the characteristics of global ideas. Global ideas facilitate the organization of transnational governance networks because they tend to be what Ansell (2011) calls "meta-concepts." Concepts like sustainable development, human rights, community policing, and IWM present a desirable end goal to be achieved, identifiable by certain general conditions. Yet, they are ambiguous enough to allow different actors to imbue them with multiple interpretations, meanings, or values. This reflects both the ongoing effort to build knowledge and the attempt to forge consensus among individuals and organizations with fundamentally different values and priorities. It is this combination of plasticity with what Levy and Wissenburg (2004, 786) call "policy telos"—"shared conceptions giving direction to cooperative political ventures"—that allows certain global ideas to have wide appeal. Global ideas become banners for connecting and rallying a diverse set of actors, providing an accepted common point of reference, even as different actors argue over their precise meaning. This encourages communication and collaborative action among individuals and organizations that might otherwise view themselves as pursuing unrelated or even conflicting enterprises.

Sustainable development provides one of the clearest illustrations (Ansell 2011). Most people agree that sustainable development is a good thing worth promoting, yet there are many visions for how it should be practiced. Economic development programs to reduce poverty, technological development to increase efficiency of consumption, the conservation of natural resources, and efforts to reduce health problems caused by pollution are all characterized as "sustainable development." While some scholars critique the ambiguity of the concept, others note that this ambiguity is constructive. According to Kates, Parris, and Leiserowitz (2005, 20),

> sustainable development draws much of its resonance, power and creativity from its very ambiguity. The concrete challenges of sustainable development are at least as heterogeneous and complex as the diversity of human societies and natural ecosystems around the world. As a concept, its malleability allows it to remain an open, dynamic, and evolving

idea that can be adapted to fit these very different situations and contexts across space and time.

One consequence is that even as various international actors engage in acrimonious debate over the exact meaning of a global concept, different transnational networks rally around a global idea—identified by general principles—and call for it to be institutionalized in countries around the globe. On the ground, however, members of different networks advocate quite different institutional changes. When it comes to managing water-related resources, for example, the World Bank advocates water privatization and stresses engineering projects managed by experts to improve physical infrastructure (Olleta 2007; World Bank 1993). By contrast, the World Wildlife Fund focuses on changing land management through participatory programs to conserve and restore a watershed's natural resources (Jones et al. 2003). While these policy proposals are quite distinct, and can even be seen as contradictory, they are all interpreted as fitting within the broad set of principles known as integrated watershed management.

Therefore, when thinking about how global ideas influence local governance arrangements, part of the puzzle is why and how distinct applications of a global concept get promoted in particular localities. For example, why do IWM programs in Brazil focus more on water infrastructure projects controlled by experts, while in Ecuador you more often see participatory land management projects to conserve forests in watershed catchment areas? Answering these questions requires explaining the varying influence of different transnational networks that carry competing versions of a global concept. Not all international actors are equally successful in expanding their governance networks nationally and diffusing their preferred policy prescriptions. Indeed, this constitutes the first breakdown point in the grassroots global governance process.

Filters and Firewalls

Why do some transnational governance networks flourish domestically while others wither? The network activation strategies detailed earlier play a role, as I will discuss. But part of the answer is that a country's national context—the existing cultural norms, rules, practices, political institutions, and sociopolitical alliances—shapes the opportunity of transnational networks to expand and diffuse global ideas domestically. Scholars of international policy diffusion show that a country's domestic context can act as a "firewall," causing policy diffusion to fail (Solingen 2012). This is particularly true when global policies and practices clash with local cultural norms, leading domestic actors to reject them altogether (Acharya 2004; Checkel 1999). Social movement theorists similarly recognize that contextual factors shape opportunity by empowering some actors while inhibiting others, and constraining some courses of action while enabling others (Kriesi 2007; McAdam et al. 1996; Tarrow 1996).

Of course, the domestic context is not static, nor is its effect deterministic. Members of governance networks can adapt their strategies to try to navigate the national context. I therefore conceptualize a country's national context as a "filter" that affects the influence of rival global policy networks by shaping their ability to use different strategies.[7] The existing rules, norms, practices, and relationships in a country constitute a kind of "toolkit" available to network members to construct strategies of action (Berk and Galvan 2009; Swidler 1986). Some network members have a hard time using this toolkit; for them the national context looks like a firewall. Others find it easier to employ these tools to expand their network domestically. Consider the pathways by which transnational governance networks might influence grassroots policies and practices. Policy advocates might try to leverage the power of national governments, corporations, NGOs, or social movements. Domestic norms, rules, political institutions, and sociopolitical alliances determine which, if any, of these paths are open to different networks.

Often, foreign policy advocates first try to influence local practices by working with national government bureaucrats and politicians to change national policy. Sometimes this works. But as noted in chapter 1, national policy is no guarantee of action on the ground; politicians, bureaucrats, and various private actors often block new policies from being implemented (Abers and Keck 2009; 2013; Hochstetler and Keck 2007). When one pathway closes, transnational actors may pursue another, for example by tapping into formal and informal domestic social networks (Abers and Keck 2009; 2013; Hochstetler and Keck 2007). This will be easier for some than others. Some, for example, can utilize cultural norms to frame their preferred policies in a way that resonates with influential domestic actors, while others find this virtually impossible. The difference in this ability to employ domestic norms affects not only the degree to which domestic groups mobilize to oppose particular transnational networks, but also the ability of transnational advocates to tap into domestic social and political networks. Contextual factors therefore structure the contestation around a global idea in a given country. They empower some transnational networks and disempower others. This explains why one version of a global idea rather than another gets pursued domestically.

---

[7] Diffusion scholars like Falkner and Gupta (2009), Klingler-Vidra and Schleifer (2014), and Solingen (2012) similarly conceptualize domestic institutions as filters through which external ideas and practices must pass.

National Brokers

Even for those transnational networks that are not "filtered out," navigating the national context and expanding the governance network to reach the local level remains a key challenge. Foreign members of transnational governance networks are disadvantaged when it comes to influencing national policy. Paul Steinberg (2001) notes that they lack the domestic political resources and knowledge needed to navigate domestic political systems and get things done. They therefore need domestic brokers who have ties to transnational networks, thereby accessing policy ideas and resources available in global arenas, but who also possess the domestic political resources and skills needed to effectively contest global ideas in national arenas. These are Steinberg's "bilateral activists" (2001, 10).

While Steinberg demonstrates the importance of bilateral activists within national governments, I argue that similar national-level brokers are equally important for helping transnational governance networks shift arenas when opponents block national policymaking. Like their political counterparts, these are highly educated, cosmopolitan professionals who have strong international ties. They are aware of global ideas like IWM and embrace them as solutions to problems they care about. But rather than navigating governmental arenas, these bilateral activists have the knowledge, resources, and network connections to access, navigate, and mobilize action within domestic social networks. This makes them among the most powerful members of transnational governance networks in phase 1.

In the case of Ecuadorian IWM reform, these national brokers were usually environmental engineers and environmental activists who were educated abroad but had strong ties to domestic social, environmental, and development networks. Bilateral activists are natural allies for transnational policy advocates at the national level. They become key brokers, facilitating the national expansion of transnational governance networks. They do so by working with foreign partners to employ the network activation strategies described earlier.

Chapter 4 describes, for example, how foreign and national IWM advocates developed multiple national programs for training grassroots actors (e.g., small-holder farmers, community activists, and municipal bureaucrats) in IWM principles and practices. They used these programs to build national networks of watershed stakeholders trained in IWM principles and practices. National linking institutions like Ecuador's National Water Resources Forum connected these stakeholders, along with social movements, NGOs, government representatives, and others. These linking institutions became powerful sites for disseminating information, expanding network connections, increasing technical capacity through training, generating new ideas and collaborative initiatives, and mobilizing resources for advancing the IWM policy agenda nationally. Over time, the number of Ecuadorians connected to transnational IWM networks steadily expanded through community training programs, conferences, education campaigns, academic programs, and the creation of municipal environmental management units.

The Ecuadorian cases illustrate how these network activation strategies are like planting seeds. Over time, grassroots networks of local policy advocates (i.e., local knowledge communities) grow and alter local sociopolitical alliances in ways that create windows of opportunity for pursuing local policy change. Members of local knowledge communities become natural allies for external policy advocates, both domestic and foreign. Together, they form local coalitions dedicated to institutionalizing a particular version of a global idea in a given locality.

Phase 2: Local Adaptation and Experimentation

The formation of a local coalition constitutes the expansion of a transnational governance network to a particular locality and marks the beginning of phase 2. These coalitions are transnational in that domestic and foreign actors coordinate "shared strategies or sets of tactics to publicly influence social change" (Khagram et al. 2002, 7). However, I refer to these coalitions throughout the book as "local coalitions" to emphasize their local focus and local members, and to distinguish them from the national-level coalitions formed during phase 1.

Local Brokers

In this phase, contestation over global ideas occurs in local arenas. The challenge is explaining why some attempts to apply global principles, policies, and practices break down while others lead to adaptation and experimentation with innovative institutional arrangements. As in phase 1, brokers are needed to navigate domestic arenas, mobilize action, and get things done. However, brokers in local arenas look quite different from national brokers. These are not highly educated, urban globetrotters like Tarrow's "rooted cosmopolitans" or Steinberg's "bilateral activists." They are normal people living in rural communities and small towns—smallholder farmers, neighborhood association leaders, community organizers, municipal bureaucrats, and others. For reasons discussed later, these grassroots actors take the lead in transnational governance networks as efforts turn to implementing global ideas locally. This matters because these grassroots advocates rarely follow the standard, international script.

Local Contestation and Experimentation

The fact that some grassroots actors join a local coalition means that some local stakeholders do not wholly reject the global idea in question. However, they often recognize that elements of the policies and practices initially proposed by outsiders are ill-suited to their local context. Moreover, they must contend with other local stakeholders who are far more resistant. As a result, local coalition members contest, translate, and adapt global ideas to fit local realities and experiment with unique institutional applications.

The model's assumption of adaptation and experimentation, rather than acceptance or rejection, is supported by recent research on international policy diffusion. While much of this literature focuses on explaining policy convergence, many studies "show that, as they diffuse, norms, ideas, and practices often change in form and content" (Klingler-Vidra and Schleifer 2014, 264).[8] One reason is structural; it results from the filtering effect of the domestic context described earlier and illustrated in chapter 4 (Falkner and Gupta 2009; Solingen 2012; Yeo and Painter 2011). In their review of the diffusion literature, Klingler-Vidra and Schleifer (2014, 271) find that "scholars point to the mediating effect of local norms, political institutions, and economic structures on diffusion outcomes."

Checkel (1999, 87) argues that there must be a high degree of congruence with local culture for external norms to diffuse and be adopted. Since perfect matches almost never exist, the degree of difference becomes important. So does agency. If the difference is too great, local actors will reject the external norm outright. But numerous diffusion studies show that if the difference is moderate, local actors reinterpret and adapt external norms, policies, and practices to fit local conditions (Acharya 2009; Falkner and Gupta 2009). Yeo and Painter (2011), for example, show how policymakers in China and Vietnam neither fully accepted nor fully rejected the global model of telecom regulation that by 2002 had diffused to approximately 120 states. While they accepted many features as suitable for local contexts, they rejected a fully privatized regulatory body with independent oversight. They adapted the model by transforming state-owned telecom companies into joint stock companies.

These and similar cases challenge the impression given by some studies of institutional diffusion that ideas first develop coherence and then are imposed or copied internationally (e.g., DiMaggio and Powell 1983; Molle 2008). Rather, they show that ideas and related institutions continue to be reconstructed domestically throughout the policymaking process due to creative action by

---

[8] Klingler-Vidra and Schleifer (2014) and Solingen (2012) provide excellent reviews of studies showing that policies and practices vary as they diffuse.

local actors. The need to navigate unique local environments spurs policy advocates to engage in bricolage—recombining elements of external and local institutions, procedures, and practices and using them in new, creative ways.

Recent studies of institutional change similarly highlight the importance of creative action by local actors engaging in bricolage.[9] These studies challenge the notion that institutional outcomes can be explained by structural conditions. Instead, they point to creative practices by actors inside and outside of government. One important practice is experimentation, which involves "combining and using ideas, resources, and relationships in new ways" (Abers and Keck 2013, 17). Berk and Galvan (2013, 29) call this process "ramshackling" to highlight the fact that new institutions tend to be created improvisationally (Ansell 2011; Schickler 2001). Experimentation resembles ramshackling because it typically occurs in complex environments characterized by uncertainty, overlapping and conflicting sources of authority and power, limited access to resources, and many other challenges. Those seeking better ways to address pressing problems must cobble something together with what they have to work with at the moment.

A second reason experimentation involves bricolage is that ideas, policies, and practices continue to get (re)constructed and (re)negotiated throughout the policy process.[10] As Abers and Keck (2013, 12) explain, "policy ideas grow out of a combination of debates among specialists (in which contesting ideas are defended), political struggle (in which ideas that are not specific to the specialist community get into the discussion), and practical experiments in particular locations." Institutional change is therefore a political and relational process as much as it is a technical process. This is why network activation practices are important.[11]

The question, then, is why some local experiments break down while others endure long enough to produce innovative institutional adaptations of global ideas. The answer lies in the ability of transnational governance networks to incorporate a diverse group of local, influential stakeholders with the motivation and capacity to push the process of institutional change forward. To explain why some networks are more successful at doing this than others, it is useful

---

[9] E.g., Abers and Keck (2013); Ansell (2011); Berk and Galvan (2009, 2013). This work is inspired by earlier pragmatist scholars like John Dewey (1927; 2002 [1922]) and Hans Joas (1993; 1996).

[10] Policy scholars have long noticed that the stages of the policy process do not proceed linearly, but are iterative and interconnected (Hill 2009; Jenkins-Smith and Sabatier 2003; Sabatier 1986).

[11] Abers and Keck (2013, 17) call these practices "engagement," which occurs "when actors start connecting with other actors in their networks, using those connections to move resources and ideas around."

to first discuss why it is important to incorporate representatives of each local stakeholder group.

Pressure from Beside

Changing local rules, institutions, and practices is an inherently conflictual process. Coalitions of local, national, and foreign policy advocates identify individuals engaging in "bad" behaviors and pressure and persuade them to change. Inevitably, some individuals resist these efforts. To overcome resistance, transnational governance networks must be able to project power across network ties. This requires expanding governance networks (through network activation) to include organizations with the ability to influence resistant stakeholders.

As discussed earlier, the power available to governance networks depends on the mix of member organizations. There are multiple pathways for exerting influence, and different actors have access to different kinds of power. Transnational networks seeking to influence local policies and practices are more successful to the extent they incorporate a diverse array of local actors able to exercise multiple forms of power. One reason is that this allows governance networks to steer events locally by leveraging influence in multiple local arenas, including legal-political and social arenas, in both rural and urban parts of a watershed. A second reason is that applying global ideas locally requires the exertion of pressure from multiple sources in multiple arenas simultaneously. To understand why, it is useful to consider where pressure comes from in phase 2 and how this differs from conventional models of pressure in transnational politics.

Existing models of transnational politics focus on policy change at the national and international levels, and therefore stress the importance of pressure from "above" and "below." Pressure from "above" comes from more powerful external actors like states and IGOs, or the structural forces of globalization. For example, political and economic pressures from powerful states are credited with compelling governments in Latin America and elsewhere to adopt global human rights policies in the 1980s (Keck and Sikkink 1998; Lutz and Sikkink 2001; Risse et al. 1999). Integration into the global economic system compels governments of countries and megacities to embrace global policies associated with "good governance," including high levels of fiscal discipline and accountability (Kaplan 2013; Kaufmann et al. 2004; Mosley 2003). Pressure may also come from "below," for example when subnational groups mobilize to pressure national leaders or representatives of international organizations. Picture the antiglobalization rallies in front of World Bank offices around the world.

As chapter 1 discussed, however, global efforts to solve many local-cumulative problems seek policy change at the local level. These efforts often target grassroots actors with relatively weak connections to the global system, which make conventional models based on pressure from above and below inappropriate. Efforts to reform local watershed management are illustrative. Watershed stakeholders are typically grouped into three broad categories: members of local government (e.g., politicians and bureaucrats), landowners (e.g., those owning or using the land in the watershed—particularly in catchment areas), and water users (e.g., households, irrigation councils, and hydroelectric companies). In rural communities (the kind that exist in and around most watershed catchment areas), these individuals' connections to the global system are at best weak and indirect. Unlike leaders of states, megacities, or international companies, these actors are much less vulnerable to the forces of globalization or the political and economic pressure from above described in the literatures on transnational advocacy networks and norm diffusion. Threats of sanctions from foreign governments would ring hollow to smallholder farmers, if they were ever heard. Most poor farmers are unaware of the effects of capital flight from banks in far-away capital cities.

Sure, international organizations can provide and then threaten to withdraw economic aid and other "carrots." But the rural poor are skillful at exploiting outside resources for a time while maintaining the status quo or reverting back to it when these resources disappear. In the case of IWM reform, threats to withdraw funding do not pose serious consequences since a primary goal is to develop local revenue sources rather than rely on external donations (see chapter 3). Local stakeholders are often dismayed to find that there are few opportunities to extract external rents.

As chapter 1 noted, pressure from above by national governments is also frequently limited, whether due to a lack of political will, conflict among national policymakers and bureaucrats, weak state institutions, and/or neoliberal norms advocating third-party outsourcing of many government functions. Since local stakeholders exist at the most local level, there is also no pressure from below.

Under these conditions, when faced with resistance, transnational governance networks must rely on local supporters (i.e., local stakeholders who join the governance network) who can access local sources of power and are better situated to exploit resistant stakeholders' local vulnerabilities. Through the network activation strategies described earlier, local coalitions expand their governance network by recruiting members from each targeted stakeholder group and persuading them to pressure resistant members of both their own and other groups.

When successful, this creates a mutually enforcing circle of pressure, as illustrated in Fig. 2.3. In the case of IWM reform, for example, supportive local government representatives use their authority to pressure resistant landowners and water users to change their use of natural resources. They leverage coercive power through the use of ordinances, sanctions, and threats to expropriate land.

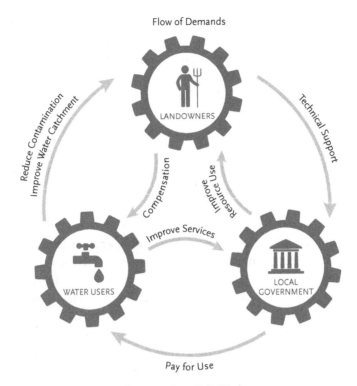

Figure 2.3 Pathways of Pressure from Beside in IWM Reform.

Supportive landowners use their control over natural resources to pressure resistant water users and local politicians to provide the material resources necessary for reform. At the same time, supportive water users use their economic clout and power of mobilization to pressure resistant politicians and landowners to improve their access to water-related services. In short, the pressure on resistant targets does not come from "above" or "below," but from "beside."[12] The leverage for exerting pressure from beside comes from the interdependence of local stakeholders and the fact that each can draw on different sources of power to exploit particular vulnerabilities of others.

[12] By "beside," I am referring to the fact that the actors exerting pressure on one another exist at the subnational level, rather than at the national or international levels. This does not deny differences in power that create hierarchies, particularly among individuals. It simply acknowledges that each of the targeted groups exists within the same level of analysis. While they may not be perfectly equal, they each draw on different sources of power that allow them to pressure the other groups. Lily Tsai (2007; 2002) similarly notes the importance of local, horizontal pressures by citizens, who use local social norms to hold local politicians accountable. The Ecuadorian cases of IWM reform build on this insight by examining the effects of multidirectional pressures among multiple local stakeholder groups that employ material as well as normative sources of power.

Given these mutual, self-reinforcing pressures from beside, the cogs in a clock provide a useful metaphor for the pathways of pressure in the second stage of grassroots global governance. In this metaphor, the clock represents the process of institutionalizing a global idea locally (e.g., implementing a local IWM regime) and the cogs represent the local stakeholder groups (e.g., those in each watershed). The main insight of this metaphor is that, like cogs, each local stakeholder group has to push the others to make the reform process advance. So long as each cog (stakeholder group) is in place and exerts pressure, the "clock" runs, meaning the IWM reform process continues. If one of the cogs is unaligned or stops working (i.e., one stakeholder group is not mobilized and fails to exert pressure), the reform process breaks down.

A coalition of local, national, and foreign policy advocates is like a clockmaker that synchronizes the cogs and winds the clock by creating the motivation and capacity to reform among influential members of all local stakeholder groups. There are two important lessons of the clockmaker metaphor. First, policy advocates must leverage the interdependencies among local stakeholder groups to exert influence. Second, the delicate balancing act required to maintain pressure from beside means advocates cannot focus on one stakeholder group at the expense of others. Mobilizing different groups sequentially is also risky because one of the groups may not yet be mobilized to exert pressure from beside at crucial points of the policy process, particularly the implementation phase. This is akin to throwing the proverbial wrench into the cogs and leads to a breakdown of the reform process.

Why Local Experiments Endure or Break Down

How do coalition members build the metaphorical clock? How do they expand their governance network locally and mobilize pressure from beside so that local experiments endure? And why do some experiments endure longer than others? The answers to all these questions lie in the combination of network activation strategies coalition members employ locally. Various combinations explain not only whether experimentation with institutionalizing global ideas endures long enough to succeed, but also at what stage of the policy cycle failed efforts break down (i.e., the breakdown points in phase 2 illustrated in Fig. 2.1).

For reasons discussed earlier, grassroots global governance theory argues that local experiments are more likely to endure when coalitions employ a frame-displacement strategy, and less likely when they employ a counter-framing strategy. The frame-displacement strategy is more likely to motivate local stakeholder groups to join the coalition, contribute their resources and efforts to the cause, and exert pressure from beside.

A second hypothesis is that local experiments are more likely to endure when policy advocates engage in a high level of network capacity building with all stakeholder groups. This allows coalitions to mobilize and combine the diverse array of resources and sources of pressure available to various coalition members and to direct these toward experimenting with unique institutional applications of global ideas. I distinguish between a high and low level of network capacity building, defined operationally by: (1) the amount of time and resources put into the capacity-building strategies described earlier (e.g., training and organizing local knowledge communities and creating new linking and governance institutions); (2) the number of local stakeholder groups which the coalition targets for network activation; and (3) whether the coalition takes a technical or participatory approach to information gathering and rule making.

Because building network capacity is a difficult, long-term process that requires sustained investments of time and resources, some coalitions engage in a low level of network activation. They spend little time, energy, and resources developing deep connections with a wide array of stakeholder groups. Rather than spending years training and organizing local knowledge communities and connecting them through linking institutions, some coalitions build and utilize ties with one or two groups seen as particularly instrumental. In Ecuador's IWM reform efforts, for example, some coalitions responded to resistance by landowners and water users by withdrawing from these groups and working primarily with local government experts and politicians. These coalitions gave short shrift to agenda setting and social mobilization. Instead, they focused on gathering information, formulating rules, and designing institutions. These activities were carried out by a small number of technical experts, usually from external organizations and the municipal government.

By contrast, other coalitions engage in a high level of network capacity building. They devote ample time and resources to training, organizing, recruiting, and ultimately incorporating into the coalition members of each major stakeholder group. These coalitions typically employ a participatory approach to information gathering and rule making as a network activation strategy. In this approach, a technical team formed by coalition partners collaborates with community members from each stakeholder group to identify problems, gather information, jointly analyze the information and assess needs, and then use this information to design new institutions and formulate rules. These activities typically happen in conjunction with the training and organizing of local knowledge communities and are structured by newly created linking institutions.

The expected outcomes for different combinations of strategies are shown in Table 2.1. I expect successful cases (i.e., those that endure) to be characterized by a frame-displacement strategy combined with high levels of network capacity building. This combination should produce a broad coalition comprised of

Table 2.1 **Explaining Outcomes during Phase 2**

	Frame-Displacement (Motivation)	Counter-Framing (No Motivation)
High Network Capacity Building	Successful Reform	Breakdown During Rule making
Low Network Capacity Building	Breakdown During Implementation	Breakdown During Political Agenda Setting or Social Mobilization

many different stakeholder groups with the motivation and capacity to maintain pressure from beside. In contrast, a counter-framing strategy combined with low levels of network capacity building (producing a narrow coalition) should fail at the initial agenda setting and/or social mobilization stages (the first two breakdown points on the process model in Fig. 2.1). This combination fails to mobilize one or more key stakeholder groups, undermining the process.

Other combinations should produce mixed results (i.e., breakdown at later points in the policy process). I expect high levels of network capacity building combined with a counter-framing strategy to produce breakdown at the rule-making stage. In this scenario, a diverse array of stakeholders is initially mobilized, but they reject proposed policies because they are perceived to conflict with local norms and the dominant framing of the issue in question. By contrast, the combination of a frame-displacement strategy with low levels of network capacity building should break down at the implementation stage. In this scenario, the motivation to reform is successfully cultivated among some targeted groups, but one or more key stakeholder groups are not incorporated into the coalition. This obstructs the simultaneous, mutual pressure among local stakeholder groups needed to sustain the implementation process. One or more of the cogs is not synchronized and becomes stuck, stopping the process.

Phase 3: How Local Experiments Drive the Evolution of Global Ideas

Phase 3 of grassroots global governance begins when local experiments are perceived as successful. Local experiments that endure long enough to produce innovative institutions and practices are frequently perceived as successful even before their outcomes are fully known. Research on the cognitive-psychological mechanisms behind decision making suggests this is because people use cognitive shortcuts, or heuristics, to deal with complexity and make decisions efficiently (Gilovich et al. 2002; Kahneman et al. 1982).

Two heuristics—representativeness and anchoring—are particularly important to policy diffusion, generally, and for explaining why some local experiments have global repercussions. As Weyland (2005, 24) explains,

> [the representative heuristic] leads people to see firm, clear patterns in a limited set of data. Therefore, they overestimate the importance of an initial stretch of success that an innovation may attain. Jumping to conclusions, they quickly emulate a seemingly promising innovation.

Due to the anchoring heuristic, people tend to accept and base future decision making on initial information. Early judgments about the success of policy innovations influence later judgments and limit subsequent revisions in people's evaluations. Therefore, local experiments that are labeled as successful early on tend to keep this reputation over time.

Because local experiments adapt global ideas to fit local conditions, the resulting institutional innovations reflect local norms and practices that sometimes challenge existing global ideas. In some cases, the difference is relatively small; local experiments produce minor tweaks to global practices. In other cases, the challenge to global norms is quite significant. In either case, successful local experiments lend credibility to local ideas about how to solve global problems. They provide "proof of concept" that an alternative to existing global approaches is not only possible, but practically viable. In phase 3, local norms and practices reflected in local experiments diffuse to the global level, where they challenge existing global ideas. In some cases, this either leads to the emergence of new global ideas or the evolution of existing ones.

Phase 3 paints a very different picture from conventional stories of how local actors interact with international norms through transnational activist networks. This is not a case where local actors frame their claims to fit with accepted international norms to gain international attention and support (Bob 2005; Tarrow 2005). On the contrary, grassroots global governance is propelled by local actors who are not satisfied with international norms and "who formulate alternative norms and mobilize to institutionalize them" (Martin 2011, 30). Nor is this primarily a story about "rooted cosmopolitans" building alliances with international actors at international meetings. Rather, international actors learn from their interactions with local actors at the grassroots level.[13] The contestation, experimentation, and learning that occurs between global and grassroots actors—through the process of trying to institutionalize global

---

[13] Research shows that social interaction produces learning in ways that impact institutional and normative change at both domestic and international levels (e.g., Abers and Keck 2013; Ansell 2011; Checkel 2001; Martin 2011).

ideas locally—leads some international organizations to alter their thinking and strategies for addressing global problems. Together with grassroots actors, they engage in network activation to scale up innovative local governance models nationally and internationally.

Global governance from the grassroots is fueled by an interactive effect between successful local experiments and network expansion, documented in recent studies of institutional change (Abers and Keck 2013; Ansell 2011). Local experiments initially have modest goals and involve few people and resources. However, when experiments are perceived as successful, they change ideas, relationships, and available resources. People gain confidence, new skills, and knowledge in the process. Successful experiments also attract wider audiences, making it easier to expand the network of people involved and the resources they commit. These factors combine to produce experimentation on a larger scale with more ambitious goals.

Phase 3 is therefore the mirror image of phases 1 and 2. It starts with a relatively small group of organizations (domestic and foreign) who advocate a new way to deal with global environmental problems based on local ideas, policies, and practices. These organizations use the resources at their disposal and the network activation strategies described earlier to influence organizations with which they have network ties, and which in turn have the ability to influence policy internationally. As these governance networks expand internationally, they carry local norms and practices to the global level where they challenge existing global policies and practices. These networks often become strong enough to influence global discourse surrounding a global problem. In some cases, they may even produce new global institutions and "best practices." In this way, innovative institutional adaptations of global ideas reverberate back to the global level.

Just as influential local actors are key to phase 2, success in phase 3 requires activating networks of organizations influential in international arenas. These include states, international NGOs, IGOs, expert networks, and multinational corporations. There are therefore multiple pathways by which local experiments can impact global ideas. In one pathway, domestic actors engage their national government, which partners with them in a campaign to institutionalize new norms, first nationally and then internationally. As the campaign moves to the international realm, the state becomes the primary coalition representative due to its unique power to influence international policy. Martin (2011, 31) describes this as a "counter boomerang effect." She shows, for example, how Ecuadorian activists allied with the Ecuadorian state to push a new global mechanism to pay for avoided emissions by keeping oil in the ground. The financing to avoid oil exploitation in Ecuador ultimately fell through. However, the international organizing and negotiating around

Ecuador's initiative did produce new international structures and mechanisms to pay for preserving the Amazon and other biodiversity hotspots in the
developing world.

Alternatively, lessons from local experiments may reverberate internationally by virtue of the transnational activities of the international actors involved.
International NGOs, donor agencies, academics, and others learn from their
local experience and consequently adjust their international programming.
Local experiments seen as successful quickly gain international recognition
through conferences and publications, prompting other international organizations to incorporate the new policies and practices into their own programming. This is, for example, how a local experiment with participatory budgeting
in Porto Alegre, Brazil, changed international actors' strategies for promoting
"good governance." After it gained international attention as a successful strategy,
numerous international NGOs, donor agencies, and IGOs worked to promote
participatory budgeting around the world. Since Porto Alegre's experiment in
1989, participatory budgeting has been implemented in more than 1,500 cities
worldwide.[14]

In addition to engaging states and changing their own global programming, transnational actors involved in local experiments also lobby IGOs to
change their policies and practices based on learning from these experiences.
This explains, for example, the World Health Organization's (WHO) decision to change their global strategy for combating tuberculosis (TB), known
as DOTS (Ansell 2011; Kidder 2009). Paul Farmer and other international
health experts learned, by working in local clinics in Haiti and Peru, that
DOTS had negative side effects. They worked with local partners to experiment with new strategies for combating TB without these side effects, and
succeeded. Farmer and his colleagues used their professional networks to
launch an international campaign to change WHO's global policy. While
their struggle was conflictual, they ultimately succeeded in persuading WHO
to adopt the new practices.

Sometimes, the evolution of global ideas does not originate from a single
local experiment. Rather, international actors simultaneously learn from multiple local experiments. When these point in a similar direction, they can have
a cumulative effect and shift international actors' thinking and practices. These
local experiments will inevitably vary in their details, since they operate under
different local conditions. International actors give them coherence by grouping
them together under a new global idea, or meta-concept. As Ansell (2011, 52)

---

[14] "Where Has It Worked?" Participatory Budget Project (website) www.participatorybudgeting.
org/about-participatory-budgeting/where-has-it-worked (accessed January 28, 2016).

explains, these global ideas, or meta-concepts, are "the boundary object around which local experiments accumulate and knowledge and experience is shared." Linking local experiments to meta-concepts with broad appeal is an example of how policy advocates use framing to activate networks in phase 3. It expands the audience that cares about local experiments by framing them as promising strategies for tackling problems of broader concern.

Sustainable livestock is a good example. During the 1990s, farmers across Latin America experimented with ways to make livestock production more efficient and ecologically sustainable. Each produced unique practices by improvising under different ecological, political, and socioeconomic conditions. Local NGOs formed around successful experiments and promoted these to international donors. In 1999, the UN Food and Agriculture Organization partnered with two such NGOs to create the Latin American Network on Agroforestry for Animal Production. This linking institution was formed to create international knowledge communities "through the exchange, training and popularization of knowledge and experiences."[15] In international discussions, these various local practices were grouped together under a new meta-concept "sustainable livestock." This new meta-concept facilitated collaboration among actors who were engaged in quite different practices, but who were attempting to address a similar kind of problem—deforestation due to livestock production. Sustainable livestock emerged as a truly global idea in the late-2000s, promoted by new international institutions like the Global Agenda for Sustainable Livestock.[16]

Just as attempts to apply global ideas locally are marked by contestation, so too are efforts to institutionalize local norms and practices at the international level. Whether or not they succeed depends on advocates' ability to expand transnational governance networks to include organizations with the motivation and capacity to influence international policies and practices. Even when efforts to replicate local experiments internationally do not succeed, the international organizing and contestation surrounding these efforts can change international discourse in important ways. In some cases, these efforts produce new international institutions and governance networks dedicated to a new global idea—like the Global Alliance for the Rights of Nature, the UN's Interactive Dialogues on Harmony with Nature, and the Global Agenda for Sustainable Livestock. And the cycle of grassroots global governance begins again.

[15] "Red Latinoamericana De Agroforestería Pecuaria." Centro para la investigación en sistemas sostenibles de producción agropecuaria, www.cipav.org.co/red_de_agro/red.html (accessed January 25, 2016).

[16] Global Agenda for Sustainable Livestock, www.livestockdialogue.org/en/ (accessed January 28, 2016).

Summary of Argument

In chapter 1, I presented the two questions motivating this book. First, when states fail to address a global problem, either through multilateral agreements or national laws, why and how do you nonetheless get things done on the ground? Second, how do ideas regarding the best way to tackle global problems evolve? I argue these two questions are linked because global governance of local-cumulative problems occurs through a cyclical process comprised of three phases: (1) the diffusion of policies and best practices from the global to the local level via transnational governance networks; (2) local adaptation of these global ideas and experimentation with unique institutional applications; and (3) the evolution of global ideas resulting from the reverberation of local experiments. Consequently, the process of getting things done locally partially drives the evolution of global ideas. This is why I call the process *grassroots global governance*.

The cyclical nature of grassroots global governance means that the answer to both questions lies in the ability of governance networks to ensure the process endures. Things get done on the ground when transnational governance networks successfully diffuse global ideas to particular localities and provide the necessary resources, pressure, and persuasion to ensure that experimentation with institutionalizing these ideas endures. Similarly, local experiments contribute to the evolution of global ideas when transnational governance networks diffuse lessons learned and new policies and practices to the international level.

Success in both instances depends on the ability of governance networks to expand by activating networks of actors who are influential in the arenas where contestation occurs at each phase of the process. Thus, the difference between success and failure depends on the network activation strategies employed by network members. Governance networks are more successful to the extent they: (1) provide information and employ frame-displacement strategies to motivate influential actors to join the network; and (2) engage in high-level network-capacity-building activities, particularly training knowledge communities and creating new linking and governing institutions. These latter strategies enhance a network's governance capacity by connecting various stakeholders, concentrating the distinct resources available to each, and providing a focal point for converting these into action. When networks do not employ these strategies, or employ some but not others, the grassroots global governance process breaks down at different points, as discussed earlier.

Network activation is crucial because of the need to shift arenas throughout the grassroots global governance process. Since each arena has a unique set of rules and resources, different arenas privilege different organizations. For this reason, power shifts within governance networks as the process advances. As power shifts to domestic brokers, they use this power to adapt global ideas to fit domestic realities. This is why global ideas evolve as the process advances. Because local actors have the greatest power to control events during phase 2, and this is the phase where global ideas are put into practice, they are influential global governors.

The remainder of the book shows how this works by comparing successful and failed attempts by multiple transnational governance networks to implement local integrated watershed management programs in Ecuador. After setting the stage in chapter 3, the subsequent chapters analyze the three phases of grassroots global governance in sequence, showing how the network activation strategies employed explain variation in outcomes at each phase.

3

Ecuadorian Watershed Management Reform in Context

On August 15, 1962, 13 members of the Salasaca indigenous group in Ecuador's Tungurahua province were shot to death by police as they took water from an irrigation canal. The police were acting on orders from a powerful local landowner who claimed ownership of the canal's water even though a 1960 water law made water a public good and guaranteed access to all farmers. The Salasaca massacre was but one of many severe water conflicts in Ecuador in the decades following the 1960s agrarian reform.[1] Conflicts were particularly common around Ambato, Tungurahua's capital, due to large water deficits and inequitable distribution. Contamination and the exploitation of natural resources, particularly in the páramos (high Andean grasslands serving as water catchment areas), reduced the quality and quantity of water. Water conflicts often had ethnic undertones since indigenous peoples tend to live in the páramos that collect water for the Ambato River, while mestizos (people of mixed European and indigenous ancestry) have historically controlled distribution through the canals that channel water for irrigation and consumption. By the mid-1990s, local communities, water user groups, and the province's three indigenous movements were highly divided over what to do. The municipal and provincial governments had done little to address the problem.

Just a decade later, community organizations, indigenous movements, local businesses, water councils, and local government agencies were collaborating to better manage the Ambato River's watershed resources. The three historically divided indigenous movements merged under a single organization to better address water resource issues. They worked with indigenous communities to develop community-level páramo management plans. Many communities living in the páramos agreed to limit their advance of the agricultural frontier, in some

---

[1] For details of the Salasaca massacre see Poeschel-Renz 2001; Zapata 2009. See Blankstein and Zuvekas (1973) for the history of agrarian reform in Ecuador.

cases relocating homes and animals to less fragile areas. Indigenous people living in the páramos and mestizos living below worked together both to protect and restore the páramos and to improve irrigation and production in lower areas. A Water Parliament was created to allow citizens, businesses, and NGOs to work together with government representatives to develop strategies for managing watershed resources in an integrated, sustainable manner. One result was the creation of a local fund to finance watershed management projects. The Fund for Tungurahua's Páramos and Fight Against Poverty was formed through voluntary contributions from water users, including indigenous farmers, the municipal water company, two hydroelectric companies, and the provincial government.

The extent to which Tungurahua's watershed management reforms changed long-standing land-use practices, sociopolitical relations, and local governance arrangements is striking. Yet, Tungurahua's experience is not entirely unique. During the 1990s and 2000s, dozens of similar local watershed management reforms cropped up across Ecuador and in countries as diverse as India, Philippines, Indonesia, Guatemala, Colombia, Kenya, and South Africa, among many others (Huang and Upadhyaya 2007; Porras et al. 2008; Smith et al. 2006). Each local watershed governance regime has unique characteristics owing to distinct circumstances. Yet, each implements in its own way the set of global principles and practices known as Integrated Watershed Management (IWM) described in chapter 1.

It is hard to appreciate the changes brought by IWM reform and the degree to which reform proposals challenged vested interests and engendered struggle without understanding the contexts in which they were pursued. This chapter sets the stage for the rest of the book by describing the local IWM reforms implemented in Ecuador and comparing them with preexisting watershed management practices. The first section describes Ecuador's national system for managing watershed resources during the 1990s, when transnational coalitions formed to promote IWM reform (i.e., phase 1 of grassroots global governance). Ecuador's system was highly fragmented through a complex and uncoordinated system of weak institutions and regulations. This meant that in practice decisions on how to use watershed resources were left to those living in and around watersheds.

Phase 2 of grassroots global governance involves efforts to apply global ideas like IWM at the local level. Therefore, the chapter's second section describes the local IWM reforms that were implemented in successful cases (i.e., those where phase 2 endured) to highlight how these reforms changed watershed management practices and governance systems. Of course, not all reform attempts were equally successful. The third section describes the degree to which IWM reforms were implemented in six cases and explains the methodology for measuring variation in outcome. In so doing, it identifies both the cases where the grassroots global governance process endured through phase 2 and the points in the process where failed cases broke down.

Interestingly, success and failure did not correlate with local conditions. This is surprising given that the literature on common pool resources emphasizes the importance of local environmental, demographic, and socioeconomic conditions to explain the creation of local governance systems that sustainably manage natural resources.[2] Subsequent chapters show that success and failure is instead explained by the network activation strategies used by IWM advocates (discussed in chapter 2). The final section of this chapter sets the stage for discussions of network activation in phase 2 by describing the various local conditions in which IWM reforms were attempted. It introduces the six case study locations, including the various environmental and socioeconomic conditions and stakeholders involved, as well as the distinct environmental problems they faced. In so doing, the chapter shows that IWM reform attempts succeeded under varied local conditions, even as other attempts failed under similar conditions.

Ecuador's Weak, Fragmented Watershed Management Regime

Ecuador's experience with watershed management in the late twentieth century (the eve of global IWM reform efforts) was representative of most less-developed countries.[3] Authority for managing watershed resources was centralized but fragmented through a complex and uncoordinated system of institutions and regulations, each responding to a different sector. Different government agencies were responsible for managing potable water and sanitation services, national irrigation systems, hydroelectric projects, and other water-related issues, from aquaculture to recreation to navigation. Complicating matters, regional development corporations were created in the 1990s to oversee water infrastructure projects. And this was just for water, which is but one of a watershed's many natural resources. A host of other institutions were responsible for additional resources, like forests, soil, biodiversity, and minerals.

---

[2] For summaries, see Agrawal (2002); Dinar et al. (2005); Leach and Pelkey (2001); Ostrom (1990); Sabatier et al. (2005); Wade (1988). Propitious conditions include institutional arrangements (e.g., clear rules and ability to sanction violators); characteristics of local social groups (e.g., group size, mobility, interdependence among group members); characteristics of the natural resource system (e.g., size, definition of boundaries); and external structural conditions (e.g., state of technology; relationships with the state).

[3] See Vallejo (2008) and Boelens et al. (2015) for the historical evolution of water management in Ecuador.

This fragmented system produced a duplication of responsibilities, resulting in much confusion, little coordination, and a lack of accountability. The issue of water quality provides a telling example. Ecuador's Water Resources Council was created in 1994 to centralize planning and administration. But responsibility for water quality remained disbursed among the Ministry of Agriculture (for agricultural waste), various environmental agencies (for industrial discharge), and the Ministry of Energy and Mines (for hydrocarbon pollution). Enforcement of national water quality standards fell to municipal governments, since they provided drinking water.

Duplicating responsibilities across scale as well as sector added to the problem. Different laws assigned responsibility for watershed management to provincial governments, the forest service within the Ministry of Agriculture, and regional development corporations. A lack of coordination and capacity meant that important aspects of watershed management were simply ignored. As a 2004 review notes, "in practice, few [watershed management] activities are implemented at the ministerial or provincial level, and there is little or no coordination with the development corporations or municipalities to address watershed issues" (Echavarria et al. 2004, 10). In other words, while authority legally lay with central government authorities, the weakness of central government institutions and confusing regulatory structure meant most decisions on how watershed resources were used ultimately lay with local stakeholders.

Yet, municipal governments also played only a limited role in managing watershed resources, largely due to unclear lines of authority and limited capacity. Their main responsibility was providing water and sanitation services in urban areas. Municipal governments were therefore among the first to feel the effects of deteriorating watershed ecosystems on water quantity and quality. Yet, managing watersheds' rural areas, including water catchment areas, was traditionally seen as outside their purview. Most local governments had never developed the capacity to manage watershed ecosystems, and many were not sure they had the authority to do so. Before the mid-1990s, provincial and municipal governments lacked an agency responsible for environmental management. They also lacked a strategy for land use planning and agricultural development policies designed to alleviate watershed degradation. There was little environmental awareness, insufficient planning and political support, and little coordination among institutions, whether public or private (IEDECA 2006b, 13–15).

To summarize, watershed resources were not managed in a centralized or integrated fashion, but simply used by various groups of people living in and around watersheds. Most used these resources much as their ancestors had done for decades or even centuries. Smallholder farmers deforested the land to raise livestock and crops. In dry areas, they relied on decades-old, hand-dug canals to bring water for irrigation. Some families supplemented their income through logging, mining, or fishing. Households and businesses used the watershed to absorb their waste, dumping it directly into rivers and streams. In many places, hydroelectric projects added to these more traditional demands. By 1997 hydro power plants generated 55% of Ecuador's electricity (Salazar and Rudnick 2008, 1). These and similar practices created a variety of problems, including deforestation, biodiversity loss, soil degradation, declines in water quality and flow, and conflict over access to watershed resources (e.g., water, land, trees, minerals, etc.).

The specific problems faced in each watershed varied by the type of ecosystem, demographic patterns, and economic activities (described in subsequent sections). In each case, however, some local stakeholders became concerned and looked for solutions. Chapter 5 describes how local activists connected with outsiders advocating IWM reform as the best solution and allied with them to promote IWM reform locally. This marked the beginning of phase 2 of grassroots global governance. However, the proposed reforms required changing land use practices and creating new systems for governing watersheds in an integrated manner. The next two sections describe the key changes associated with local IWM reform and the degree to which they were implemented in the book's six case studies (i.e., the degree to which phase 2 of the grassroots global governance process endured).

How IWM Reform Changed Local Watershed Management

Chapter 1 described the principles and practices associated with the global idea IWM. Among these was the principle of subsidiarity—the idea that watershed management should be decentralized to the local level to allow for meaningful participation by local stakeholders and a flexible approach tailored to the unique needs of each watershed ecosystem. This principle was one reason transnational IWM networks promoted IWM reform at the local level. Because local watershed management institutions were lacking, IWM reform required creating new governance arrangements and institutions. Through these institutions, local government authorities, landowners, water users, and other interested groups were to collaboratively manage watershed resources according to watershed management plans that viewed watersheds as complex ecosystems and treated its component parts as integrated. Given the fragmented nature of Ecuador's preexisting watershed management regime, getting to this point required several significant changes in the way decisions were made.

Perhaps the biggest change seen in cases of successful IWM reform was that watershed stakeholders managed watershed resources through a collaborative process that relied on consensus decision making. This process was structured by new participatory decision-making institutions comprised of local government authorities, those that live or work in the areas where ecosystem services are produced (e.g., water catchment areas) and various beneficiaries of ecosystem services (e.g., water and irrigation councils, farmers associations, indigenous and environmental movements, municipal water companies, hydroelectric companies, households, etc.). Examples of participatory decision-making institutions include Tungurahua's Water Parliament, El Chaco's Environmental Management Committee, and Celica's Environmental Services Committee (discussed in chapters 6 and 7). Through these new governance institutions, local stakeholders jointly identified needs, set priorities and action plans, and oversaw watershed management activities.

A second change was that stakeholders made decisions based on both traditional knowledge and new technical knowledge of how each watershed functioned. To do this, they gathered information on the watershed's physical features, climate, soil and water systems, plant and animal communities, land use, demographics, as well as the values and economic activities of the communities living there. They identified the various uses of watershed resources, the stakeholders using them, the problems with ecosystem functioning, and the obstacles to stakeholders realizing their goals. Local stakeholders then used this information to identify the nature and scope of problems, set future resource use targets, and design specific projects meant to promote the well-being of both the watershed ecosystem and local communities. This required reconciling competing political, cultural, technical, and economic considerations—no small feat.

Achieving consensus on a watershed management plan and related projects was only the first hurdle. Implementing the plan required overcoming other obstacles. Not the least of these were the problems of changing long-standing land-use practices and financing projects. To deal with the financing issue, IWM advocates created financing mechanisms in which local stakeholders paid into funds used to finance watershed management activities identified in watershed management plans. Examples include The Fund for Tungurahua's Páramos and Fight Against Poverty and the Environmental Services Funds created in El Chaco and Celica.

While often referred to as "payment for ecosystem services," these financing mechanisms included a much broader array of instruments for regulating watershed ecosystem services.[4] They varied in terms of the source of funds (e.g.,

---

[4] For definitions of payment for ecosystem services and its relation to other financial instruments for regulating ecosystem services, see Cordero (2008); Porras et al. (2008); Wunder (2008).

obligatory environmental taxes vs. voluntary contributions), the structure of the mechanism (e.g., trust funds vs. municipal bank accounts), and the array of expenditures allowed. Expenditures ranged from providing cash or in-kind compensation to landowners in exchange for restoring water catchment areas to financing economic development projects, conservation and reforestation projects, land purchases for conservation, and environmental education and training campaigns.

Despite these differences, Ecuador's financing mechanisms all share two characteristics. First, they are all local in that they draw on local sources of revenue and are controlled by local stakeholders. They assign a value to a watershed's ecosystem services, and local beneficiaries pay to protect these services. Beneficiaries may include water users, environmentalists who value a watershed's biodiversity, indigenous groups who value watershed resources for their spiritual significance, or any other group that values functioning watersheds. Second, the financing mechanisms provide a stable source of funding for IWM activities, making them less dependent on the vagaries of outside donors. This financial stability comes either from a permanent environmental tax (e.g., levied on water use) and/or interest income from a capitalized trust fund.

Arguably the biggest changes brought by successful IWM reform, however, were the changes to long-standing land-use practices and economic activities. Projects to conserve and restore water catchment areas required smallholder farmers to remove crops and animals from significant portions of their land. Many farmers switched to more ecologically friendly economic activities. In some cases, whole households and farms relocated to less fragile areas. Restrictions were placed on logging, the burning of forest and páramo vegetation, and various forms of pollution. Throughout each watershed, areas along the banks of rivers and streams were fenced off to prevent pollution from animals, households, and industry, as well as to allow vegetation to regenerate in order to reduce sediment runoff. Education campaigns were launched to encourage and teach people how to use water more efficiently and reduce pollution. Water users and other beneficiaries of watershed ecosystem services paid more to finance all these activities.

In addition to the participatory decision-making and financing institutions, new administrative systems were created to support the changes just described. Systems for monitoring compliance and sanctioning violators were created to increase transparency and build trust. All of these changes were backed by voluntary, written community agreements, legal contracts among stakeholders, and/or municipal ordinances, which provided the basis for resolving conflicts. Finally, systems for monitoring the restoration of vegetation, soil, and water flow and quality were created. Improvements in ecosystem functioning come slowly.

Nevertheless, stakeholders in each of the successful cases have documented improvements in the quantity and/or quality of vegetation, soil, and water in critical areas.

Measuring the Success of Local IWM Reform

The extent to which these changes were implemented varied among the six Ecuadorian cases. IWM reform is a process that takes time; new watershed management systems are built over years, not days. In some cases, this process endured long enough to achieve all of the desired conditions. In other cases, the process lasted long enough to create some conditions, but broke down before new governance arrangements were fully functional. In some cases, IWM reform efforts never got off the ground. Reform "success" is therefore a function of whether the local IWM reform process (i.e., phase 2 of grassroots global governance) endures or not.

To measure this in the Ecuadorian cases, I developed an index of 15 indicators based on four concepts commonly used to measure the quality of governance: consensus, inclusiveness, effectiveness, and sustainability.[5] The indicators reflect a series of conditions that are realized as a case advances through phase 2 of the grassroots global governance process (see Fig. 2.1): problems are defined and are placed on the agendas of consequential political and social groups; strategies and plans for solving the problem are created; new governance institutions are designed; and finally these institutions and plans are implemented.

Using the index, I scored the six Ecuadorian cases on a scale ranging from 0 (low success) to 15 (high success). A higher score means a case reached a later stage in the IWM reform process. As Table 3.1 shows, Tungurahua, Celica, and El Chaco were successful in that new IWM governance institutions and action plans were implemented and functioned as intended. Tungurahua is the only case where an initial IWM reform effort broke down but a subsequent effort succeeded (see chapter 7). For the three unsuccessful cases, the lower the score, the earlier in the process reform efforts broke down. Efforts in both Ibarra and

---

[5] These measurements are consistent not only with those found in studies of watershed management (Ostrom 1999; Peña and Solanes 2003; Sabatier et al. 2005), but also with indicators used by scholars studying local governance in general. Effectiveness is at the core of most definitions of good governance (e.g., Crook and Manor 1998; Grindle 2007; World Bank 2007). Consensus and inclusiveness capture the elements of responsiveness, participation, deliberation, and equitable distribution of resources that are included in most definitions of democratic governance (Avritzer 2009; Fung and Wright 2003; Grindle 2007; Moreno-Jaimes 2007; Van Cott 2008). Sustainability reflects the recognition by these and other studies that local governance reforms are fragile and easily undone if not rooted in institutionalized mechanisms.

Table 3.1 **Measuring Success of IWM Reform**[a]

Governance Concept	Indicator	Tungurahua	Celica	El Chaco	Zamora	Ibarra	Pastaza
Consensus	General consensus among local authorities, water users, and landowners on broad principles and goals for watershed management (reflected in statements by group representatives and surveys).	1	1	1	1	0	0
Consensus	General consensus among local authorities, water users, and landowners on specific projects and work plans (e.g., work plans developed with broad social participation and endorsed by members of all three groups).	1	1	0.5	0.5	0	0
Consensus	Compensation for conservation agreements between local authorities and landowners exist for at least 20% of landowners in the prioritized areas of the watershed. This includes sales of land for conservation.	1	1	1	0.5	0.5	0
Effectiveness	Development of a relatively comprehensive watershed management plan with specific projects (reflecting planning capacity).	1	1	1	1	0.5	0

(continued)

Table 3.1 **Continued**

Governance Concept	Indicator	Tungurahua	Celica	El Chaco	Zamora	Ibarra	Pastaza
Effectiveness	Creation of a local financing mechanism with an initial capital investment (i.e., the institution exists and has funds).	1	1	1	1	0	0
Effectiveness	Implementation of the watershed management plan has begun, according to the timetable set forth in the plan.	1	1	1	0.5	0	0
Effectiveness	Abatement or prevention of point or non-point sources of pollution (e.g., fencing off streams, restricting animal presence and commercial waste).	1	1	1	1	1	0.5
Effectiveness	Restoration of vegetation, reforestation, and decline in deforestation in critical areas.	1	1	1	1	1	0.5
Effectiveness	A monitoring system exists with capacity to sanction violators.	0.5	0.5	0.5	0.5	1	0
Inclusiveness	Creation of a participatory mechanism linking various actors (e.g., local authorities, landowners, user groups) for decision making on watershed management; effort made to involve representatives of affected groups.	1	0.5	0.5	0	0	0

(continued)

Table 3.1 **Continued**

Governance Concept	Indicator	Tungurahua	Celica	El Chaco	Zamora	Ibarra	Pastaza
Inclusiveness	Members of local government, user groups, and landowners collaborate on key decision-making processes.	1	0.5	0	0	0	0
Inclusiveness	Members of local government, user groups, and landowners share responsibility for implementing watershed management projects.	1	0.5	0.5	0	0.5	0
Sustainability	Local actors make regular contributions to the local financing mechanism.	1	1	1	0	0	0
Sustainability	Local government ordinance allows regulation of watershed land use.	0	1	1	1	0	1
Sustainability	Watershed management well-institutionalized (institutional mechanisms exist for planning, implementation, monitoring, and evaluation of management projects, facilitated by trained technical experts).	1	1	1	0.5	0	0.5
Total Score		13.5	13	12	8.5	4.5	2.5

[a] Scoring rules: 0 = absence of criteria; 1 = presence of criteria; 0.5 = criteria are only weakly present or were present at one time but not sustained.

Pastaza broke down at the initial agenda-setting stage. While the indigenous group living in Ibarra's watershed catchment area took some unilateral efforts, IWM reform never made it on to the local government's agenda and the process soon collapsed (see chapter 5). In Pastaza, advocates got local authorities to buy in and design new institutions, but these remained empty paper reforms due to a lack of agenda setting with social groups. In Zamora, new institutions and an IWM plan were created and funded, but efforts broke down at the implementation stage. Chapter 6 describes the collapse of IWM campaigns in Pastaza and Zamora.

One interesting thing about Ecuador's successful cases is that IWM reform succeeded despite the fact that it seemingly went against the status quo interests of politically powerful actors. IWM reform is not just about improving efficiency, but achieving a more sustainable balance among competing interests. It requires new arrangements for deciding who gets access to resources like land and water, how much each person gets, and how they can use these resources. More important, these new governance arrangements expand the array of stakeholders who participate in decision-making. As a result, they inevitably challenge powerful interests and tap into long-standing political, class, and ethnic tensions. This is perhaps best illustrated by the way Tungurahua's IWM reforms resulted in marginalized indigenous groups assuming leadership positions within irrigation councils and dominating the new Water Parliament. This challenged the historical dominance of wealthier, mestizo landowners (described later).

Local Contexts of IWM Reform

It is tempting to assume that powerful actors were simply responding to extreme situations, like declines in water quantity and quality, and that variation in success relates to variation in local conditions. After all, the literature on common pool resources stresses the importance of local conditions for determining whether local communities develop governance systems for sustainably managing their natural resources. However, as Table 3.2 shows, both successful and failed cases varied on a range of local conditions cited as important in this literature. These include ecosystem characteristics, including the quantity of available water, land tenure and land-use patterns, the poverty rate, population size, and the degree of homogeneity. In addition, both successful and failed cases vary in their political organization (e.g., party affiliations among mayors, municipal councilpersons, and the national government); the level of social organization (e.g., the presence of irrigation councils, indigenous movements,

Table 3.2 **Select Case Study Characteristics**

	Tungurahua	Celica	El Chaco	Zamora	Ibarra	Pastaza
IWM reform results	Score: 13.5 Success after initial breakdown at rulemaking	Score: 13 success	Score: 12 success	Score: 8.5 breakdown at implementation	Score: 4.5 breakdown at agenda setting with politicians	Score: 2.5 breakdown at agenda setting with civil society
Capital city	Ambato	Celica	El Chaco	Zamora	Ibarra	Puyo
Canton population[a]	329,856	14,468	7,960	25,510	181,175	62,016
Region	Andean	Andean	Amazon	Amazon	Andean	Amazon
Watersheds targeted	Upper Ambato	Quilluzara and Matalanga	San Marcos, Santa Rosa, Linares, Sardinas, & Rumipamba	El Limón	Tahuando	Pambay and Puyo
Watershed size (miles²)	1,200	2	8	4	132	6
Ecosystem (catchment area)	Páramo	Dry Montane Forest	Cloud Forest	Tropical Rainforest	Páramo	Tropical Rainforest
Water scarcity	High	High	Low	Low	High	Low
Landowner location[b]	Catchment Area	City	Catchment Area	City	Catchment Area	City
Poverty rate[a]	50%	76%	65%	61%	40%	67%
Irrigation, water councils	Yes	No	No	No	Yes	No

(continued)

Table 3.2 **Continued**

	Tungurahua	Celica	El Chaco	Zamora	Ibarra	Pastaza
Farmers associations	Yes	Yes	No	No	Yes	No
Indigenous movements	Yes	No	No	No	Yes	No
Hydro-electric companies	Yes	No	Yes	No	Yes	No
Conservation NGOs	No	No	Yes	Yes	No	Yes
National park guards	No	No	Yes	Yes	No	No
Other key stakeholder groups	Local governments; municipal water companies; landowners (e.g., those owning or using the land in the watershed); urban water users (households & businesses)					
Key problems identified by local stakeholders	Water scarcity; unequal distribution; conflict over access	Water scarcity; unequal distribution; conflict over access	Threats to biodiversity; poor water quality; contaminated rivers	Threats to biodiversity; poor water quality; contaminated rivers	Water scarcity; unequal distribution; conflict over access	Poor water quality; contaminated rivers

[a] Source: 2010 Census, Integrated System of Social Indicators in Ecuador (SIISE), www.siise.gob.ec.
[b] Whether landowners live in the watershed, which affects their interest in and use of watershed resources.

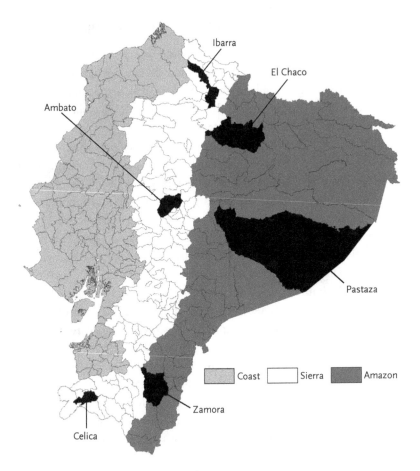

Figure 3.1 Map of Ecuadorian Case Studies.
Source: Author.

and environmental and farmer associations); and the stakeholders involved (e.g., whether hydroelectric companies, indigenous groups, and conservationists, among others, are present).

The Ecuadorian cases show that the outcome of local IWM reform attempts cannot be explained primarily by local power dynamics or other local conditions. Reforms succeeded in wildly different local contexts, yet some reform attempts failed under conditions similar to those of successful cases. I demonstrate this in the next sections by comparing the local conditions in the six case studies. The following description of the local conditions in which IWM reforms were pursued and the local actors involved sets the stage for the analysis of local IWM reform attempts in subsequent chapters. Because local conditions vary greatly between Ecuador's mountainous Sierra region and the tropical Amazon region, I examine regionally similar cases together.

Local Conditions and Stakeholders in the Andean Cases

The Andean cases include the most successful case, Tungurahua, and one of the least successful cases, Ibarra. Despite their diverse outcomes, Tungurahua and Ibarra are extremely similar in terms of ecological, demographic, socioeconomic, and political conditions. The third Andean case, Celica, shows how IWM reform succeeded under different Andean conditions.

In all three cases, IWM reforms targeted watersheds providing water to the capital cities of each canton (which share the same name as the capital cities). However, the size of these cities and the watersheds serving them vary greatly (see Table 3.2). Ambato and Ibarra are large, vibrant cities that double as provincial capitals (for Tungurahua and Imbabura provinces, respectively). While the rural hinterlands are important agricultural centers, the cities are industrial and transportation hubs for Ecuador. Not surprisingly, the watersheds serving them are relatively large. The Upper Ambato Watershed, for example, covers 1,200 square miles. In both cases, the water catchment areas exist high in the Andes Mountains (more than 11,000 feet above sea level) and consist of páramo— spongy, grass-like vegetation that captures and stores moisture from the air and regulates the flow of water to lower areas. By contrast, Celica is a small town of 6,611 people nestled in a remote area of Ecuador's Dry Forest ecoregion, sandwiched between the western foothills of the Andes and the Pacific Ocean. Its economy is predominantly agricultural. Most people have a few cows they use for both meat and dairy, and many also grow corn and/or coffee, which they export to Ecuador's major cities. The micro-watersheds serving the city cover just over two square miles.

Tungurahua and Ibarra share similar land tenure and socioeconomic patterns because both were shaped by Spanish colonial land systems. Throughout Ecuador's Sierra region, Spain granted its colonists rights to both land and the indigenous peoples living there. Over time, a feudal system emerged in which mestizo descendants of Spanish colonists owned haciendas (large plantations) worked by indentured indigenous workers, who were bought and sold with the hacienda. Indigenous families worked without salary in exchange for the right to farm small plots of land on the hacienda. This feudal system survived largely intact until 1964, when it was outlawed by the Land Reform, Idle Lands, and Settlement Act. In the 1960s, Ecuador's government broke up the haciendas and redistributed land. However, land ownership in the Sierra remained extremely unequal. In the 1980s, 80% of farms were small plots of less than 10 hectares; but these accounted for only 15% of cultivated land (Flores and Merrill 1989).

The local politics surrounding IWM reform in Tungurahua and Ibarra are shaped by this legacy of Spanish colonialism and the fact that for many indigenous rights activists the páramo has come to symbolize their historic struggle for access to land and water. Even after land reform, hacienda owners and their descendants retained large farms in the most fertile land, while indigenous families were given poorer land high up in the páramo. While the páramo is an excellent water catchment system, its soil is less well suited to agriculture. Nevertheless, indigenous families practicing subsistence farming tend to populate the upper areas of the watersheds. The more fertile lands in the watersheds' lower areas tend to be farmed by wealthier, mestizo families, although there are some indigenous communities there as well. Further down, the watersheds are populated more by mestizo families and become more urban.

In addition to land, access to water needed for irrigation was also unequally distributed in Tungurahua and Ibarra, partly because the system of irrigation canals and water concessions remained the same as before the 1964 land reform. Water canals were built with "ovals"—enclosed, circular distribution networks that branch off a main canal (see Fig. 3.2). Originally, an oval might have served a single hacienda. But after the land reform, multiple landowners relied on water from a single oval. Importantly, water concessions from the state were given to an oval as a whole. Decisions on how to manage water within an oval were made by water councils comprised of landowners connected by an oval. In practice, this preserved economic and ethnic hierarchies. Wealthier mestizo owners of large farms (often the descendants of hacienda owners) typically owned the land where the oval connected to the main canal, and therefore controlled the water that flowed throughout the oval. They occupied the leadership positions in water councils and dominated management decisions. This resulted in unequal distribution, with poorer, often indigenous, smallholders receiving less access to water.

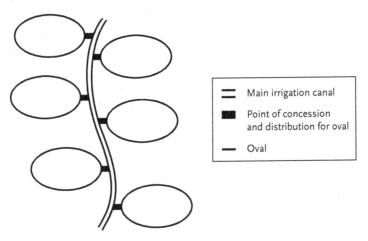

Figure 3.2 Andean Irrigation Ovals.

Because indigenous communities tend to live in the páramos, organized indigenous groups were important players in Tungurahua's and Ibarra's IWM reform processes. Most of Ibarra's watershed catchment area (the páramos of Angochagua) is populated by the Zuleta indigenous community, which is highly organized and owns and manages the land communally. The indigenous communities populating the much larger Upper Ambato watershed are also highly organized, but are represented by three provincial-level indigenous movements that are often divided over political and religious issues. The first—the Indigenous Movement of Tungurahua (MIT)—formed in the 1970s to support the indigenous struggle for land reform. The movement soon split in two amid leadership struggles. One movement retained the name MIT, while the other took the name Indigenous Movement of Tungurahua-Atocha (MITA). In the 1980s, the Association of Evangelical Indigenous Peoples of Tungurahua (AIET) formed to represent the growing number of evangelical communities. While all three movements represent Kichwa peoples, they compete as rivals in elections and often differ on policy. Each represents a different set of Kichwa communities in the watershed, creating an obstacle to collective action.

Of course, mestizo and indigenous farmers are not the only water users in Tungurahua and Ibarra. Thousands of businesses and households in and around the capital cities require water for consumption. In addition, Tungurahua relies heavily on hydroelectric power, and two hydroelectric plants generate power from water provided by the Ambato watershed. To a lesser degree, Ibarra also relies on hydroelectric power.

While Celica was also established by the Spanish in the sixteenth century, its land tenure and socioeconomic patterns differ from those in Tungurahua and Ibarra, mainly because the region's indigenous peoples migrated out after the Spanish arrived. Today, less than 1% of Celicans self-identify as indigenous. Rather, the canton is populated by mestizos whose families go back generations. Nearly half the canton's population lives in the town of Celica. Because of its small size and remote location (nestled high in the mountains and accessible only by winding dirt roads), Celica's families know each other well. There are neither the ethnic tensions nor strong class divisions you see in Tungurahua and Ibarra. Seventy-six percent of Celicans live under the poverty line, working mainly as smallholder farmers.

In contrast to Tungurahua and Ibarra, the families that farm the land in the catchment areas of Celica's watersheds do not live on their farms. Rather, most live in town and travel each day to tend their farms. Most of Celica's families cannot survive on farming alone, so the men migrate seasonally to Ecuador's coast to work on large-scale banana and shrimp farms at harvest time. They return to Celica to plant their own crops during the rainy season, since the vast majority of Celicans lack irrigation. Without irrigation canals, there are no irrigation councils to institutionally link water users. Nor does Celica have the hydroe-lectric companies or indigenous movements seen in Tungurahua and Ibarra. Indeed, Celica historically had very low levels of organizing among social groups (Bustamante 2004, 39).

What the three Andean cases did share was serious problems with access to water, which often produced conflict. Tungurahua's experience is representative. By the 1990s, demand for water was 40% greater than supply, creating a water deficit of 900 million cubic meters per year (IEDECA 2006b, 3). In addition, Ambato's water delivery infrastructure lost more than 50% of water due to leak-age. Highly unequal distribution exacerbated problems of access, particularly for poorer farming communities. As poor farmers found it increasingly difficult to subsist on their land, they advanced the agricultural frontier higher into im-portant water catchment areas. Burning páramo vegetation to convert land for agriculture exacerbated problems of soil erosion and reduced the ecosystem's capacity to store and release water. This was one of many reasons the flow of water in the watershed decreased an estimated 40 to 60% between the mid-1980s and 2000 (Mesa de Trabajo Provincial 2001, 4, 8). Government studies similarly estimate that the water flow to Ibarra decreased around 50% between the 1970s and late 2000s.[6] By the early 2000s, the amount of water available in the city of Celica was reduced to just two hours per day during the dry season (Cuenca 2008).

Another common feature of the Andean cases was that before IWM reforms were implemented, neither the national nor local political authorities had a strategic plan for addressing the water deficit, the inefficient and unequal distri-bution of land and water resources, or the resulting conflicts. In fact, the frag-mented national system for managing watershed resources exacerbated water conflicts. Lack of coordination and monitoring meant central government agencies issued concessions for more water than was available. By 2000, con-cessions equaled an estimated 150% of actual water amounts in Tungurahua (Mesa de Trabajo Provincial 2001, 15). In practice, the Ecuadorian state was not involved in day-to-day water management decisions; these were left to local water councils that controlled access to the canals. The central govern-ment only became involved when conflicts were brought to the national Water Resources Council to be adjudicated. More often, local stakeholders handled these matters themselves. This system privileged wealthy landowners and in-dustry heavyweights, like hydroelectric firms, who converted their economic power into local political power.

---

[6] University professor and member, Imbaburan Provincial Consortium for Water Resources Management (COIMBAGUA), interview by author, Ibarra, Ecuador, June 1, 2010.

Even when state institutions did try to intervene, their efforts were often undermined by a lack of local support. A failed reforestation project in Celica during the early 1990s illustrates the national government's limited ability to change traditional agricultural practices. Concerned by deforestation in the Dry Forest region, the Ecuadorian Institute for Forestry, Natural Areas, and Wildlife (INEFAN), planned a reforestation project. Lacking adequate resources, INEFAN contracted Ecuador's armed forces to carry out the project. The military implemented the reforestation program in a top-down fashion, without working with the local communities. Landowners resisted the program because it restricted the amount of land available for livestock and agricultural production. The military nevertheless carried it out. But when the military left, community members immediately cut down the newly planted trees and resumed their prior activities. This experience epitomizes many local stakeholders' resistance to changing their use of watershed resources, despite the problems they faced. This resistance was one of the major obstacles facing IWM reform across Ecuador and makes the successful cases all the more surprising.

Local Conditions and Stakeholders in Amazon Cases

There are many reasons to expect that IWM reform would be more difficult in the Amazon compared to the Sierra. There is plenty of water, so it should be harder to demonstrate the need for reform and cultivate a sense of urgency among local stakeholders. For a variety of historical and geographic reasons, most of Ecuador's Amazonian communities have fewer social organizations and less social trust compared to Andean communities (Lucero 2008, 147–48). This makes it difficult to organize collaborative efforts even if groups become motivated. The Amazon cases are particularly interesting because they show that IWM reforms can succeed under very different conditions, including those that can be considered unfavorable. El Chaco, the Amazon's most successful case, provides a stark contrast to Tungurahua. Yet, IWM reform attempts failed in Zamora and Pastaza, where local conditions were similar to those in El Chaco.

All three Amazonian cantons are largely rural with relatively small populations. Consequently, the watersheds providing water to the capital cities are also quite small. Another difference with the Andean cases is that the Amazonian cantons are situated in lush cloud or tropical forest ecosystems that are rich in biodiversity, roaring rivers, and spectacular waterfalls. In fact, El Chaco and Zamora contain some of the most biodiverse areas on the planet. Consequently, ecological preserves cover much of their territories. Eighty-eight percent of El Chaco falls within three of Ecuador's most important protected areas: the forest

La Cascada San Rafael, the Cayambe Coca Ecological Reserve, and Sumaco Napo-Galeras National Park (the latter two are part of Ecuador's Condor biosphere reserve). Most of Zamora falls within Podocarpus National Park (also a UNESCO-recognized biosphere reserve). While Pastaza province is also rich in biodiversity, there are no national parks in the canton Pastaza.

In the Amazon cases, IWM reform sought to address different environmental problems from those in the Sierra. Because water scarcity was not a major problem, local stakeholders were more concerned with poor water quality and threats to biodiversity, particularly in the ecological preserves. These problems stemmed from a common pattern of historical development. All three cantons are relatively new, established in the twentieth century, and were settled primarily by mestizo smallholder farmers who migrated from the Sierra region to convert the forests to pasture for livestock and tillage. This process continues today. Perceiving no limit to the agricultural frontier, many settlers in the Amazonian cantons farm the land until the soil is exhausted and simply move on to new land. This has spurred rapid deforestation in the watersheds feeding the cantons' capital cities.

Rapid deforestation put tremendous pressure on both watershed ecosystems and the cantons' limited physical infrastructure. Before the 2000s, for example, Pastaza had few paved roads and just one third of households had access to basic infrastructure like public water, sanitation, and electricity services.[7] As deforestation increased soil erosion, frequent hard rains increased sediment runoff, obstructing and overloading the water distribution infrastructure. This forced municipal authorities to turn it off, producing the ironic situation where the more it rained, the less water was available to city residents. The same occurred in El Chaco and Zamora. Locals in all three cantons also noticed with alarm the increased contamination of rivers, which are a center of social activity in the Amazon.

Land tenure and socioeconomic patterns in the Amazonian cases are also quite different from those in Tungurahua and Ibarra, due to their distinct historical development trajectories. The three Amazonian cantons are populated mainly by mestizo smallholder farmers who either settled the land since the mid-twentieth century or who later bought settled land. In 2000, each of El Chaco's 1,363 families owned 50 hectares on average, squeezed into the 12% of El Chaco's territory not protected as ecological reserves. Eighty percent of this land went toward raising cattle, 6% was used to grow subsistence crops, and 14% was forest that was fast disappearing (Yaguache et al. 2004, 6). In Zamora,

---

[7] According to Ecuador's 2001 census, 34.4% of Pastaza's households had access to Ecuador's Index of Basic Infrastructure (IMIB); data available online, Sistema de Indicadores Sociales del Ecuador, www.siise.gob.ec (accessed January 29, 2016).

agriculture accounts for 98% of the economy—mainly smallholder farmers growing coffee, sugar cane, oranges, and plantain.

Roughly half of El Chaco's families live on their farms in the watersheds' upper areas, while half live in the city below and commute to their farms. By contrast, in Zamora and Pastaza, most families that farm the watersheds' upper areas live in the cities below and commute to their farms. In each case, landowners living in the city supplement their income by working for local businesses or as teachers, firemen, and government employees. Some local entrepreneurs capitalize on the region's natural beauty by promoting ecotourism. Thus, the watersheds serve households and businesses by providing water for consumption as well as supporting economic activities like fishing and rafting. Residents also use the watersheds as a waste disposal system, discharging waste directly into rivers.

Because these cantons were founded as mestizo settler colonies, the three Amazonian cases lacked the extreme economic and ethnic divisions found in Tungurahua and Ibarra. However, they also lacked the Andean history of social organizing. This may be because of the strong individualistic ethic found in these cases, likely due to these being young cantons made of settlers searching for their own land. Regardless of the reason, there were few social organizations that brought stakeholders together around a common cause. Since rain was plentiful, there were no irrigation councils linking farmers. Nor were there producer or water user associations or indigenous movements. Despite the presence of ecological preserves, there were not even local environmental NGOs in the watersheds serving El Chaco and Zamora. Typically, the only civic association in a watershed was a gathering of "heads of family." This relative lack of civic organizing presented a different challenge for IWM advocates.

Another challenge was the lack of institutional capacity for regulating land use among national and local governments. Ecuador's central government had difficulty protecting the ecological reserves in El Chaco and Zamora. Settlers continued to deforest large areas for illegal logging, to expand the agricultural frontier, and for artisanal mining in the case of Zamora. As with many low-income countries, Ecuador's central government lacked the human, financial, and political resources needed to effectively monitor and conserve these areas. In the early 1990s, only a handful of local park rangers were assigned to protect the one million acres in the Coca Cayambe reserve. Their job was complicated by historically poor relations between local communities and INEFAN, the central government agency responsible for managing protected areas. INEFAN viewed local communities as a threat to the protected areas, while local communities viewed INEFAN as a threat to their economic interests (Ulfelder 1998). Ecuador's Environment Ministry, which replaced INEFAN in 1996, has had similar difficulties. By 2010, nearly 30 years after Podocarpus National Park was created, the Environment Ministry still had only delineated 60% of the park's boundaries.[8]

National and international conservation NGOs tried to fill the void left by weak state institutions. Several have been active in El Chaco and Zamora since the 1980s, working to conserve the biodiversity and integrity of the ecosystems in the ecological reserves. Over the decades, conservation NGOs worked with local communities to prevent deforestation and pollution. In El Chaco, they also opposed the Coca Codo Sinclair hydroelectric project. While this project does not draw water from the micro-watersheds included in this study, dam construction did negatively impact water quality and quantity for El Chaco's residents. On the other hand, the project provided jobs and electricity for some residents. The debate over hydroelectric power in El Chaco illustrates the tension seen in each case between the desire to exploit watershed resources to make a living and the desire to protect a canton's natural treasure.

Municipal governments were even less equipped to regulate land use than the national government. Before IWM reform attempts began in the late 1990s, municipal governments lacked a strategy for managing watershed resources or combating pollution. Indeed, Amazonian municipal governments struggled to fulfill their basic responsibility of providing reliable water and sanitation services. Pastaza's experience is representative. In Puyo, Pastaza's capital city, the water distribution system was frequently turned off. When water did come out of the tap, it was often thick with sediments. As mentioned above, part of the problem was related to land use in the watershed's catchment areas. Deforestation increased the amount of sediments flowing into the water distribution system, which was overwhelmed and shut down during heavy rains.

However, part of the problem was political. Candid politicians admitted to me that they had resisted fixing Puyo's deteriorated water infrastructure because they did not see it as politically advantageous. While public water service was poor, the municipal government subsidized 75% of the cost. Fixing the system would be tremendously expensive. Even if the municipality could raise the money, it would then have to charge people more for the improved service, which would be politically unpopular. Because the improvements would be underground, and therefore invisible, politicians feared they would not get credit at election time. Yet, they would certainly get blamed for the higher cost of water. Therefore, they perceived a political incentive to do nothing.

In this, Pastaza was similar to the other five cases. Local politics in Ecuador tends to be clientelistic. At election time, mayors feel the need to point to highly visible construction projects, like paved roads or recreation centers, that

---

[8] Ministry of Environment official representing Region 7, interview by author, Loja, Ecuador, January 20, 2010.

advertise they have "done something." While voters may complain about water-related problems, politicians often view the solutions as politically risky. Water catchment areas are not readily visible, and voters typically lack a clear understanding of how land use in upper areas affects water quality and quantity in lower areas. Therefore, politicians fear voters will not credit them for undertaking projects to improve conditions in these areas. Moreover, projects to improve watershed management and water delivery can breed resentment. Asking landowners to change their land use practices will likely be unpopular. So will asking water users to pay to finance improvements in infrastructure and ecosystem conditions. Because water subsidies were traditionally very high throughout Ecuador, most water users perceive water access to be inexpensive. It is common for Ecuadorians to fiercely protest price increases. For all these reasons, many local politicians perceive political incentives to not undertake dramatic changes in watershed management.

Conclusion

The descriptions of the six case studies show that transnational networks advocated local IWM programs as the solution to various types of problems, from water scarcity and conflict to pollution and threats to biodiversity. They also promoted IWM in watersheds characterized by different ecosystems and land tenure patterns, different arrays of stakeholders, and different demographic and socioeconomic conditions. In each case, IWM advocates sought to address these problems by replacing Ecuador's centralized but fragmented system for watershed management with decentralized watershed management regimes that took an integrated approach to watershed management. To this end, they worked to create new local participatory decision-making, financing, and administrative institutions that could design, finance, and implement integrated watershed management plans.

By comparing IWM reform proposals to the way watershed resources were previously used and managed, this chapter highlighted how IWM reform required significant changes to land use practices, which challenged vested interests. Given this, one might expect success and failure to be explained by preexisting power relationships and other local conditions. Yet, reform attempts succeeded under varied demographic, political, socioeconomic, and environmental conditions, even as some attempts failed under similar conditions. The Ecuadorian cases therefore highlight the need to look beyond structural conditions to the strategies of various actors to explain success or failure. The remainder of the book examines transnational efforts to promote IWM in Ecuador in order to analyze the interaction of strategy and structure throughout the grassroots global governance process. The following chapters show how variation in the network activation strategies employed explain whether or not the process endures through each phase, as well as the point where failed attempts break down.

4

Phase 1

National Network Activation

Efforts to build a global governance system around IWM principles took off in the 1990s when these principles were incorporated into the global sustainable development agenda.[1] The 1992 International Conference on Water and the Environment in Dublin was held to formulate sustainable water policies in advance of the 1992 Conference on Environment and Development in Rio de Janeiro. The IWM principles set at Dublin and subsequent international conferences soon made their way into state, IGO, and NGO development agendas. They were consolidated into Chapter 18 of Agenda 21, the action plan to promote sustainable development that emerged out of the 1992 Conference on Environment and Development. They were reaffirmed at the 2002 Johannesburg World Summit on Sustainable Development (United Nations 2002), and later included in the Millennium Development Goals (Third World Water Forum 2003). At the turn of the century, IWM was a dominant global strategy for achieving sustainable development.[2]

By the Second World Water Forum in 2000, a group of water experts and policymakers had shifted the focus of global discourse over water toward the need to improve governance systems (Turton et al. 2007a). They argued that the global water crisis was not about having too little water to satisfy needs, but rather a crisis of how to manage the available water resources. As a result, the Forum's World Water Vision and Framework for Action called for all countries

[1] Conca (2006) details the rise of integrated water resources management as a global idea and the formation of transnational networks to promote it.

[2] The emergence of a global IWM agenda did not mean there was universal agreement on either the value of IWM or the best way to implement it. Some academics and activists criticized the validity of IWM on social justice grounds (Conca 2006; Terán 2005). Critics from the developing world in particular argued that the IWM agenda was hijacked by powerful economic interests who used the language of sustainable development to advance their economic agenda at the expense of the poor (Goldman 2009; Terán 2005).

to enact comprehensive policies and strategies for integrated water resources management by 2015. The 2002 World Summit on Sustainable Development placed integrated water resources management at the top of the international agenda and provided specific targets and guidelines for implementing it worldwide (United Nations 2002).

With IWM recognized as an important mechanism for achieving sustainable development, many multilateral and bilateral development agencies and NGOs committed themselves to implementing IWM programs throughout the developing world. The World Bank, UN Development Programme (UNDP), and the UN Food and Agriculture Organization (FAO) served as critical network nodes for global organizing around the IWM agenda (Conca 2006). Each emphasized a different set of policies for implementing IWM, discussed later. Thus, during the late 1990s and 2000s, multiple transnational networks were promoting various IWM reform agendas in developing countries like Ecuador, with varying degrees of success.

This chapter examines phase 1 of grassroots global governance by comparing the ability of different transnational IWM networks to expand within Ecuador and diffuse their preferred IWM policies to the local level where they could be implemented. The chapter's first section describes three transnational networks promoting IWM programs in Ecuador, each linked to one of the three main nodes for global IWM organizing: the World Bank, FAO, and the UNDP. Each saw IWM as a way to advance different institutional goals, and therefore took a different approach to IWM and advanced a different policy agenda.

In phase 1, grassroots global governance theory explains why some versions of global ideas like IWM diffuse to particular localities while others do not. Part of the explanation is that a country's national context acts as a filter, affecting the ability of rival governance networks to expand and exert influence domestically. The chapter's second section identifies two sets of conditions that coalesced in the 1990s to shape the politics of IWM reform in Ecuador, and thus the opportunity for transnational IWM networks to expand. The first was the weakening of national government institutions, due to economic and political crises and neoliberal policies designed to shrink the government. The second was the rise of powerful indigenous and environmental social movements demanding changes to how natural resources were managed.

Navigating a country's national context is the first challenge for transnational governance networks and constitutes the first breakdown point in grassroots global governance. The chapter's third section shows how structural features of Ecuador's national context—including its institutions, sociopolitical alliances, and cultural norms—undermined efforts to implement IWM through national government policy. The section describes how ascendant social movements blocked the World Bank network's efforts to implement IWM through a new water law. It then shows how IWM advocates incorporated IWM reform into Ecuador's new environmental decentralization regime, only to have its implementation obstructed by political instability and opposition by national politicians and bureaucrats.

While IWM advocates were unsuccessful in Ecuador's national political arenas, this did not foreclose the possibility of local IWM reform. Grassroots global governance theory argues that a country's national context does not constitute a deterministic opportunity structure, but rather a kind of toolkit available to network members to construct strategies for action. The chapter's fourth section illustrates this by showing how FAO's conservation-focused approach to IWM allowed it to tap into networks of Ecuadorian indigenous, development, and environmental activists, using the network activation strategies discussed in chapter 2. Members of the UNDP's network similarly capitalized on popular mobilization against water privatization to organize Ecuadorian social movements around an alternative approach to IWM. However, doing so required them to adapt their approach to fit the norms and interests of Ecuador's dominant social groups.

By contrast, the World Bank network found Ecuador's social arenas as closed as its political arenas. Its approach to IWM focused on privatizing and creating new markets for water resources. Because privatizing and commodifying nature deeply violated the cultural norms of Ecuador's ascendant indigenous and environmental movements, the World Bank network could not activate domestic social networks to exercise power outside the national political arena. In essence, its influence was filtered out by Ecuador's national context.

Together, the third and fourth sections show how national context does not just affect the degree to which domestic groups mobilize against different transnational networks. It also affects the ability of foreign network members to tap into domestic social and political networks in order to shift arenas of contestation. In this way, the national context empowers some transnational networks and disempowers others. This, in turn, explains why some versions of a global idea like IWM are pursued domestically while others are not.

In tracing the domestic expansion of transnational IWM networks, the fourth section highlights the key role played by Ecuadorian professionals with strong ties to both foreign IWM advocates and domestic social networks. These Ecuadorian brokers guided the national network activation process. They created national networks of domestic IWM advocates by training local knowledge communities and organizing them through national linking institutions. These linking institutions were powerful sites for disseminating information, expanding network connections, increasing technical capacity through training, generating new ideas and collaborative initiatives, and mobilizing resources for advancing the IWM policy agenda nationally. Just as important, these national-level brokers adapted global IWM principles to fit Ecuador's national context.

The chapter's final section completes the analysis of phase 1 by tracing the expansion of transnational IWM networks, and thus the diffusion of IWM principles, to the grassroots level. The national network activation strategies employed by those transnational IWM networks not filtered out by Ecuador's national context produced two pioneering experiments with local IWM reform. These experiments presented distinct models of local IWM reform and catalyzed the formation of two rival national-level IWM networks, one tied to the FAO network and the other tied to The Nature Conservancy and the UNDP network. Each national IWM network was dedicated to replicating one of these distinct models of local IWM reform across Ecuador, including in the six case studies analyzed in this book. By tracing the relative expansion of rival IWM networks, the chapter shows how structure and strategy combine during phase 1 to explain why some approaches to IWM were pursued while others were not, and why specific models of local IWM reform were advocated in each of the book's six case studies.

Rival Transnational IWM Networks

During the 1990s, three main transnational governance networks worked to implement IWM programs in Ecuador. However, each advanced a different policy agenda based on distinct policy goals (see Table 4.1). One transnational IWM network centered on the World Bank, which like other international financing entities focused on increasing the efficiency of water distribution. Viewing IWM through the lens of neoliberal economic theory, network members stressed privatization, deregulation, and water markets as the best strategies. In the 1990s, the World Bank and International Monetary Fund pushed Latin American policymakers (including in Ecuador) to adopt new water management systems based on five pillars:

(a) privatization of water resources, rights and services so as to create tenure security, stimulate investments and generate efficient water use; (b) commodification of water resources, rights and services so as to create opportunities for trading them; (c) opening of markets and creation of market rules and mechanisms for selling and purchasing water rights and services; (d) reduction of the State apparatus and subsidies, drastic cuts on public spending, and withdrawal of direct State intervention from market transactions; and (e) deregulation and reorganization of the water governance structure, for example, decentralization and

Table 4.1 **Three Transnational IWM Networks in Ecuador**

Transnational IWM Network	Goal of IWM	Policy Focus
World Bank Network	Efficient Water Distribution	Privatize and commodify water resources; create markets for water rights and services; deregulate and transfer water management and administration to local governments and nonstate actors.
FAO Network	Sustainable Forest Management	Community forestry management programs that strengthen civil society organizations, promote social capital and participatory planning, and conserve natural resources through agro-ecological techniques.
GWP-ECLAC-GTZ Network	Agricultural Development	Conserve water catchment areas; technical improvements to irrigation and agricultural production; create participatory watershed governance institutions to mitigate social conflict.

transfer of water management and administration to local government authorities and non-State actors (Boelens et al. 2015, 4).

A second transnational IWM network emerged from FAO's watershed management efforts in Latin America. Given its institutional mission, FAO espoused a very different vision of IWM to that of the World Bank, one rooted in forestry and forestry-related hydrology (FAO 2006). With the rise of the sustainable development agenda, FAO adopted new goals, such as poverty reduction and environmental sustainability (Pérez-Foguet et al. 2005). Community-level forestry management, based on integrated natural resource management, became an essential component of FAO's poverty reduction strategy (Téllez 2008). Community forestry development programs were prioritized as the best way to implement Agenda 21's action plan for sustainable agriculture and rural development (Espinoza et al. 1999). FAO was appointed task manager for implementing Chapter 13 of Agenda 21, which deals with sustainable mountain development and is among Agenda 21's most extensive statements on watershed management (FAO 2006). Beginning in the 1990s, FAO oversaw a rapid, worldwide diffusion of community forestry projects that incorporated IWM concepts and practices.

FAO's community forestry projects reflected new norms in international development circles during the 1990s that embraced community-led, culturally appropriate, and environmentally sustainable approaches to development. The projects utilized new strategies in international development investment designed to promote socioeconomic change and "good governance" by strengthening civil society organizations (particularly among indigenous populations), promoting social capital and participatory planning, and conserving natural resources through ecologically friendly agricultural techniques. These were the policies at the heart of the FAO network's approach to IWM reform.

A third transnational network promoting a distinct vision of IWM in Ecuador was tied to the UNDP. It viewed IWM reform through the lens of agricultural development. A central node in this global IWM network is the Global Water Partnership (GWP). GWP was created in 1996 as a joint initiative of the UNDP, the Swedish International Development Agency, and the World Bank. GWP is a global linking institution, connecting IGOs, development banks, professional associations, research institutions, NGOs, and the private sector. Its activities initially focused on establishing regional Technical Advisory Committees as "start engines" for raising awareness of integrated water resources management in each region (Global Water Partnership 2010). The Global Water Partnership's South American Technical Advisory Committee (GWP-SAMTAC) was housed in the UN Economic Commission for Latin America and the Caribbean (ECLAC). Thus, the GWP network in Latin America centered on ECLAC.

When created, GWP-SAMTAC was staffed by water experts based in ECLAC's Natural Resources and Infrastructure Division. These ECLAC experts—most notably, Axel Dourojeanni, Miguel Solanes, and Humberto Peña—were highly influential in developing and diffusing IWM concepts among Latin American development specialists. Through conferences, publications, and personal consultancies, their ideas significantly influenced the thinking of water experts in Ecuador's public and private sector, as well as environmental and agricultural development NGOs.[3]

The influential role played by ECLAC water experts meant that GWP-SAMTAC's approach to IWM in Latin America was more in line with UNDP's mission of socioeconomic development, rather than the World Bank's focus on water privatization or FAO's emphasis on community forest management. This often translated into a greater focus on IWM as a response to problems of

---

[3] This point was frequently stressed during interviews with Ecuadorian water and development specialists. It is supported by numerous publications, including Burau (2002); Boelens and Zwarteveen (2005); Cabrera Haro (2008); Cremers et al. (2005); Crespo (2003); Global Water Partnership (2003). Influential writings by this team of ECLAC experts include Dourojeanni (1994); Dourojeanni and Jouravlev (1999); Dourojeanni et al. (2002); Solanes and Dourojeanni (1995).

agricultural production, including conflicts over access to water and reduced flows for irrigation. Writings by Dourojeanni framing IWM as a way to address water conflicts prompted many development NGOs and bilateral cooperation agencies to shift their focus from technical improvements of water delivery systems toward a holistic approach that incorporated the social component of resource management and linked the conservation of watershed resources to improved irrigation and production.

Another key member of this network was the German Organization for Technical Cooperation (GTZ; now GIZ), which partnered with ECLAC to promote development policies based on IWM principles throughout Latin America.[4] GTZ provided important connections between IWM advocates in the GWP network and national governments across Latin America. During the 1990s, GTZ closely consulted with many Latin American governments on their plans for state modernization, decentralization, and environmental management. As I describe later, GTZ attempted to use this influence to incorporate IWM reform into these plans.

Ecuador's National Context

Two sets of conditions coalesced in the 1990s to shape the politics of IWM reform in Ecuador, and thus the opportunity for these transnational IWM networks to expand. The first was the weakening of national government institutions, due to economic and political crises and neoliberal policies to shrink the size of the state. Like most Latin American countries, Ecuador embraced neoliberal policies promoted by international organizations like the World Bank and Inter-American Development Bank beginning in the 1980s. These policies included privatization, decentralization, and state "modernization" (a euphemism for state downsizing) as a way to improve government efficiency and shrink state expenditures to address the region's debt crisis.

Ecuador's neoliberal reforms in the late 1990s coincided with the country's worst economic crisis in history, which analysts attribute in part to the weakness of state institutions (Jacome 2004). The collapse of the banking system produced a financial crisis that in 1999 cost an estimated 20% of GDP (Hoelscher and Quintyn 2003). On the brink of hyperinflation, bank accounts were frozen and the economy was dollarized in January 2000. The loss of wealth and resulting job losses sparked the largest emigration wave in the country's history

---

[4] In January 2011, GTZ merged with German development organizations DED and Inwent to form GIZ. For information on the partnership between GIZ and ECLAC, see www.giz-cepal.cl (accessed January 29, 2016).

(Jacome 2004). The handling of the crisis produced accusations of government corruption, which triggered increasing social unrest and led to the ouster of President Jamil Mahuad in 2000. Mahuad was the second Ecuadorian president to be toppled in three years.

Political instability was a constant feature of the decade between 1997 and 2007 (the period when Ecuador's local IWM reforms were initiated). Three Ecuadorian presidents were removed through mass uprisings. None of the six presidents serving between 1996 and 2006 finished their term. This upheaval resulted in frequent ministry level changes that further weakened state institutions (Barrera 2007).

The second key feature of Ecuador's national context during the 1990s was the empowerment of indigenous, campesino, and environmental groups. Economic crises combined with neoliberal reforms to weaken the Ecuadorian state and political elites just as the country returned to democracy. This allowed historically marginalized groups to gain political strength and legitimacy (Bebbington et al. 1992). Indigenous and environmental movements emerged to play influential roles in Ecuadorian politics, generally, and IWM reform specifically.

Indigenous groups became one of the most powerful political forces in Ecuador during the 1990s. After years of regional organizing, indigenous groups from the Andes and Amazon agreed in 1986 to merge under the Confederation of Indigenous Nationalities of Ecuador (CONAIE, *Confederación de Nacionalidades Indígenas del Ecuador*).[5] While CONAIE is Ecuador's largest indigenous organization, two other national federations compete to represent the concerns of Ecuador's many different indigenous peoples. These include the National Federation of Indigenous, Peasant, and Black Organizations (FENOCIN, *Federación Nacional de Organizaciones Campesinas Indígenas y Negras*) and the Ecuadorian Federation of Evangelical Indigenous People (FEIE, *Federación Ecuatoriana de Indígenas Evangélicos*). All three sit atop national networks connecting local and provincial indigenous organizations.

In 1990, CONAIE led a National Indigenous Uprising, the largest in the country's history. Participants paralyzed much of the country for more than a week by blocking highways and occupying cities. The event helped unify Ecuador's diverse indigenous populations around a common political agenda that included legal recognition of Ecuador's nations, cultural autonomy, recuperation of land and water rights, environmental sustainability, opposition to neoliberalism, and a new development approach rooted in indigenous culture.

---

[5] On the history and politics of Ecuador's indigenous mobilization, see Andolina et al. (2009); Becker (2008; 2011b); Lucero (2008); Yashar (2005).

Over the next 15 years, CONAIE and other indigenous organizations repeatedly demonstrated their power by leading national "uprisings" (*levantamientos*) of indigenous peoples, poor mestizo farmers, and other disaffected groups. Spurred by their success, some indigenous leaders formed a political party known as Pachakutik to contest the 1996 elections. While the party was (and remains) controversial among indigenous peoples, some of whom question the benefits of working within the political system, Pachakutik's electoral success in 1996 was striking. It won 70% of the races it entered (Pallares 1997, 544). In 1997 CONAIE led a successful movement to oust President Abdalá Bucaram and force the convocation of a constituent assembly to reform the political system (Andolina 2003). By working inside the system through Pachakutik and outside the system through social movements, indigenous leaders were able to exert a great deal of influence over the resulting 1998 Constitution, which recognized Ecuador's many nations and expanded their rights.

Ecuador's indigenous movements were a dominant social and political force during the period of IWM reform. Despite divisions, they frequently used their capacity to mobilize indigenous and mestizo campesinos to great effect. Indigenous and campesino uprisings repeatedly forced Ecuador's government to renegotiate laws, toppled three presidents, and twice contributed to the rewriting of Ecuador's Constitution (in 1997 and 2007).

During this same period, Ecuador's environmental movement emerged as a second powerful social force. Ecuador's environmental movement developed around a conservationist agenda closely linked to the creation of national parks, an agenda that was strongly pushed by international environmental actors. During the 1970s a number of IGOs, NGOs, and development agencies launched a transnational campaign to protect tropical forests in Latin America.[6] These organizations promoted the creation of national parks as a way to balance human resource use and environmental protection (IUCN 1980). Ecuador's first environmental NGO, Fundación Natura, was created in 1978, two years after Ecuador created its National System of Protected Areas. Fundación Natura grew rapidly due to grants from USAID and The Nature Conservancy as well as money from debt-for-nature swaps engineered by the World Wildlife Fund (WWF). During the 1990s, the number of Ecuadorian environmental NGOs exploded, fueled by a growing interest in conservation and a desire to access external resources (Ortiz Crespo 1998).

Ecuador's environmental movement is divided between those that work with mainstream international conservation NGOs, like The Nature Conservancy

---

[6] Participating institutions included the World Bank, FAO, the International Union for Conservation of Nature and Natural Resources, The Nature Conservancy, WWF, and U.S. Agency for International Development, among others.

and WWF, and more radical organizations that criticize their tolerance of market-based approaches and the exploitation of natural resources, however "green" these may be. Radical NGOs like Acción Ecológica oppose a development strategy based on the privatization, marketization, and exploitation of natural resources, blaming these for both environmental degradation and social inequality. They advocate instead a development strategy based on environmental justice, the rights of nature, coexistence with the land, and the Andean indigenous "cosmovision" of the universe. Since its founding in 1986, Acción Ecológica has mobilized popular opposition to industrial mining, logging, and oil exploitation, particularly in the Amazon rainforest, as well as attempts to privatize water. In this, it found common cause with Ecuador's powerful indigenous movement. The alliance between urban environmental groups and indigenous and campesino organizations made Ecuador's environmental movement one of the strongest in Latin America.

Failed Network Activation in National Political Arenas

Amid the above conditions, international IWM advocates initially contested IWM principles and policies in national political arenas. The international organizations at the center of the transnational IWM networks described earlier already had ties to Ecuadorian policymakers, forged through previous contracts and international meetings. They naturally tried to leverage these ties to incorporate IWM principles and practices into Ecuadorian law and government policy. However, Ecuador's national context made Ecuador's national legislature and executive agencies ineffective arenas for implementing local IWM reform. To illustrate, this section examines failed efforts to implement IWM through new national water and decentralization laws and policies.

Pursuing IWM Through New Water Legislation

In the early 1990s, the World Bank and its allies used the resources at their disposal, particularly the financing of Ecuador's debt, to pressure Ecuadorian policymakers to adopt their preferred IWM policies through a new water law. The World Bank made new loans to Ecuador conditional on its acceptance of a water law modeled on Chile's 1981 Water Code, which effectively privatized water by creating a market for tradable water use rights (Donoso Harris 2003). The World Bank even hired Chilean technical experts to train Ecuadorian policymakers on how to design the system (Boelens et al. 2015).

In 1994, Ecuador's government approved the Agrarian Development Law, which introduced several changes to the 1972 Water Law. The Agrarian Development Law and related executive decrees expanded the potential for private sector participation in water management and created a more decentralized structure. With World Bank support, the Ecuadorian government decentralized administrative responsibilities to 12 Regional Water Authorities and transferred management of some national irrigation systems to newly created water user associations. Most important, the Agrarian Development Law put into question the public nature of water guaranteed by the 1972 Water Law. It created a registry of water rights (concessions granted by the state) based on property titles and allowed water rights to be automatically transferred when land was sold or inherited. Furthermore, it provided water rights in perpetuity, making it like private property.[7]

The Agrarian Development Law and possible opening of a Chilean-style water market prompted widespread social protest. Ecuador's three national indigenous movements led a national protest, which they labeled a "Mobilization for Life," to block the law's implementation. Hundreds of thousands of people from more than 3,500 indigenous, campesino, and other popular organizations blocked the country's roads, paralyzing the country and bringing commerce virtually to a halt for two weeks. After enduring military repression, the protesters forced the government into negotiations and eventually achieved significant revisions to the law, including keeping water ownership public (Andolina 1999; 1994).[8]

The ferocity of social protest and criticism of the government kept the World Bank's proposals for water privatization and related land reform from being implemented. The World Bank's influence waned considerably over the following decade as Ecuador's state weakened while its social movements grew in strength. The latter's anger toward neoliberal economic policies, from water privatization to free trade to industrial oil exploitation in the Amazon, was fueled by the perception that these were enriching corrupt Ecuadorian elites and foreigners while Ecuadorian society paid a horrible price, both economically and environmentally. Three times between 1997 and 2005 social uprisings toppled Ecuadorian governments and demanded governance changes. The experience of Lucio Gutierrez, the third president to be ousted, is telling. Having risen to

---

[7] By contrast, the 1972 Water Law had fixed time periods for water concessions, such as 10 years for irrigation. For the history of water laws and reform in Ecuador, see Boelens et al. (2015); Vallejo (2008); Zapata (2005).

[8] Other key changes included: (1) allowing communitarian and cooperative forms of agrarian organization to continue; (2) privileging food production for internal consumption; and (3) recognizing indigenous agricultural knowledge and respect for the cultural and social values of indigenous and campesino farmers.

power via indigenous support, CONAIE soon broke with Gutierrez after he signed a Letter of Intent with the IMF pledging to, among other things, "privatize the petroleum sector, electricity, telecommunications, and natural resources like water."[9] Experiences like these kept Ecuador's social movements vigilant against the pressures of international financial institutions and signaled a warning to aspiring Ecuadorian politicians.

In 2006, Rafael Correa was elected president after tapping in to this social anger. Leading a social movement called Alianza PAIS (Proud and Sovereign Fatherland Alliance), Correa initially gained the support of indigenous, environmental, and other social movements based on campaign promises to restore Ecuador's political sovereignty, protect the environment, and provide economic relief to Ecuador's poor, all by reversing the neoliberal agenda of the 1990s. Shortly after taking office in 2007, Correa demonstrated his popular credentials by expelling the World Bank's representative and threatening to remove the World Bank and the IMF from the country. That same year, a constituent assembly wrote a new constitution (passed in 2008) that, among other things, specifically prohibits the privatization of water, declares water access a human right, and recognizes both public and community water management.

Despite its significant economic resources, the World Bank network was blocked by historically marginalized groups within Ecuadorian society. These groups effectively closed the national political/legal arena as a space through which the World Bank and its network members could project power locally. It is a powerful example of how national context filters the ability of transnational governance networks to govern domestically.

Pursuing IWM Through Environmental Decentralization Legislation

A second attempt at national political network activation occurred when members of both the transnational forest conservation network and the GWP-ECLAC-GTZ network tried to implement IWM programs through Ecuador's environmental decentralization laws. By 1997, decentralization dominated Ecuador's national agenda due to pressure from above and below. The country's worsening economic situation led several Ecuadorian provinces to call for autonomy. The indigenous uprisings grew to include other social groups demanding expanded rights, economic justice, and participation in the political process. International and domestic proponents advocated decentralization as a

[9] Letter from CONAIE, available online at www.en-camino.org/node/13 (accessed February 13, 2016).

way to both ease the state's fiscal burdens while increasing democracy through expanded social participation in public policy.

The country's framework for decentralization was codified in a series of laws, including the 1997 Decentralization and Social Participation Law (*Ley de Descentralización y Participación Social*), the 1997 Law of 15% (*Ley de 15 percent*), and the 1998 Constitution. Ecuador's decentralization regime had the unusual condition of making decentralization obligatory for the state and voluntary for local governments. This meant that local governments chose whether or not to request decentralization in one or more of 10 areas.[10] Of the 10 sectors eligible for decentralization, the environment (which included watershed management) received the greatest number of requests from municipal governments—77, compared to 107 requests for the other nine sectors combined (López 2005, 85–86). The central government was legally obliged to transfer related responsibilities and resources following a period of negotiation.

Ecuador's environmental decentralization process effectively began in 1998 when President Jamil Mahuad tapped long-time environmental activist Yolanda Kakabadze to be environment minister. Kakabadze was both a founder of Ecuador's environmental movement and a leader in the transnational conservation network. Before serving as Ecuador's Environment Minister, Kakabadze was President of the International Union for Conservation of Nature (IUCN), "the world's oldest and largest global environmental network."[11] Among Kakabadze's first steps was to oversee the passage of Ecuador's 1999 Environmental Management Law, which called for the creation of a National, Decentralized System for Environmental Management. This reflected the prevailing wisdom in international conservation and development circles that decentralization and local citizen participation were the best way to effectively and efficiently manage natural resources.

Kakabadze had strong ties with local and international NGOs and donor agencies, many of which advocated IWM as a sustainable development strategy. Given the Environment Ministry's limited human, technical, and financial resources, she asked these IWM advocates to help design Ecuador's environmental decentralization process. While many international IWM advocates were involved, GTZ played a particularly influential role. Ecuador's government contracted GTZ to provide technical assistance on decentralization and natural

---

[10] These included agriculture, environment, social welfare, economy, education, health, tourism, transportation, housing, and roads and airports (López 2005). See Frank (2007) for the origin of Ecuador's unique decentralization regime.

[11] See www.iucn.org/about (accessed March 14, 2016). IUCN's membership includes "more than 1,000 government and NGO member organizations, and almost 11,000 volunteer scientists in more than 160 countries."

resource management, and GTZ became a close advisor. In 1998, GTZ established its Watershed Management Project, PROMACH, with the goal of implementing a strategy for decentralized integrated watershed management to more efficiently manage natural resources in Ecuador (Biederbick 1999, 1).

Since leaders of the global sustainable development agenda (including Kakabadze) designed Ecuador's environmental decentralization policy, it is no surprise that IWM principles were included from the beginning. Various environmental management policies issued between 1998 and 2000 all contained key IWM policies like decentralizing decision making to local participatory organizations, valuing ecosystem services, and creating payment for ecosystem services programs to finance management activities.[12] Ecuador's Decentralized System for Environmental Management specifically called for creating local payment for ecosystem services programs with local financing mechanisms and participatory decision-making bodies for integrated watershed management (Yaguache et al. 2005; MAE 2003).

Efforts to implement local IWM reform through the environmental decentralization process began in 2000. Since national legislators never specified a process for transferring responsibilities and resources, the Environment Ministry, GTZ, the National Council for State Modernization (CONAM), and the Consortium of Ecuadorian Provincial Councils (CONCOPE) jointly developed a five-stage plan for transferring responsibilities.[13] However, the process never advanced beyond the first stage. In the end, responsibilities for environmental management were only transferred to one local government.[14] In 57 cases contracts were signed but never fulfilled; national politicians and bureaucrats obstructed the transfer of responsibilities and resources. In the remaining cases negotiations failed to produce agreement for decentralization.

By the mid-2000s Ecuadorian experts widely viewed this decentralization process as failed (Barrera 2007; Carrión 2007; Falconí and Muñoz 2007; López 2008). The process was undermined by opposition among national-level politicians and bureaucrats (Frank 2007; Faust et al. 2007). Congress never passed the secondary laws needed to implement the process due to disagreement on the responsibilities to be assumed by subnational governments and the resources to be transferred (Carrión and Dammert 2007, 2). Rather, national political elites

---

[12] Examples include the 1998 Presidential Executive Decree No. 340 (GTZ 1999); the Environment Ministry's Strategy for Sustainable Forestry Development in Ecuador (MAE 2000b); and the Environmental Strategy for Sustainable Development in Ecuador (MAE 2000a).

[13] National Decentralization Plan, Executive Decree 1616, Official Registry Number 365, July 10, 2001. See Number 4: Application and Sector 9.

[14] López 2005, 86. Responsibility for managing Cajas National Park was transferred to the municipal government of Cuenca, Ecuador's third-largest city.

made ad hoc deals with local elites to maintain power (Ojeda 2004). This led to a system of overlapping functions, fragmentation in political and territorial organization, and a lack of clear mechanisms for transferring powers and resources (Falconí and Muñoz 2007, 25–26).

As a result, the Environment Ministry's decentralization efforts lacked a legal basis. This produced confusion regarding what powers could be transferred, particularly regarding natural resources, as well as the criteria and process for doing so. For example, in September 2002 Ecuador's Constitutional Court declared the ministry's outsourcing of forestry management to be unconstitutional, creating uncertainty over whether natural resources could be decentralized (López 2005, 26). As I show in chapter 5, this made it necessary for IWM advocates to strategically frame natural resource management as a legal power of local governments when trying to establish local IWM coalitions and launch phase 2 of grassroots global governance.

Ministry bureaucrats also blocked decentralization by resisting the transfer of powers and resources. Despite the constitutional requirement to transfer responsibilities requested by municipalities, ministry bureaucrats engaged local leaders in lengthy political battles (Cameron 2003; Lalander 2005). Many bureaucrats unwilling to engage in decentralization simply avoided responding to petitions by local governments (Faust et al. 2007). Similar problems existed with the transfer of resources. Mayors complained that the national government often did not remit the 15% of state resources as required by the 1997 Law of 15% (Van Cott 2008, 37).

Social Network Activation and Ecuador's Pioneering IWM Reforms

While local IWM reforms were never implemented through national water and environmental decentralization laws as initially planned, these unimplemented laws did have an important, if unintended, effect. Members of some transnational IWM networks used them as tools for activating domestic social networks to pursue local IWM reform through informal processes. I show later how members of the GWP-ECLAC network capitalized on popular mobilization against water privatization to organize Ecuadorian social movements around an alternative approach to IWM. GTZ took advantage of this national social network activation to promote local IWM reform in Tungurahua's Ambato River watershed, which it chose as a pilot project for its Watershed Management Program, PROMACH. FAO similarly activated national social networks to promote local IWM reform through its community forestry program.

However, some IWM advocates had a hard time employing network activation strategies in social arenas. Members of the World Bank network found Ecuador's social arenas as closed as its political arenas. Because commodifying and privatizing nature deeply violated the cultural norms of Ecuador's ascendant social movements—indigenous and environmental groups—the World Bank network could not activate domestic social networks to exercise power outside the national political arena. Its influence was filtered out by Ecuador's national context.

In the next sections, I trace the expansion of two networks not filtered out by Ecuador's national context—the GWP-ECLAC-GTZ and FAO networks. I show how they used network activation strategies to navigate Ecuador's national context and diffuse their preferred IWM policies to the grassroots level. The case studies highlight the importance of national-level brokers who train, organize, and activate networks of domestic IWM advocates. They also (re) frame IWM to fit the goals of influential domestic stakeholder groups. In this way, global ideas begin to evolve.

Social Network Activation by
the GWP-ECLAC-GTZ Network

The GWP-ECLAC-GTZ network initially expanded within Ecuador by activating networks of domestic development NGOs and water experts in Ecuador's Sierra region. As chapter 3 described, Ecuadorian development and water specialists working in the Andes were struggling to address severe water conflicts. Many became interested in IWM after reading articles by the Global Water Partnership's South American Technical Advisory Committee (GWP-SAMTAC), which framed IWM as a way to address water conflicts. These and other articles on IWM coming out of ECLAC prompted Ecuadorian development and water experts to shift their focus from technical improvements of water delivery systems toward a holistic approach that incorporated the social component of resource management and linked the conservation of watershed resources to improved irrigation and production. This shift in mentality and strategy led them to advocate IWM reform throughout Ecuador's Sierra region.

Several Ecuadorian development and water specialists became crucial national brokers, facilitating the GWP-ECLAC-GTZ network's expansion within Ecuador. One such national broker was Pablo Lloret, an Ecuadorian water expert who became president of GWP-SAMTAC. Lloret is what Sidney Tarrow (2005) calls a rooted cosmopolitan—a domestic expert with strong international ties and exposure to global ideas like IWM. Lloret received a masters degree in environmental sciences from Navarra University in Spain and was a member of several transnational expert networks regarding watershed management. Lloret illustrates how such national brokers facilitated connections between the GWP-ECLAC-GTZ network and Ecuadorian development NGOs, universities, social movements, and local government agencies. They used these connections to activate domestic IWM networks.

In 1994, Lloret became Director of Environmental Management in the municipal water company for Cuenca, Ecuador's third largest city. Faced with severe water conflicts, he contacted ECLAC for conceptual support. Over time, Lloret developed a close relationship with Dourojeanni, Solanes, and other members of GWP-SAMTAC. He embraced ECLAC's ideas and invited Solanes and Dourojeanni to Ecuador to advise on the creation of local watershed management institutions. Over time, he developed a strong relationship with ECLAC and was named the Global Water Partnership's representative in Ecuador. Lloret became well known in Ecuador for his visionary role in creating Ecuador's first Watershed Council, a participatory decision-making body that integrated the stakeholders in Cuenca's Machangara watershed.

National brokers like Lloret played key roles in diffusing IWM principles and policies. They did so by employing network activation strategies, like training knowledge communities of domestic IWM experts and organizing them through national linking institutions and newly created IWM governance institutions. For example, in late 1994, amid the social contestation surrounding the Agrarian Development Law, Lloret and other Ecuadorian academics and development specialists founded a consortium as a national social space for debating natural resource management. This consortium, called CAMAREN (Consortium Training in Management of Renewable Natural Resources; *Consorcio Capacitación en Manejo de Recursos Naturales Renovables*), constituted a new governing node in the transnational IWM network.

The idea behind CAMAREN was that training would provide a neutral way to convene people around the controversial topic of natural resource management. Because he had established Ecuador's first university program on watershed management (at the University of Cuenca), CAMAREN's members asked Lloret to manage the consortium's efforts on water. In the late 1990s, he and others developed training materials on watershed management, based on IWM principles. Focused on under-served rural areas, the training program became a powerful source of network activation across Ecuador. Over the next decade, CAMAREN trained and organized 1,500 technical experts working in rural areas and 1,450 campesino community organizers.[15]

[15] www.camaren.org/quienes-somos/ (accessed February 13, 2016).

CAMAREN also created a national linking institution to organize the local knowledge communities that were forming around the country. In 2000, Lloret helped CAMAREN found Ecuador's national Water Resources Forum (*Foro de Recursos Hídricos*) as a space where a diverse array of stakeholders could jointly analyze, discuss, respectfully debate, and develop policy proposals for IWM. From the beginning, the forum was meant to democratize water governance by incorporating community-level campesino, indigenous, and environmental groups into discussions typically dominated by engineers and policymakers. To this end, the national Water Resources Forum helped develop provincial-level forums and local working groups to develop ideas that were discussed at national meetings. The Forum's inclusive culture and decentralized structure combined with the country's social mobilization around water to produce high levels of participation by a diverse spectrum of Ecuadorian society.

The treatment of IWM within Ecuador's Water Resources Forum illustrates how national brokers use their influence to adapt global ideas to fit national contexts in order to activate domestic networks. As the Global Water Partnership's representative in Ecuador, Lloret used the Water Resources Forum to promote IWM policies and drew on the GWP-ECLAC network for support. However, Lloret expressed IWM principles through the lens of Ecuador's sociocultural context. While many GWP members focused on privatization and market incentives to improve efficiency of water use, Lloret and the Forum's other creators emphasized the need to democratize decision making to reduce inequality of access. They also linked water management with "the conservation of nature, respect for the rights of nature, and the development of populations traditionally forgotten by the state."[16] These priorities reflected a desire by Lloret and his South American counterparts on GWP-SAMTAC to pursue what Lloret called "a more South American way of managing GWP policies in the world."[17]

This adaptation of GWP's approach to IWM put Lloret at odds with GWP's directorate in Sweden and institutional members like the World Bank. Frustrated by the GWP director's efforts to manage SAMTAC's activities from Sweden, Lloret and SAMTAC's other South American members established the South American Water Forum (*Foro Sudamericano del Agua*) as an alternative to SAMTAC. This rift ultimately caused the GWP to break formal ties with its South American representatives, but the latter continued to utilize their extensive network ties to promote IWM principles in their home countries in a way that fit domestic values.

---

[16] www.camaren.org/foro-de-los-recursos-hidricos/ (accessed February 13, 2016).
[17] Interview by author, Quito, Ecuador, April 8, 2011.

Due to the efforts of Lloret and other national-level IWM advocates, Ecuador's Water Resources Forum became a place where the concept of IWM was broadly accepted, but adapted to fit Ecuadorian values. Rather than debating the need for IWM, debate focused on how to design IWM systems that remained true to values held by local stakeholders. Among other things, these included the public's right to equitable water access; participation by local social groups in water resource management; respect for indigenous knowledge, rights, and traditions; and differentiated fees for different resource uses and users with different economic conditions.[18]

The policy proposals adopted at the Water Resources Forum's first meeting reflect members' acceptance of IWM principles. The members issued four policy proposals designed to achieve "participatory and decentralized action for the holistic and integrated management of water resources" (CAMAREN 2002, 8). Among other things, the proposals called for:

1) organizing management systems at the watershed level (recognizing the need for decentralized systems with local management at the micro-watershed level);
2) valuing full inclusion of all stakeholders over "rational and efficient administration" (a euphemism for control by technical experts);
3) designing and implementing new local IWM systems through decentralized, participatory processes (e.g., creating new organizations that allow local stakeholders to participate in planning, implementation, and oversight of activities);
4) establishing transparent and sustainable financing mechanisms where those benefiting from watershed ecosystem services pay to ensure the continuation of these services. Importantly, the proposal demanded that social and environmental values of water be recognized in addition to economic values, and that all resource users—including the hydroelectric industry—contribute to financing watershed management activities.

The adopted proposals do not mean there was no disagreement among Forum members. Among the fiercest debates were those surrounding the concept of payments for ecosystem services (e.g., Isch López 2005; Isch López and Gentes 2006). Some indigenous groups, environmental NGOs, and others criticized this as the commodification of nature and feared it would lead to privatization (Acción Ecológica 2006). A number of IWM advocates, both foreign and

---

[18] These themes appear repeatedly in discussion documents produced by the Water Resources Forum (e.g., Arévalo 2003; Arroyo 2005; CAMAREN 2002).

Ecuadorian, learned from their participation in these debates. They adapted their language and strategy so as to reconcile core IWM principles and practices with those of other stakeholders. Chapters 6 and 7 provide examples of how this was done in specific cases. They describe, for example, how IWM advocates adapted their strategies in response to bargaining with local stakeholders to produce innovative financing mechanisms that maintained core IWM principles while overcoming concerns about the privatization and commodification of nature.

To summarize, foreign and Ecuadorian IWM advocates affiliated with the GWP-ECLAC network took advantage of the national social mobilization that occurred in response to concerns about water privatization. They tapped into campesino and indigenous networks by framing IWM reform as an agricultural development strategy, training community experts and organizers in rural communities, and providing an organizational space for these groups to participate in water governance, both locally and nationally. Foreign and domestic IWM advocates willing to work with these groups as genuine partners were able to use this space to develop and strengthen their own connections with social networks, helping to extend their reach to the grassroots level. These social networks proved valuable for IWM advocates seeking to overcome obstruction by national political elites and advance their agenda through informal processes at the local level.

Social Network Activation by the FAO Network

The FAO network similarly expanded within Ecuador by training and organizing local knowledge communities through national linking institutions. FAO's network activation occurred through its Community Forestry Development Program for the Ecuadorian Andes, popularly known as DFC (*Desarrollo Forestal Comunitario*). FAO created DFC in 1993 to help Ecuador's Institute for Forestry, Natural Areas and Wildlife (INEFAN) develop a Forestry Action Plan that would promote food security and reduce poverty. As mentioned earlier, the program reflected new norms in international development circles embracing community-led, culturally appropriate, and environmentally sustainable approaches to development. This dovetailed neatly with indigenous demands for greater participation in local development, particularly regarding natural resource management. DFC's focus on forest conservation also resonated with Ecuadorian environmental groups. Therefore, in contrast to the World Bank's experience, social movement leaders did not mobilize opposition to the FAO network's IWM efforts, but rather sought to construct ties with network members to pursue their own agendas. So while Ecuador's national context filtered out the World Bank network's influence, it provided fertile ground for the FAO network to expand through network activation.

Like its counterparts in the GWP network, FAO created a new governing node to guide IWM reform through social network activation: the DFC program office. With funding and technical support from the Dutch government and FAO, DFC staff provided training and capacity assistance to indigenous communities and small farmers to design and carry out their own community forest plans. Faced with the need to balance communities' desire for expanded agricultural production with INEFAN's focus on sustainable forestry management, DFC's technical experts (including trained Ecuadorian experts as well as those from the Netherlands and FAO) advocated IWM principles as the best approach.

Among the DFC's strategies was to "support the construction of a new organizational architecture" that would "facilitate the relationship among organizations ... with the goal of coordinating complementary actions" among a watershed's stakeholders (Salazar et al. 2004).[19] A key component of this strategy was the training of local organizers who were connected through an interlocking system of social networks. Over time, the network connections became dense, and local organizers moved into influential positions within local and national governments, indigenous movements, development NGOs, and civil society organizations. DFC created a national committee that served as an organizational node linking representatives of these networks. The dense network connections of organizers trained through the DFC program sustained this national committee informally even after the DFC program formally ended.[20] As I show in this and in subsequent chapters, this FAO-DFC network became an influential force promoting local IWM reforms across Ecuador focused on financing community forest management through local payment for ecosystem services programs.

As in the GWP-ECLAC network, national-level brokers with strong international ties played a key role in expanding the FAO-DFC network in Ecuador. One such broker was William Zury, an Ecuadorian forestry engineer who studied watershed management in Costa Rica. From 1993 to 2003 he worked in FAO's DFC program, where he developed his ideas about local, participatory strategies for integrated watershed management. He helped incorporate IWM concepts into the environmental management program in Loja National University, one of Ecuador's premier technical universities. During the 2000s, Zury personally trained a corps of young environmental engineers who became key actors in many of Ecuador's local IWM reforms, including several analyzed in this book.

---

[19] My translation. Throughout the book, all translations of text originally in Spanish are my own.
[20] Former DFC staffer currently with FAO-Ecuador, interview by author, Quito, Ecuador, February 22, 2011.

Pioneering IWM Reforms and Rival National IWM Networks

Ecuador provides a useful lens for studying IWM reform because it is the site of two of the world's first voluntary, decentralized mechanisms for protecting watershed ecosystem services (Albán and Wunder 2005). In 2000, Pimampiro municipality launched the world's first voluntary, decentralized, payment for ecosystem services program, designed to protect the watershed where its water originates (Echavarria et al. 2004). That same year, the city of Quito established the Water Protection Fund (*Fondo para la Protección del Agua*—FONAG) to sustainably finance the management of surrounding watersheds (Troya and Curtis 1998; Krchnak 2007). FONAG was innovative in that it pioneered the use of trust funds in a voluntary, decentralized mechanism for financing watershed conservation.

In this section, I show how these innovative models of local IWM reform emerged from the national network activation described in the previous sections. These pioneering experiments with local IWM reform are important because they catalyzed the emergence of two rival national-level IWM networks, each dedicated to replicating one of these models of local IWM. The six local IWM reform campaigns analyzed in subsequent chapters constitute their initial efforts.

Network Activation around Pimampiro's PES Program

Pimampiro's payment for ecosystem services program grew out of DFC's efforts to create a community forest management plan that would protect the watershed providing Pimampiro's water. Like many of the small Andean farming communities where DFC worked, Pimampiro suffered from high poverty rates and severe water shortages, exacerbated by deforestation in the watershed to expand agriculture.[21] Beginning in 1994, DFC technicians worked with the local farmers' association to develop a forest management plan for farmers' land, located in the catchment area of the watershed feeding Pimampiro. Given farmers'

---

[21] Pimampiro is a municipality in Ecuador's Imbabura province, one of nine provinces in Ecuador's highlands where DFC operated. The institutions working on the DFC program in Imbabura included the municipality of Pimampiro, CEDERENA (an Ecuadorian NGO created by Ecuadorian DFC technicians to facilitate community management of natural resources, local development, environmental services, and institutional development), and the Red MACRENA (an Ecuadorian NGO created by ex-DFC technicians for training in natural resources management); these organizations received funding from the Inter-American Foundation, FAO, and the Dutch government (Echavarria et al. 2004).

desire to increase production, the plan combined forest and soil conservation with agroforestry projects (e.g., fruit trees, commercial orchid cultivation, and medicinal plant collection), as well as environmental education (CEDERENA 2002). DFC also helped create a new Environment and Tourism Unit within the municipal government. The unit constituted a new local governing node in the transnational IWM network. It was staffed by experts trained through DFC and charged with designing and implementing the municipality's environmental strategy.

While DFC's program ended in 1997, Ecuadorian experts trained through DFC founded the local NGO CEDERENA (the Ecological Corporation for the Development of Renewable Natural Resources) to continue DFC's work in Pimampiro (illustrating the power of network activation). By 1999, CEDERENA's technicians had become quite concerned. Various tactics to convince local farmers to stop cutting down trees had failed, and deforestation in the watershed continued. Studies showed this contributed to reduced water flow, and water access was down to two hours per day. Moreover, studies showed the watershed was the only viable water supply.

Desperate to find something that would work, CEDERENA proposed creating a payment for ecosystem services fund. After reading about Costa Rica's recently established national-level payment for ecosystem services system, CEDERENA developed the idea of adapting it to be a voluntary local program. CEDERENA sold the idea to experts in the municipal Environment and Tourism Unit, and worked with them to design the program and sell it to landowners and politicians. Pimampiro's municipal government launched the program in 2000, with support from FAO, the Inter-American Foundation, and CEDERENA.[22]

The program's logic is that beneficiaries of ecosystem services (in this case, water users) voluntarily "buy" these services (i.e., the flow of clean water) from "providers" who enact land-use practices designed to ensure that the services continue. The municipal government acts as the "buyer" of watershed services on behalf of the city's water users. The municipal Environment and Tourism Unit manages the program. It negotiates voluntary agreements with farmers to conserve and sustainably manage the forest on their land in exchange for cash payments. To finance the payments to farmers (the ecosystem service "providers"), the government passed an ordinance levying a 20% fee on drinking water (The Inter-American Foundation and CEDERENA also made initial donations for start-up costs). This money is held in a municipal government account in the National Development Bank. Decisions on how to use these funds are made

---

[22] For details of Pimampiro's program, see Echavarría (2004); Kauffman (2014). For definitions and descriptions of payment for ecosystem services, see Goldman-Benner et al. (2012); Wunder (2005).

by Pimampiro's Mayor and the directors of the municipality's Financial Unit, Environment and Tourism Unit, and Environmental Commission.

During the early 2000s, Pimampiro became known nationally as a pioneering case of decentralized payment for ecosystem services. Its perceived success raised CEDERENA's stature as a leading authority on watershed management. By 2003 CEDERENA was devoting its energy and resources to replicating the Pimampiro model in other municipalities. Drawing on the FAO-DFC network, CEDERENA organized coalitions of local, national, and international organizations to implement payment for watershed services programs in various Ecuadorian municipalities, including Celica and El Chaco (see Fig. 4.1).

Network Activation around Quito's Watershed Trust Fund

Ecuador's second pioneering local IWM program—Quito's Water Protection Fund (FONAG)—developed from the merging of three trends in the late 1990s: (1) the rise of ecosystem services as part of the global IWM agenda; (2) the transnational movement to promote national parks; and (3) the rise of Ecuador's environmental movement around the conservation of national

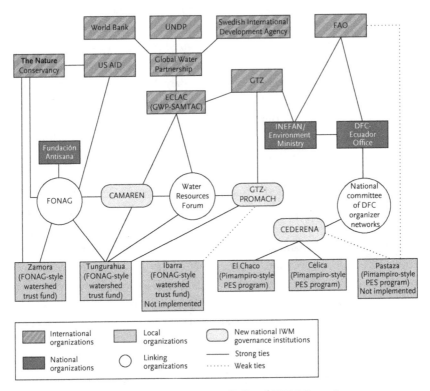

Figure 4.1 Global Grassroots Connections in Six Local IWM Campaigns.

parks.[23] The idea to create FONAG originated with Juan Black, an Ecuadorian conservationist who in 1992 became The Nature Conservancy's Latin America director. At the time, Ecuadorian conservationists and their foreign allies were concerned with how to fund Ecuador's parks system. Like many developing countries, Ecuador's government devoted few resources to conserving protected areas. It was Black who first proposed that the Cayambe-Coca and Antisana ecological reserves should be compensated for the water they funnel to Quito.

When Black died in 1996, the director of Fundación Natura (Ecuador's first environmental NGO), Roberto Troya, replaced him as head of The Nature Conservancy's Latin American office. Troya worked with María Helena Jervis of the local NGO Fundación Antisana to promote Black's idea. They hired Marta Echavarría, a Colombian woman with experience setting up water associations in Colombia, to explore options for how to design such a financing mechanism. Echavarría analyzed experimental financing mechanisms for protecting watersheds in Colombia, Costa Rica, Brazil, and New York. In this way, concepts related to IWM and ecosystem services coalesced with Ecuador's emerging movement to fund national parks.

Troya, Jervis, and Echavarría designed the proposal for FONAG drawing on ideas from national-level programs in other countries as well as publications by ecosystem services scholars like Robert Costanza (e.g., Costanza et al. 1997; Costanza and Folke 1997). The innovation was adapting these ideas to fit Ecuador's need for a voluntary, decentralized program (given the country's political instability and weak national government institutions). The proposal received strong political support in Quito, largely because the transnational conservation network reached far into the municipal government. Then-mayor Roque Sevilla was an environmental activist who had served as director of the World Wildlife Fund (WWF) and president of Fundación Natura. With Sevilla providing the political will, FONAG was created in 2000, with the municipal water company taking a strong leadership role.

FONAG's water trust fund model has several features that make it different from Pimampiro-style payment for environmental services programs.[24] First, money collected from water consumers is used to capitalize the trust fund, which is invested in financial markets to provide a sustainable revenue stream through interest income. Rather than direct compensation to individual farmers, income generated by the trust is used to finance a variety of watershed management and conservation activities specified in the trust's contract. The two models also differ on the role of local governments. The FONAG model calls

---

[23] I am indebted to Marta Echavarría for providing this insight.

[24] For details of FONAG and the differences between water trust funds and payment for environmental services programs, see Goldman-Benner et al. (2012); Kauffman (2014).

for the trust fund to be managed by financial institutions that are independent of local governments and other watershed stakeholders. Decisions on how to use the interest income generated by the trust are made by a board of directors with representatives from local government and various private stakeholder groups. Thus, local governments do not have unilateral control over the funds. This is meant to depoliticize the watershed management process and prevent the diversion of funds for other purposes. This contrasts with the strong local government control in Pimampiro. Those advocating the Pimampiro model argue that local governments, as the legitimate local authority, should control the funds, which are usually held in one of the municipality's bank accounts.

FONAG quickly gained international attention for pioneering the use of trust funds in a voluntary, decentralized mechanism for financing watershed conservation. As with Pimampiro, FONAG's perceived early success prompted transnational efforts to replicate the model through a series of campaigns. At least 15 similar local water trust funds have since been created or are under development across Latin America, 7 of which are in Ecuador. The story of FONAG's replication illustrates how Ecuadorian and international conservation organizations connected with the GWP-ECLAC-GTZ network and used network activation strategies to expand their conservation-oriented IWM network to local communities across Ecuador.

The intention to replicate FONAG throughout Ecuador was present from the beginning, and The Nature Conservancy began organizing campaigns almost immediately (Troya and Curtis 1998). Advocates first promoted FONAG through a series of publications and conferences, including through CAMAREN and Ecuador's national Water Resources Forum. With funding from USAID, experts from The Nature Conservancy, FONAG, and Ecuadorian technical universities began identifying important watersheds and working with local governments, NGOs, and communities to establish FONAG-style water funds. Many of these experts, including Pablo Lloret, were members of the GWP-ECLAC-GTZ network.

Based on his pioneering role advocating IWM in Ecuador, Lloret was hired as FONAG's first technical secretary. He immediately implemented a series of national programs to train local stakeholders in IWM policies and practices and to replicate FONAG in other Ecuadorian watersheds. FONAG has since become a national linking institution that connects and mobilizes resources from IGOs, donor agencies, NGOs, private companies, and community organizations to promote local IWM reforms throughout Ecuador. Importantly, individual brokers like Pablo Lloret, as well as common organizational nodes, like FONAG, CAMAREN, and the Water Resources Forum, produced strong ties between The Nature Conservancy and the GWP-ECLAC-GTZ network. This increased the networks' ability to mobilize resources and exert influence.

By 2009 this combined network helped create water trust funds and related governance institutions in five other localities, including Zamora and Tungurahua.[25]

Conclusion

This chapter examined phase 1 of grassroots global governance—the diffusion of particular IWM policies and practices from the global to the grassroots level through the expansion of transnational IWM networks. It showed how structural features of Ecuador's national context—including cultural norms, socioeconomic conditions, political institutions, and sociopolitical alliances—determined the opportunity for various transnational networks to expand. Ecuador's national context acted as a filter, empowering some transnational networks (like FAO) and disempowering others (like the World Bank). By shaping network expansion, Ecuador's national context explains why local IWM reforms in Ecuador reflected The Nature Conservancy's and FAO's focus on forest conservation, community management, and equitable access rather than the World Bank's emphasis on market incentives, expert-designed engineering projects, and efficiency.

The chapter also traced the network connections and strategies by which transnational IWM networks expanded to the local level within Ecuador. Figure 4.1 illustrates the main network connections tying the two transnational IWM networks that expanded in Ecuador to the six cases of local IWM reform analyzed in this book. The figure also illustrates the top-down network activation that occurs during phase 1. Each network diffused its preferred model of IWM to specific localities by creating and activating new national governing nodes (e.g., FONAG, CAMAREN, and CEDERENA) and linking institutions (e.g., Water Resources Forum and National Committee of DFC-trained networks). Figure 4.1 also shows how the IWM model pursued in a given locality resulted from the pattern of network expansion, which tied that locality to a particular IWM network. Localities with strong ties to The Nature Conservancy-GWP-GTZ network pursued FONAG-style watershed trust funds while those tied to the FAO-DFC-CEDERENA network pursued Pimampiro-style payment for ecosystem services programs.

Ecuadorian professionals with strong international ties were key brokers facilitating network expansion nationally. Ecuadorians like Juan Black, Pablo Lloret, and William Zury embraced IWM concepts as a promising solution for local problems related to water scarcity and ecosystem conservation. Along with foreign IWM advocates, these national brokers built networks and organizations

---

[25] The three other localities were Paute, Riobamba, and Espíndola.

for linking various stakeholders throughout Ecuador around the issue of watershed management. These linking institutions were powerful sites for disseminating information, expanding network connections, increasing technical capacity through training, generating new ideas and collaborative initiatives, and mobilizing resources for advancing IWM policies nationally. The number of Ecuadorians connected to transnational IWM networks steadily expanded through community training programs, conferences, education campaigns, new university programs, and the creation of municipal environmental management units. Like planted seeds, grassroots networks of IWM advocates grew over time, altering local sociopolitical alliances and creating windows of opportunity for governance changes at the grassroots level.

Of course, not all localities were equally touched by national network activation. Transnational IWM networks focused their efforts on some localities and neglected others. As chapter 5 shows, Ibarra and Pastaza did not experience the national network activation described above. Yet, IWM reform campaigns were launched by organizations with weak ties to transnational IWM networks (indicated by the dotted line in Fig. 4.1 and described in chapter 5). Not surprisingly, these were the least successful cases. To illustrate the impact of national network activation for local IWM reform campaigns, chapter 5 examines phase 1 from the grassroots perspective. It shows how IWM advocates' national network activation strategies not only produced local IWM coalitions but conditioned their ability to expand locally.

5

Local Legacies of National
Network Activation

This chapter examines phase 1 of grassroots global governance from the grass-roots perspective. Chapter 4 described how transnational IWM networks cre-ated national-level programs to promote IWM across Ecuador. By training local knowledge communities, organizing them through linking institutions, and creating new local governance institutions, IWM advocates shifted contestation over IWM from national to local arenas. This chapter shows what national net-work activation looked like at the local level and analyzes its effects in the book's six case studies. I call this local network activation during phase 1 "early local network activation" to contrast it with the local network activation carried out by local IWM coalitions during phase 2. Looking at early local network activa-tion focuses the analysis on the transition between phase 1 and phase 2, which begins when local IWM coalitions form and launch local IWM reform cam-paigns. I analyze this transition for two reasons.

The first purpose is to demonstrate a key feature of nodal governance—how organizations govern indirectly, projecting influence across network ties through network activation. During phase 1, foreign and national-level members of transnational IWM networks spent years activating networks of local stakehold-ers, facilitating the rise of local IWM coalitions. Interestingly, the foreign and national organizations that spurred local network activation during phase 1 were typically absent during local IWM reform campaigns (phase 2); they left these localities either before or soon after local IWM coalitions formed. Yet, IWM re-form campaigns continued without them, led by local IWM advocates who were trained and organized during phase 1. This indirect influence through network activation is the essence of nodal governance.

The chapter's second purpose is to highlight an interesting relationship be-tween phase 1 and phase 2 of grassroots global governance: the level of local net-work activation during phase 1 influences the prospects for success during phase 2. The six cases vary in the degree to which they were touched by the network activation described in chapter 4. Four cases (Tungurahua, Celica, El Chaco, and Zamora) experienced high levels of early local network activation, while two cases (Ibarra and Pastaza) experienced very little (see Table 5.1). The level of early local network activation is positively correlated with success in phase 2. The four cases with high levels of early local network activation are the most successful. The two without early local network activation are those that broke down during the initial agenda-setting stage of phase 2.

This correlation supports grassroots global governance theory. The theory argues that success in phase 2 requires simultaneous pressure from beside among multiple stakeholder groups, which is created by activating networks of IWM advocates representing all major local stakeholder groups. Simultaneous network activation in multiple stakeholder groups requires local IWM coalitions to expand their network connections in multiple directions rapidly. This is difficult to do. Early local network activation makes it much easier.

Early local network activation means that at the time local IWM coalitions form, watershed management is already identified as an important issue, social groups are organized around this issue, new local governance institutions provide a platform for promoting IWM, and there exists a community of local experts and organizers representing various stakeholder groups. These local experts and community organizers become natural allies for outside IWM advocates. Together, they create local IWM coalitions with strong ties to a diverse set of stakeholders, allowing coalitions to expand more quickly. In this way, early local network activation during phase 1 creates fertile conditions for rapid local network activation (and thus the mobilization of pressure from beside) in phase 2.

By contrast, IWM coalitions in localities untouched by early local network activation face far less propitious conditions when they launch their campaigns. They have few if any natural allies in local stakeholder groups, watershed management is likely not a salient issue, and there is likely no local governance institution to guide reform efforts. Of course, local IWM coalitions can work to create these conditions, but this takes time and slows down the coalition's ability to expand through network activation. This makes it difficult to mobilize the simultaneous pressure from beside needed to sustain the process as the campaign wears on.

Results from the six case studies support this expectation of grassroots global governance theory. As Table 5.1 shows, local IWM coalitions formed in all six cases during 2004 and 2005. In just a few years, three coalitions had created basic IWM institutions and were putting them into practice. Of the failed cases, Zamora advanced the furthest; its coalition created a watershed trust fund in 2006 but failed to make it operational. The difference between these cases and the two where reform efforts collapsed early on was the presence of early local network activation by foreign IWM advocates between 1997 and 2003.

Table 5.1 Early Local Network Activation and Success in Phase 2

Case	Early Local Network Activation Initiated (Phase 1)	Local IWM Coalition Formed	Initial Coalition Members	IWM Institutions Put in Practice	IWM Reform Results in Phase 2
Tungurahua	1997 (GTZ-PROMACH)	Reconstituted in 2004 after initial attempt broke down in 2002	Provincial government; CESA and IEDECA (national NGOs); GTZ (German development agency); National Council for Water Resources	2006 (Water Parliament); 2007 (Fund for Páramo Management)	Score: 13.5 Success
Celica	1998 (Dry Forest Project)	2004	CEDERENA (National NGO); Municipal environmental management unit	2005 (PES Program and Environmental Services Committee)	Score: 13 Success
El Chaco	2000 (TNC-Parks in Peril; GTZ)	2004	CEDERENA (National NGO); Municipal environmental management unit	2005 (PES program and Environmental Services Committee)	Score: 12 Success
Zamora	1997 (Podocarpus Program)	2004	Arcoiris (local NGO); The Nature Conservancy (international NGO); Municipal environmental management unit	2006 Procuencas (watershed trust fund)	Score: 8.5 Breakdown at implementation
Ibarra	N/A	2004	PROFAFOR (National NGO); Municipal Water Company (EMAPA-I)	N/A	Score: 4.5 Breakdown at agenda setting with politicians
Pastaza	N/A	2005	CODEAMA & Amazon Forest Service (Local NGOs); Municipal sustainable development unit	N/A	Score: 2.5 Breakdown at agenda setting with civil society

Through programs like FAO's community forest program (DFC), GTZ's watershed management program PROMACH, and The Nature Conservancy's Parks in Peril program, outside IWM advocates worked for years to build local communities' motivation and capacity for managing watershed resources. It typically took seven years or more for local IWM coalitions to form. Once they did, however, these coalitions were able to get basic IWM programs up and running within two to three years. This seemingly quick turnaround is deceptive. It occurred only because IWM advocates had already worked for a decade to train and organize local IWM advocates within each watershed stakeholder group.

By contrast, transnational IWM networks were absent in Ibarra and Pastaza between 1997 and 2003. While local IWM coalitions did form through a confluence of events, these coalitions had only weak ties to transnational IWM networks. More important, there was no prior network activation to make local sociopolitical conditions more conducive to IWM reform. Local IWM coalitions were starting from scratch. While this did not predestine failure, it meant IWM advocates faced a much more challenging environment.

The timing of early local network activation in Ecuador (1997–2003) is not coincidental. Foreign and national IWM advocates were working to prepare local governments and communities to take on watershed management responsibilities in anticipation of environmental decentralization (see chapter 4). By incorporating IWM reform into Ecuador's decentralization process, transnational IWM advocates created a platform for pursuing their agenda in communities across the country. The fact that local IWM coalitions formed (and in some cases succeeded) after the decentralization process stalled in 2003 demonstrates the power of nodal governance. The impact of early local network activation lasted far beyond the foreign programs and national processes that prompted these activities. Once activated, local IWM networks took on lives of their own. Local IWM advocates trained and organized during phase 1 worked to pursue IWM reform during phase 2 through local processes that did not involve formal transfers of authority or even much participation by the national government.

To illustrate the importance of early local network activation, the rest of this chapter traces the transition from phase 1 to phase 2 in two Andean cases: one where local IWM reform efforts succeeded (Celica) and one where they failed (Ibarra). The first section describes early local network activation in Celica and shows how this produced both a local IWM coalition and propitious conditions for its rapid expansion among local stakeholder groups. The Celica case highlights the important role played by national-level brokers in expanding transnational IWM networks to the local level, in particular by training local knowledge communities and organizing them through linking institutions. Equally important was the creation of environmental management units within local governments. These new governing institutions provided a space for building the capacity of local governments and citizens to implement IWM programs.

The Celica case shows how combining newly trained knowledge communities with new local governance institutions creates a multiplier effect. As in other cases, Celica's environmental management unit was staffed by a new generation of local IWM experts trained through environmental management programs established in Ecuadorian universities by national brokers like Pablo Lloret and William Zury (see chapter 4). These local experts became important brokers between transnational IWM networks and local stakeholder groups. They were uniquely situated to incorporate representatives of multiple stakeholder groups into the IWM coalition. They therefore took the lead in guiding local IWM reform processes. By showing how this occurs, the Celica case demonstrates both how outside organizations govern indirectly through network activation and how power shifts from national brokers to local brokers during the transition from phase 1 to phase 2.

The second section contrasts Celica's experience with that of Ibarra, whose watershed was ignored by transnational IWM networks in the late 1990s and early 2000s. The Ibarra case describes how a local IWM coalition formed in Ibarra despite the lack of early local network activation. This coalition had only weak ties with Ecuador's national IWM networks and was weakly embedded in local stakeholder groups. The Ibarra case also highlights the importance of strategic framing during phase 1. Given the obstruction of environmental decentralization (described in chapter 4), outside IWM advocates had to strategically frame unimplemented decentralization laws to justify local governments' assumption of new authority for watershed management. This was an important condition for building local governments' motivation and capacity to pursue IWM reform. The chapter's third section compares this framing strategy in successful and failed cases. It explains how in successful cases outside IWM advocates strategically interpreted unimplemented decentralization laws to justify the expansion of local government authority for the planning, regulating, financing, and implementation of watershed management activities. The failure to do so in Ibarra, combined with the failure to employ other network activation strategies, obstructed the IWM coalition's ability to place IWM reform on the political agenda (producing breakdown at the first stage of phase 2).

Early Local Network Activation in Celica

The idea of Integrated Watershed Management first emerged in Celica through the Dry Forest Project (*Proyecto Bosque Seco*), which was part of FAO's community forestry development program, DFC, described in chapter 4. Severe drought and soil degradation from deforestation and corn monoculture attracted the attention of two outside IWM advocates. One was Tjalling Postma, a member of the Dutch development agency SNV. The second was William Zury, an Ecuadorian watershed management expert who coordinated FAO's DFC program in Loja province (where Celica is located). In chapter 4, I noted Zury's role as a national broker for the FAO-DFC network. Zury's role in diffusing IWM to Celica, described in this section, illustrates the crucial role national brokers play in expanding transnational governance networks to the local level and beginning the local network activation process during phase 1 of grassroots global governance.

Concerned by Celica's drought, Zury and Postma came to Celica in 1997 to assess the feasibility of creating a more participatory and sustainable approach to watershed management. After conducting a baseline study of natural resource management, they developed a project called Community Management of the Dry Forests and Micro-Watersheds in the Southwest of Loja Province. The project, known as the Dry Forest Project (*Proyecto Bosque Seco*), was created in December 1997. It was financed by the Dutch government, administered by SNV in collaboration with Ecuador's national forestry department, INEFAN, and directed by Postma.[1]

Program documents reveal the strategies the project's creators used to build local motivation and capacity for implementing local IWM reform (which they expected would be implemented through Ecuador's environmental decentralization process). Project experts advocated IWM as the solution to locally identified problems of water scarcity and poor agricultural production. They developed three strategies for addressing these problems: (1) organizing and training rural community members in environmental management; (2) strengthening interinstitutional coordination to link the municipal government and various local actors; and (3) providing a coherent IWM plan (Proyecto Bosque Seco 1999b). In other words, the project employed network activation strategies—training local knowledge communities and creating linking institutions to connect stakeholder groups—in order to create a new decentralized, participatory, and integrated approach to watershed management.

During its first phase, the Dry Forest Project focused on creating and strengthening municipalities' institutional structure for environmental management, particularly by creating environmental management units. Celica was among the first municipalities in Ecuador to develop an environmental management unit, which constituted a local governing node in the transnational IWM network. Celica's experience illustrates the impact made by a new generation of

---

[1] The Dry Forest Project was carried out in five cantons: Celica, Macara, Pindal, Puyango, and Zapotillo.

local experts trained in IWM at Ecuadorian universities. In addition to working for FAO's community forestry development project, William Zury taught environmental management in the National University of Loja, specializing in watershed management. In 1997, one of Zury's students, Paulo Bustamante, graduated with a degree in forestry management and returned to his native Celica to work with the municipality as part of a required rural service program. This occurred just as the Dry Forest Project was formulated, and Bustamante was involved from the beginning. With advice from Zury, Bustamante helped create Celica's first environmental management unit and became its first director.

Celica's environmental management unit was created in 1998 through a contract between the Dry Forest Project and Celica's municipal government. Under the contract, Dry Forest Project experts trained municipal personnel and provided technical and financial assistance for agroforestry and watershed management activities undertaken by the municipality with local communities (Proyecto Bosque Seco 1999a, 3). Project experts also helped create a new IWM governance institution within the municipal council (the local legislative body), the Natural Resources Commission, which was created to enhance political support for environmental management within the council. Experts from the Dry Forest Project and partnering organizations trained council members on issues like watershed management, decentralization, environmental health, waste management, and project development (Bustamante 2004, 50).

Celica's environmental management unit provided IWM advocates an important institutional basis for promoting IWM reform. As a salaried employee, Bustamante could work full-time on the issue and had the authority to institutionalize practices and influence policy. The unit also served as an important node for mobilizing resources and building a local IWM coalition. Bustamante was a key local broker due to his ties to transnational IWM networks, local politicians, and community organizations. His training by Zury at the National University of Loja made him a member of the transnational IWM epistemic community. As director of the municipality's environmental management unit he had ties to local politicians. The fact that he and his family had lived in Celica for generations also gave him strong ties to community groups. A local expert and activist, born and raised in his community, trained in global IWM concepts locally, and working in the municipality, Bustamante embodies the grassroots global governor. His personal and professional ties made him uniquely positioned to promote global principles regarding IWM within various local stakeholder groups.

From the beginning Bustamante attended monthly meetings of the Dry Forest Project's technical team as well as its training programs. The Project held workshops to define the environmental management unit's vision, values, mission, and objectives, as well as to construct a strategic plan of action. Through this process the Dry Forest Project helped provide an organizational structure and define the roles and functions of different stakeholders involved in watershed management. This included developing plans and activities to conserve and restore water catchment areas (Bustamante 2004, 42; Proyecto Bosque Seco 1999a, 8).

The Dry Forest Project also trained and organized community members in natural resource management, a task complicated by low levels of social organization and citizen participation. In fact, the Dry Forest Project's efforts to organize citizen participation were the first such efforts in Loja province (Bustamante 2004, 39). Project personnel initially organized local stakeholders by forming Agroforestry Committees (new linking institutions). To mobilize community support and participation in agroforestry activities, project experts trained and organized local agro-ecological organizers (*promotores*). Paulo Bustamante was among the first community organizers trained. Bustamante had left the municipality's environmental unit in 2000 after elections brought a change in administration. But he continued to work on watershed management issues as a community organizer (and grassroots global governor).

These local organizers, with support from the project's technical staff, helped communities develop Community Agroforestry Plans that identified priorities and planned activities (Proyecto Bosque Seco 1999b, 12). Like the other components of the Dry Forest Project, this process utilized the network activation strategies discussed in chapter 2. This included providing new information to facilitate planning, for example through diagnostic studies of communities' demographics, production practices, and natural resources. These studies were conducted through community-based participatory research; community members were highly involved in collecting information and identifying problems. This experience educated community members and government officials about the problems faced by each community and strengthened ties among them.

Network connections were further strengthened by new linking organizations created by local agro-ecological organizers. These linking institutions connected different stakeholders and mobilized informational, material, and social resources for ecologically sustainable agriculture. A leading example is UCPACE (Cantonal Union of Agricultural Producers of Celica), a linking institution that connects 18 grassroots farmers' organizations across the canton. Another important linking institution was the canton's Local Management Committee, created in 2002 to produce a Cantonal Development Plan. The committee connected local organizers from different communities and stakeholder groups with technical experts from NGOs, as well as representatives from the private sector and local government.

Celica's Local Management Committee functioned for several years, but disbanded soon after the Dry Forest Project ended in 2004. In the end, the

Dry Forest Project produced few concrete watershed management projects. However, it placed watershed management on the agenda of local organizations and created a network of trained local experts and organizers who would later be important brokers between communities and transnational networks advocating IWM reform in Ecuador. Another legacy was the municipal environmental management unit, an institutional structure that later provided legal, technical, financial, and human resources for promoting IWM reform in the canton.

The proposal to institutionalize IWM principles and practices through new participatory decision-making and local financing institutions came to Celica through technical experts from CEDERENA. As chapter 4 described, CEDERENA is a national NGO comprised of Ecuadorian experts trained through FAO's DFC program, who helped create Pimampiro's pioneering payment for ecosystem services program. Boosted by Pimampiro's perceived success, CEDERENA was looking for places to replicate the model. CEDERENA's top watershed management expert, Robert Yaguache, was a native of Celica and interested in working there. As a regional director of FAO's DFC program, Yaguache was a member of the expert network constructed through the program. He was, therefore, well aware of how the Dry Forest Project had placed watershed management on the local agenda in Celica, constructed a network of trained local experts, and created an institutional structure for natural resource management. Yaguache saw these as promising conditions for implementing a new local IWM system.

When Paulo Bustamante was again tapped to direct Celica's environmental management unit in 2004, Yaguache saw a window of opportunity. Yaguache had developed a personal relationship with Bustamante during his visits home, and in December 2004 he approached Bustamante about launching a campaign to implement a Pimampiro-style payment for ecosystem services program in Celica. Bustamante was immediately interested and agreed to advocate the idea to the newly elected mayor and council members. After six months of lobbying, in May 2005 Celica's municipal government signed a contract with CEDERENA to jointly design and implement a Pimampiro-style IWM system. The contract marked the beginning of Celica's IWM reform campaign and thus the transition from phase 1 to phase 2 of grassroots global governance.

Celica's local IWM coalition was initially rather small, comprising just the experts from CEDERENA and the municipal environmental management unit. However, the coalition quickly recruited new members thanks to the social support for IWM created by the Dry Forest Project. The rapid expansion of Celica's coalition illustrates the influence of early local network activation during phase 1 on local campaigns during phase 2. The Celica case also shows the power of nodal governance during phase 1. Both founding organizations of Celica's IWM coalition—CEDERENA and the municipal environmental management unit—grew out of FAO's community forest program, DFC. So did the Dry Forest

Project, which was the vehicle for early local network activation in Celica. Even though the Dry Forest Project formally ended in 2004, and Postma and other Dutch experts left, IWM reform efforts continued in Celica through the efforts of local IWM experts like Paulo Bustamante, who were trained through the DFC and Dry Forest Project. This lasting, if indirect, influence of network activation by external IWM advocates is the essence of nodal governance during phase 1.

The Absence of Early Local Network Activation in Ibarra

When it comes to early local network activation, Ibarra is the exception that proves the rule. Of the six cases, Ibarra's Tahuando watershed experienced the least amount of network activation during phase 1. Although there was a great deal of mobilization around watershed management reform in Imbabura province generally, this occurred in neighboring cantons and watersheds. FAO's community forestry development program DFC created many community forestry development projects in Imbabura during the 1990s. As it did in Celica, the DFC program spawned dozens of projects by local and international organizations promoting IWM in Imbabura.[2] However, IWM advocates focused on the Chota-Mira watershed, which feeds the neighboring canton of Pimampiro and surrounding areas. The Tahuando watershed, which feeds the city of Ibarra, was relatively ignored.

Since Ibarra city is the provincial capital, it is where most international and local NGOs have their offices. This creates the ironic situation of a dense network of IWM advocates located in Ibarra city but virtually no network activation to better manage the watershed that feeds the city. This is unusual given that Ibarra is a large capital city; the other five cases also involve watersheds feeding capital cities.

Organizations working on watershed management in Imbabura said they did not focus on Ibarra's Tahuando watershed because they favored areas with greater social need. Evidence supports this claim. IWM advocates were most active in Cotacachi and Pimampiro, cantons with the highest rates of social vulnerability (72 and 62% respectively).[3] By contrast, Ibarra has the lowest rate of

[2] Leading IWM advocates working in Imbabura include FAO-DFC, EU, FEPP, DRI-Cotacachi, PRODERENA, Ayuda en Acción, Prodeci Foundation, CICDA, CESA, MACRENA, AGRECO, CEDERENA, Comibagua, and the Water Resources Forum of Imbabura.

[3] Social vulnerability refers to the sum of circumstances that affect a population group's capacity to provide for their well-being. It is measured by an index of five indicators, including adult illiteracy, child nutrition, poverty rate, child mortality rate, and the presence of rural indigenous communities (DRI-Cotacachi 2005).

social vulnerability (52%) (DRI-Cotacachi 2005, 7). A second explanation is that the Tahuando watershed does not lie in the buffer zone of an ecological reserve. Some IWM advocates focused on Pimampiro's watershed because of its importance to the Cayambe-Coca ecological reserve (PRODERENA 2007, 1). Concern for ecological reserves similarly motivated IWM advocates in Quito, El Chaco, and Zamora.

Both arguments likely explain part of the general phenomenon. Regardless, both indicate the important role played by transnational IWM networks in explaining where IWM reforms occur, as well as the importance of network activation to build a successful IWM coalition. Ibarra lacked the early local network activation by transnational networks preparing the way for environmental decentralization. As I show here, this absence helps explain why Ibarra's IWM reform attempts collapsed so quickly.

The story of Ibarra's IWM coalition begins with the arrival of PROFAFOR, the first international organization to work on conservation projects in the Tahuando watershed. PROFAFOR was created by the FACE Foundation (Forests Absorbing Carbon dioxide Emissions), a Dutch organization promoting reforestation to reduce the amount of carbon dioxide in the atmosphere. PROFAFOR (the FACE Program for Reforestation in Ecuador) was created in 1993 to finance reforestation in Ecuador to store atmospheric carbon dioxide. PROFAFOR first came to Ibarra through a contract with Hacienda Zuleta, which owned much of the Tahuando watershed's catchment area, to reforest its property. In 1998 the local indigenous community, Comuna Zuleta, successfully sued for ownership of the land. After years of negotiation, in 2001 PROFAFOR and Comuna Zuleta agreed to reforest 100 hectares of páramo (PROFAFOR 2001).

The interest in creating IWM institutions came from Ibarra's municipal water company, EMAPA-I. Historically, EMAPA-I had focused on urban water delivery systems at the exclusion of managing catchment areas. This changed in 2003 when a serious accident in Ibarra's potable water system led to an overhaul of EMAPA-I's leadership and staff.[4] Alvaro Castillo became EMAPA-I's new director and provided a new focus on environmental management. Castillo is another member of Ecuador's new generation of technical experts trained in watershed management at university. As such, he saw watershed protection as integral to maintaining EMAPA-I's water delivery system. He expanded EMAPA-I's responsibilities to include conservation and reforestation of watersheds, building nurseries to grow plants, and monitoring the condition of streams that affect the quality and quantity of water. To this end, Castillo created a new Environmental Management Unit staffed by an environmental technical team.

---

[4] This accident resulted from heavy rains and led to an outbreak of gastroenteritis.

EMAPA-I's environmental unit researched the quantity and quality of water and documented a nearly 50% drop in water flow in some areas. They attributed this to deforestation and overgrazing of pasture.[5] Based on this data, the technical team proposed a series of policies oriented toward the conservation and protection of water sources. However, there was no money allotted for such activities in the budget. In 2004, Castillo and his team began searching for a way to finance its watershed conservation efforts.

When PROFAFOR director Luís Fernando Jara learned of EMAPA-I's new interest in watershed management, he saw a new business opportunity. PROFAFOR had no previous experience with protecting watershed ecosystem services; its expertise was with carbon sequestration (another ecosystem service provided by forests). However, Jara saw that payment for watershed ecosystem services programs were increasingly popular, both globally and in Ecuador, and he decided to expand PROFAFOR's business by consulting on such systems.

This decision was facilitated by the fact that Jara's wife was Doris Cordero, an internationally recognized expert on watershed management and payment for ecosystem services. Cordero is a Costa Rican who was involved in that country's national watershed management reforms. She later moved to Ecuador and worked for GTZ-PROMACH, helping design the payment for ecosystem services program proposed in Tungurahua in 2002 (see chapter 7). Cordero agreed to help PROFAFOR design a similar program to propose to Ibarra's government. Cordero once again illustrates the key role played by national brokers during phase 1, this time providing weak ties between Ibarra and the GWP-ECLAC-GTZ network.

In July 2004, Jara and Cordero presented EMAPA-I with a proposal to conduct a rapid environmental assessment that would result in a plan for establishing an IWM program to manage Ibarra's watersheds. Given Castillo's concern about financing his new conservation agenda, he eagerly accepted PROFAFOR's offer. In February 2005, EMAPA-I contracted PROFAFOR to carry out a series of diagnostic studies with the goal of creating a payment for ecosystem services mechanism and related IWM institutions (PROFAFOR 2005b, 3). With this, Ibarra's IWM coalition was formed. It had only an indirect and weak tie to transnational IWM networks via Doris Cordero, the wife of PROFAFOR's director.

Not surprisingly, given Cordero's experience with GTZ, PROFAFOR's proposed IWM system was very similar to Quito's watershed trust fund, FONAG (described in chapter 4). The centerpiece was a financing mechanism in which water users would pay into a fiduciary fund that would finance activities specified in an integrated watershed management plan. The fund was to be capitalized

---

[5] Member, Environmental Management Unit, Municipal Water Company of Ibarra (EMAPA-I), interview by author, September 11, 2009.

mainly through a fee levied on water use by EMAPA-I. Part of the money was to be invested in an endowment to ensure long-term financial stability, while part would finance watershed management activities (PROFAFOR 2005a). The proposal also called for a Fiduciary Fund Council, an independent, participatory body charged with managing the fund's money and deciding which projects were to be funded. The council was to include representatives of the watershed's various stakeholders, including the municipal government, various water user groups, and landowners in the watershed.

In the end, the coalition's efforts to institutionalize IWM in Ibarra never went beyond conducting diagnostic studies and creating a proposal. The process stalled early on because PROFAFOR and EMAPA-I were unable to get their proposal on to the municipal government's agenda. According to current and former directors of the government's Environmental Control and Management Unit, this was because natural resource management was viewed as outside the municipal government's jurisdiction.[6] As a result, the government never developed the legal framework or human and institutional capacity to manage watershed resources. Instead, the municipality's agenda was oriented toward urban pollution control.

Why did Ibarra's Environmental Control and Management Unit not address natural resource management like its counterparts in other cantons? The answer lies in the lack of early local network activation by IWM advocates. Ibarra's mayor created the municipal Environmental Control and Management Unit in 1999, when Ecuador's Environmental Management Law was passed, to prepare for environmental decentralization. He originally intended for the unit to manage natural resources as well as urban pollution.[7] However, during negotiations over decentralization, Environment Ministry bureaucrats convinced the municipality that natural resource management was outside its jurisdiction. Ibarra was caught in the bureaucratic struggles and contradictory trends regarding decentralization described in chapter 4. Although natural resource management was officially listed among the responsibilities to be transferred, ministry bureaucrats refused to concede this area for Ibarra. According to then-director of Ibarra's environmental management unit:

> We signed an agreement with the Ministry of Environment, but only for the management of certain functions, but not as a process of decentralization. Rather, it was simply for the delegation of certain responsibilities relating to environmental quality and not for the issue of natural

[6] Interviews by author, Ibarra, Ecuador, June 17 and 21, 2010.
[7] Former director of Ibarra's Environmental Control and Management Unit, interview by author, Ibarra, Ecuador, June 21, 2010.

resources, because the ministry managed natural resources and they did not want to delegate these responsibilities.[8]

As a result, natural resource management was taken off the municipal government's agenda from the beginning. The environmental management unit never developed the human, administrative, or technical capacity to address natural resources, which undermined later efforts to establish IWM reforms. Ibarra's environmental management director at the time explained this by saying "natural resources were not within the municipal government domain. . . . It's that, from the view of the constitution, what was delegated to us was environmental quality and not natural resource management." Subsequent environmental management directors also expressed this view. Yet, the statement is curious since IWM reforms were established in other cantons at the same time under the same legal framework. Local governments in the other five case studies came to see watershed management as within their domain. What explains this difference?

Strategic Framing to Establish Local Authority

The contrast between Ibarra's experience and that of the more successful cases illustrates the importance of early local network activation surrounding environmental decentralization. During the late 1990s, IWM advocates trained local knowledge communities and created environmental management units in Celica, Tungurahua, El Chaco, and Zamora to pave the way for environmental decentralization. Although Ecuador's national government never transferred responsibilities and resources to local governments as called for in Ecuador's decentralization laws, IWM advocates used these unimplemented laws to pursue their reform agenda locally even after the decentralization process stalled. These laws constituted an important resource for IWM advocates, helping them justify the expansion of local government authority for the planning, regulating, financing, and implementation of watershed management activities.

IWM advocates' use of strategic framing to establish municipal authority for watershed management was particularly important. IWM advocates strategically interpreted passages of unimplemented laws to convince local politicians that IWM reform was something they not only *should* do but legally *could* do. They were successful in five of the six case studies. Only in Ibarra did the IWM reform process break down during political agenda setting. The legal arguments justifying IWM reform in the other cases are cited in the ordinances establishing

[8] Interview by author, Ibarra, Ecuador, June 21, 2010.

the reforms. These ordinances cite the same legal passages used by IWM advocates to justify local governments' assumption of new powers related to watershed management.[9]

Program documents from Tungurahua and Celica illustrate how IWM advocates established watershed management as a municipal responsibility, in stark contrast to Ibarra's experience. When GTZ established its IWM program PROMACH in 1997, it chose Tungurahua's Ambato River watershed as the pilot project. As with its counterparts in Celica, Zamora, and El Chaco, GTZ cited the 1997 decentralization laws and 1998 Constitution to justify its efforts to expand local government authority for managing watersheds. GTZ cited Articles 224 through 233 of the 1998 Constitution and Article 10 of the 1997 Decentralization Law to argue that local governments were the "entities charged with watershed management" and that local governments were responsible for carrying out all related activities as a result of the decentralization process (REDLACH 2002, 4). A 2002 report stated that "under this mandate," GTZ-PROMACH would

> oversee a process for transferring the management of watersheds. Implementation of the political, administrative and social aspects of the Law of Decentralization and Social Participation has created a demand for strengthening local governments so they can identify their own problems and solutions, and has allowed the rationalization of administrative functions and the participation of rural actors and communities in the decision-making process. (REDLACH 2002, 8)

SNV—the Dutch organization running Celica's Dry Forest Program—similarly cited Articles 23, 225, and 226 of the 1998 Constitution; Article 9 of the 1997 Decentralization Law; and Articles 12-13 of the 1999 Environmental Management Law to justify its creation of municipal-level, participatory mechanisms for watershed management (Bustamante 2004, 8, 29–33).

Persuading local governments that they had the power to manage watershed resources was necessary because national legislation was ambiguous and contradictory, creating confusion about the responsibilities of different levels of government (see chapter 3). Political instability and the reluctance of ministry bureaucrats to cede responsibilities further complicated the situation. Municipal governments' mandate was particularly murky since municipal governments

---

[9] Passages commonly cited include Articles 23, 225, and 226 of the 1998 Constitution; Article 3 of the 1997 Decentralization Law; Articles 12 and 13 of the 1999 Environmental Management Law; and Articles 12, 15, 16, 161–165 of the Municipal Law (originally passed in 1971 and amended in 2004).

traditionally limited themselves to providing potable water and sanitation services in urban areas. Their power to manage natural resources in rural areas was
far from clear.

Nor was the incentive for local politicians to assume these responsibilities
always obvious. Since municipal governments were not normally involved in
managing watershed resources, particularly in rural areas, they did not have
the institutional capacity to do so. Because responsibilities and resources were
not formally transferred by the central government, local governments had to
develop new systems for raising the necessary resources locally. This was not
easy, given the clientelistic nature of politics in Ecuador and the tendency of
many local officials to extract rents from national patrons rather than local constituents. Assuming local authorities could be motivated to pursue IWM reform,
these officials felt the need to legally justify their assumption of authority in this
new issue area to combat local opposition.

IWM advocates were quite creative and strategic in their interpretation of
legal passages to provide this justification. One illustrative example comes from
Article 163 of Ecuador's Municipal Reform Law. This article states that municipal governments are responsible for "providing potable water and sanitation to
the canton's population, regulating its use and *doing what is necessary to ensure
the supply and distribution of water of adequate quality and in sufficient quantity for
public consumption* [italics added]." IWM advocates interpreted this call to do
"what is necessary" as a mandate to mange watershed resources in an integrated
manner. Advocates strategically framed IWM principles and practices as necessary to ensure the canton's quantity and quality of water. Among other things,
this included conserving water catchment areas, something traditionally seen
as beyond municipal governments' purview. Article 397 of the law allows municipal councils to raise revenues to recover the cost of public service provision.
IWM advocates strategically interpreted these two passages together to justify
creating local financing and decision-making mechanisms for integrated watershed management.

Ibarra was the exception and illustrates the importance of strategically framing watershed management as a power of local government. When municipal
authorities were negotiating the assumption of environmental management in
the late 1990s, there were no IWM advocates to help them contest Environment
Ministry bureaucrats' assertion that natural resource management was outside
their jurisdiction. By the time Ibarra's IWM coalition presented their watershed
management proposal in 2005, the country's decentralization process was long
stalled and the municipal government's environmental agenda was set around
pollution control. Local government representatives were reluctant to devote
more resources to watershed management and ignored the proposal. The coalition soon disbanded.

Conclusion

The Celica and Ibarra cases illustrate the importance of network activation during phase 1 for opening local sociopolitical opportunity structures to the possibility of IWM reform in phase 2. Network activation changed local conditions in ways that were conducive to both the formation of local IWM coalitions and their ability to mobilize support among local stakeholders. A leader of Celica's local IWM coalition explained how prior organizing around watershed management facilitated the coalition's ability to recruit both landowners and water users to their cause:

> The Dry Forest Project had an influence in raising awareness about the issue of environmental management and watersheds. . . . They carried out workshops to train local organizers, but also, from this emerged a social organization based on these issues, called UCPACE [Cantonal Union of Agricultural Producers of Celica]. This association resulted from the conversations the Dry Forest Project had with the communities, producing leaders who worked to organize their communities around this issue of environmental management. . . . You have to re-member that . . . some of these ideas [regarding ecosystem services] had already been planted by the Dry Forest Project and SNV [the Dutch agency overseeing the project]. . . . Basically, in [2000] this idea was developed that all the social organizations, foundations, and mu-nicipal council would collaborate to develop a Cantonal Development Plan that would identify the needs and issues to be addressed in each sector of each parish. So when the Cantonal Development Plan was published in 2002, it already mentioned ecosystem services as a goal for the municipal government of Celica; protecting water resources was part of the development plan.[10]

Network activation through the Dry Forest Program created the opportunity for IWM reform in part by placing watershed management on the agenda of local stakeholders and changing their perceptions. It created an awareness among Celica's citizens of the link between the destruction of watershed resources and their water shortage problem. This increased citizens' willingness to pay to re-store the watershed. Surveys conducted in late 2005 show that 77% of water users were willing to pay an environmental tax on water use to be reinvested in watershed protection and restoration (Cuenca 2008). These survey results gave

---

[10] Interview by author, Celica, Ecuador, March 4, 2010.

local politicians the confidence to move forward with an ordinance legislating a new IWM system. The training and institution building that occurred through the Dry Forest project—from the municipal environmental management unit to the farmers association UCPACE—greatly enhanced Celicans' capacity to design and implement this system.

In Ibarra, the lack of early local network activation around IWM reform meant Ibarra's coalition faced a relatively closed opportunity structure—one they were unable to overcome. Watershed management had not been placed on the agenda of politicians, local government experts, landowners, or water users. PROFAFOR and EMAPA-I required approval by the municipal government to move forward on their proposed IWM system. The task of gaining this approval fell to the director of EMAPA-I's Environmental Management Unit. He was never able to get the municipal council or mayor to consider the proposal. He explained the failure this way:

> I believe my words fell on deaf ears. We were not able to make the ideas stick with the three council members . . . they were not interested. Later, we met with the mayor independently, but he also was not interested in the ideas.[11]

When asked who opposed the reform proposal, the director replied, "It's not that. The project never made it to a point where it could be decided for or against. We have not yet reached that point." The IWM reform process stalled because the proposal was literally never placed on the local government's agenda. When I asked local politicians and leaders of the municipal environmental management unit why this was the case, the answer uniformly given was that natural resource management was simply not part of the municipal government's institutional mandate. Ibarra's opportunity structure was closed because IWM advocates were absent during the crucial period when Ibarra's environmental management agenda was being set.

Ibarra's challenging environment did not necessarily condemn the IWM coalition to failure. Conditions were challenging in all six cases when local IWM campaigns were launched. As the next two chapters show, success depends not only on the conditions facing local IWM coalitions when they form, but also on the network activation strategies coalitions use to expand locally—that is, to build the motivation and capacity among local stakeholders to institutionalize IWM principles.

This chapter showed how the first stage of grassroots global governance sets the conditions for the second stage. Transnational IWM networks expanded to

---

[11] Interview by author, Ibarra, Ecuador, September 11, 2009.

different localities to different degrees. Where they were active, network members altered the local conditions in which IWM coalitions formed and later pursued their agenda. This impacted subsequent efforts to expand the transnational governance network locally. High levels of network activation prior to the formation of local IWM coalitions made these coalitions' job easier. But as chapter 6 shows, local coalitions' strategies for activating local stakeholder networks still mattered a great deal.

6

Phase 2

Why Local Integrated Watershed Management
Campaigns Endure

In 2005, three organizations formed a coalition to promote IWM reform in Pastaza. The coalition included two local environmental NGOs—CODEAMA and Amazon Forestry Service (*Servicio Forestal Amazónica*)—and the municipal government's Department of Local Sustainable Development. They recognized that implementing a new IWM program required the support of local politicians, landowners farming the watershed, and various water user groups. Given limited resources, Pastaza's coalition decided to work with each stakeholder group sequentially. It first focused on gaining the support of landowners, since the ultimate goal was to change land-use practices in the watershed. In early 2006, coalition members launched an education campaign (*campaña de socialización*). They visited each property in two watersheds that were prioritized, had landowners visit the watersheds' catchment areas, and held public assemblies to discuss other communities' experiences with payment for ecosystems services.

Pastaza's IWM advocates were surprised at the level of resistance they encountered. They did not understand why landowners refused to participate in the program even though landowners could earn more income through their proposed compensation-for-conservation scheme than by raising cattle. Coalition leaders admitted, "we did not take into account that this new proposal was going to be difficult to accept and be credible [for landowners] and that it would be difficult to get a cattle rancher to leave this profession even though it is not profitable." In addition to "a lack of sympathy for the idea," coalition leaders blamed "distrust at this being a municipal initiative," due to the history of political clientelism (Garzón and Mancheno 2008, 6).

Daunted by landowners' resistance, IWM advocates switched their focus to mobilizing support among urban water users. Coalition leaders explained this change in strategy as follows:

> Due to the lack of credibility and trust between the Municipal Government and the various landowners, and the fact that there did not exist the necessary force to demand change, we decided to invest principally in raising the awareness of the problem within the population. The design for the second phase [of the education campaign] was based on the assumption that a population aware of the problem would generate a public opinion favorable to the creation of the [Watershed Management] Fund and exert "moral" pressure on landowners, which would depoliticize the problem and place it in the context of the city's structural needs. (Garzón and Mancheno 2008, 7)

In other words, the coalition's strategy was to overcome landowner resistance by cultivating pressure from beside from urban water users.

In hindsight, Pastaza's IWM advocates recognized that their efforts were complicated by the fact that they largely stopped working with landowners in order to mobilize water users. In contrast to more successful cases, there was no sustained effort to train community organizers or organize local farmers into associations dedicated to IWM reform. According to coalition leaders, "the only person who had dialogue and a permanent presence in the zone due to the task of mapping territorial boundaries was the German intern Katherine Green" (Garzón and Mancheno 2008, 6). The IWM coalition's lack of sustained contact with landowners undermined the legitimacy of reform efforts. Many landowners said that since they saw "only foreigners," they believed the program lacked support among local water users and the municipal government. Lacking pressure from other local stakeholder groups, these landowners were reluctant to change their traditional practices.

The IWM coalition's experience with urban water users paralleled its experience with landowners. Initial attempts at network activation were met with resistance. In March 2007, IWM advocates convened 25 people from six governmental organizations, six educational organizations, six indigenous and social organizations, and six neighborhood associations. At the meeting, coalition members proposed creating a Citizen Environmental Network that would mobilize public pressure for creating IWM institutions like a Puyo Watershed Fund. This local environmental network never materialized. According to participants, the March meeting became a forum for lodging complaints against the municipal government, which was reluctant to repeat the process. No further meetings were held and the citizen network never formed.

Consequently, despite some initial publicity, there was no sustained effort at network activation with either water users or landowners. Rather than persevering in their attempts to mobilize pressure from beside, coalition members turned instead to gathering information on ecosystem functioning and working with municipal politicians and bureaucrats to design IWM institutions. Pastaza's coalition arranged for municipal representatives to attend workshops with CEDERENA, the Ecuadorian NGO that developed Ecuador's first payment for ecosystem services program in Pimampiro (see chapter 4). With CEDERENA's help, municipal officials drafted regulations for an IWM system based around three new institutions: a Puyo Water Fund, a participatory Watershed Management Committee, and an Environmental Management Unit in the municipal water company charged with developing and implementing integrated watershed management plans. In 2009, Pastaza's municipal government passed an ordinance calling for the creation of a new IWM system that would function through these institutions.

Despite the ordinance, IWM reforms were never implemented. One problem was a change in administration after the 2009 elections. The new director of local sustainable development diverted the department's energy and resources to more traditional activities of agricultural development. He stalled implementation of the ordinance and declared his intention to renegotiate the terms of IWM reform. Perceiving an unfavorable political climate, Pastaza's IWM coalition disbanded. Its members turned to other projects, often in other cantons.

According to coalition members, the absence of social demand for IWM reform led municipal officials to believe they could ignore the ordinance. Given the clientelistic nature of local politics in Ecuador, laws often remain unimplemented in the absence of social demand. Political conflicts tend to be settled by mobilizing social protests to pressure reluctant politicians.[1] Without social pressure, policies often succumb to political inertia.

The break down in Pastaza illustrates how, even with initial political support, IWM reform cannot move forward without simultaneous network activation to mobilize pressure from beside. In Pastaza, the sustained network activation needed to mobilize social demand was lacking. Rather, coalition members focused on the technical components of rule making. Because the coalition had allies within the municipal government for a time, it was able to construct the legal basis for IWM reforms. When the government changed, however, the coalition lost its allies within this key stakeholder group. Given the lack of social pressure to overcome the new administration's reluctance, the coalition's efforts resulted in empty paper reforms.

---

[1] Former mayor Oscar Ledesma, interview by author, Puyo, Ecuador, December 7, 2009.

Strategies for Mobilizing Simultaneous Pressure from Beside

The challenges facing Pastaza's IWM coalition were not unique. Indeed, they were typical of the conditions facing local IWM coalitions during Phase 2 of grassroots global governance. All six IWM coalitions faced similar obstacles: distrust among stakeholders due to clientelism and/or ethnic conflict; local political struggles; a tendency to view watersheds as economic resources to be exploited rather than conserved; opposition by farmers to changing land-use practices; resistance by water users to paying more to finance watershed restoration; and a reluctance among politicians to do anything considered politically risky. Consequently, each local IWM coalition initially faced resistance among the very groups whose behaviors they sought to change and whose support they needed for IWM campaigns to succeed.

What differentiated the six coalitions was not the level of resistance initially encountered (or other local conditions), but rather the combination of framing and network capacity-building strategies IWM advocates used to overcome this resistance by mobilizing pressure from beside. IWM advocates succeeded by constructing broad coalitions linking local politicians, municipal experts, landowners, water-user groups, and other resource users. Diverse coalitions were important because they could mobilize a broader array of resources and had a greater number of access points for exerting and maintaining a mutually enforcing circle of pressure from beside. Creating this circle of pressure required the simultaneous mobilization of each main stakeholder group—that is, synching the cogs in the metaphorical clock discussed in chapter 2.

This chapter shows how mobilizing simultaneous pressure from beside required IWM advocates to: (1) *motivate* members of each local stakeholder group to join the governance network, contributing their time and resources to the cause; and (2) enhance the network's *capacity* to combine the resources accessible to each stakeholder and convert these into action. The chapter employs frame and social network analysis (described in the Methodological Appendix) to compare the framing and network capacity-building strategies IWM coalitions used to build the requisite motivation and capacity among local stakeholders. The results show that different combinations of strategies produced different outcomes during phase 2 of grassroots global governance. Variation in framing and capacity-building strategies explains not only which IWM reform processes endured, but also the stage at which failed cases broke down (see Table 6.1).

The next section compares the framing strategies used to motivate local stakeholders to join IWM coalitions. Most Ecuadorians viewed watershed resources as something to be exploited to expand production in order to reduce poverty.

Successful IWM coalitions adopted a frame-displacement strategy that redefined this dominant "production/poverty" frame (as I call it) to include IWM reform. By contrast, reform attempts were less successful to the extent IWM coalitions relied on a counter-framing strategy that challenged the "production/poverty" frame with an alternative "conservation" or "market" frame.

The following section employs social network analysis to compare the degree to which IWM coalitions employed network capacity-building strategies (e.g., training knowledge communities and creating new linking and governing institutions). Social network analysis shows that IWM campaigns were more likely to endure when coalitions engaged in a high level of network capacity building. This produced dense, cohesive networks able to mobilize resources from a diverse array of stakeholder groups and direct these toward pressure for IWM reform. Less successful coalitions engaged in a low level of network capacity building, which produced sparse networks that were weakly embedded in local stakeholder groups.

Table 6.1 shows the results of different combinations of framing and capacity-building strategies. The two least-successful cases (Ibarra and Pastaza) combined a counter-framing strategy with low levels of capacity building. This produced noninclusive coalitions that were weakly embedded within local stakeholder groups. Few coalition members were local stakeholders with the motivation and capacity to press for reform. Consequently, these coalitions lacked access points from which to exert pressure from beside and their efforts failed at the initial agenda-setting stages. Chapter 5 described how Ibarra's coalition failed to get IWM reform on the agenda of local politicians, nipping the process in the bud. This chapter's opening anecdote showed how the failure to mobilize social pressure undermined Pastaza's campaign.

Tungurahua's first failed IWM reform campaign (detailed in chapter 7) shows what happens when you combine a high level of capacity building with a counter-framing strategy. Although a diverse array of stakeholders was initially

Table 6.1 **Results of Network Activation Strategies in Phase 2**

	Frame-Displacement (Motivation)	Counter-Framing (No Motivation)
High Network Capacity Building	Successful Reform: Tungurahua, Celica, El Chaco	Breakdown at Rule making: Tungurahua's 2002 PES Proposal
Low Network Capacity Building	Breakdown at Implementation: Zamora	Breakdown at Agenda Setting (Ibarra) or Social Mobilization (Pastaza)

mobilized, they rejected the proposed rules because they were perceived to conflict with the dominant watershed management frame. As a result, the process broke down at the rule-making stage. Conversely, Zamora illustrates the results of a frame-displacement strategy combined with low capacity building. The motivation to reform was successfully cultivated among municipal authorities and some landowners, but water users were not incorporated into the coalition. This obstructed the mutual pressure among all three stakeholder groups needed to sustain the implementation process. To use the clock analogy from chapter 2, one of the cogs was not synchronized and became stuck, stopping the clock mechanism. As a result, the process broke down during the implementation stage.

IWM coalitions in the three successful cases (Tungurahua, Celica, and El Chaco) combined a frame-displacement strategy with high levels of network capacity building. This combination produces a broad coalition comprised of many different stakeholder groups with the motivation and capacity to maintain pressure for reform, allowing the process to endure. The chapter's final section analyzes local network activation in El Chaco to show how this occurs.

Creating Motivation through Framing

The first step in motivating people to take action is making them aware of a problem. When they launched their local campaigns, Ecuador's IWM coalitions used diagnostic framing to identify a problem with natural resource use and assign blame. The specific problem identified varied depending on local ecosystem characteristics. Coalitions in Ecuador's Sierra region focused on water scarcity while those in the Amazon tended to emphasize threats to ecological reserves. Nevertheless, each IWM coalition tried to create a shared conception of the watershed as a territorial site connecting different stakeholders around a collective problem of natural resource use that affected the quantity and quality of water available to stakeholders.

All six IWM coalitions blamed problems of water quantity and quality on behaviors related to economic production, particularly livestock farming, logging, deforestation to expand the agricultural frontier, and contamination of streams from pesticides and animal waste. Celica's coalition, for example, claimed that "livestock farming constitutes one of the principal problems given that it causes erosion, compacting, and damage to the natural regeneration of vegetation. Deforestation and the slash and burning of brush" to expand production were also identified as main problems (Cuenca 2008, 14). Despite the different environmental contexts, the analysis and language used by coalitions in the Amazon was almost identical. For example, Pastaza's IWM coalition blamed the lack of safe water on "bad agricultural practices, the expansion of the agricultural frontier, and the deterioration of forests and water sources" due to cattle ranching and the cultivation of *naranjillas* (a shrub producing an orange-like fruit) (Foro de Recursos Hídricos de Pastaza 2008, 1).[2]

By identifying agricultural production practices as the main problem, IWM coalitions directly challenged the existing, dominant frame regarding watershed resources. In each case, the dominant frame initially encountered by IWM advocates was a production/poverty frame. In this frame, a watershed's natural resources should be exploited to expand economic production in order to reduce poverty. Forested or vegetated areas are viewed as "unproductive" or "unused" land. Ecuadorian laws reinforced this view by allowing squatters to appropriate supposedly unused land by placing livestock or crops on it.[3] Expanding the agricultural frontier into ecologically sensitive areas, particularly water catchment areas, was seen as a natural and necessary strategy for socioeconomic development.

A second frame used by some local stakeholders was an "environmental justice" frame, which condemned the inequitable distribution of environmental "goods" (e.g., access to land and water) and "bads" (e.g., pollution). In Ecuador, as elsewhere, indigenous communities are leading advocates of the environmental justice frame due to their historic marginalization. Not surprisingly, this frame was most common in areas with large indigenous populations, like Tungurahua. In practice, the environmental justice frame was tied to an indigenous rights frame, which demanded respect for traditional values and practices as well as autonomous communal management of natural resources.[4] It also incorporated concepts from Ecuadorian indigenous cosmology, which stresses the interdependence of all living things, the value of nature for its own sake, and calls for a harmonious relationship between humans and nature. Watershed resources were seen as both life-sustaining resources to which the poor should have access and valuable cultural symbols to be protected from the vagaries of capitalist development.

Given this conflict between IWM coalitions' diagnostic framing and preexisting attitudes toward the use of watershed resources, IWM advocates realized they would need to change local perceptions. To this end, each coalition

---

[2] For similar language in Tungurahua, see Metais and Cruz (2003, 44–46); in Zamora, see Coronel and Jaramillo (2005); in El Chaco, see Yaguache et al. (2005); in Ibarra, see PROFAFOR (2005b, 34).

[3] Environmental lawyer with The Nature Conservancy-Ecuador, interview by author, Quito, Ecuador, June 23, 2011.

[4] For explanations and analysis of indigenous organizing around indigenous rights, transnationally and in the Andes, see Brysk (2000); Postero and Zamosc (2004); and Yashar (2005).

launched an education campaign—albeit to varying degrees—to raise awareness of watershed management problems and present IWM reform as a necessary solution. They did this through meetings, trainings, and workshops with stakeholders; publicity campaigns using radio, television, and print media; and hosting symbolic festivals, like those celebrating International Water Day and Earth Day. In all six cases, IWM advocates initially used these activities to counter the production/poverty frame with an alternative frame. Two main counterframes were used: "market" and "conservation" frames. As I discuss below, IWM coalitions that succeeded did so after displacing the production/poverty frame to include IWM reform. Table 6.2 compares the two preexisting watershed management frames with the three alternative frames promoted at different times by IWM advocates.

Table 6.2 **Five Watershed Management Frames**

Frame	View of Watersheds	Strategy
Production/Poverty	Natural resources to be exploited to expand economic production to reduce poverty.	Preexisting Master Frame
Environmental Justice (tied to Indigenous Rights)	Life-sustaining resources to which the poor should have access; cultural symbols to be controlled communally and protected from capitalist development.	Preexisting Frame
Market	Ecosystems producing goods and services that are inappropriately priced and thus over-consumed; sustainable use requires regulation through a market mechanism.	Counter-Framing
Conservation	Ecosystems that must be restored and protected for their inherent value and to ensure future access to ecosystem goods and services.	Counter-Framing
Displaced Production/ Poverty	Ecosystems that comprise part of the economic production chain; their destruction generates losses to production; their conservation and integrated management can reduce poverty.	Frame-Displacement

Countering with a Market Frame

Economic theories advocating markets for ecosystem services rose to global prominence in the late 1990s and diffused to Ecuador through the transnational networks described in chapter 4. As a result, many IWM advocates working in Ecuador between 1997 and 2004 initially employed a market frame. This was most evident in Ecuador's earliest IWM reform efforts—Quito's water trust fund, FONAG, Pimampiro's payment for ecosystem services program, and Tungurahua's initial campaign from 1997–2002—but also existed in later proposals in Ibarra and Pastaza.

The market frame defined the problem as the unsustainable use of natural resources due to inappropriate pricing. Because environmentally harmful behaviors were not sufficiently expensive, market failure ensued, producing negative externalities like water shortages and contamination. The proposed solution was to create a functioning market by altering the price of ecosystem goods and services. The benefits humans enjoy from watershed ecosystems were framed as "services," whose value could be converted into a price. These ecosystem services could then be sold by "producers" and purchased by "consumers," as in any other market. In this schema, landowners in a watershed, particularly catchment areas, were considered producers of ecosystem services regulating water. Downstream water users were consumers. The main challenge was calculating the appropriate price for these services so that producers had an incentive to ensure the continuation of ecosystem services by conserving and restoring strategic areas of the watershed. The benefits of forgoing environmentally harmful behaviors (e.g., expanding the agricultural frontier) must outweigh the costs.

Figure 6.1 shows a typical campaign poster using the market frame. This image was widely circulated and used by multiple coalitions. The market frame is also found in reform proposals, promotional materials, and public speeches. Those in Tungurahua are representative. Coalition documents consistently identified problems in the supply and demand for water and blamed them on the failure to place an economic value on ecosystem services (e.g., Foro Provincial de los Recursos Hídricos en Tungurahua 2002; Maldonado and Kosmus 2003). An early IWM reform proposal argued that, because natural resources constituted a form of "capital . . . it is necessary to identify and value environmental goods and services as one element of the economic system" (Comisión Ejecutiva Provincial 2002, 4). "Consumers" must make "payments" to those "producing" these goods and services. These payments represent the "opportunity cost of forgoing potential income that the land could generate through alternative economic activities" (Comisión Ejecutiva Provincial 2002, 3, 15).

Figure 6.1 Countering with a Market Frame. This image was used by Pastaza's IWM coalition in publicity materials and originally appeared in Wunder 2005. Reproduced here by permission from Belcher B, Cossalter C, and Wunder S. 2005. Exchange. Photograph. In "Payments for Environmental Services: Some Nuts and Bolts." Occasional Paper No. 42. Bogor: CIFOR, 2005.

Through publicity materials and community meetings, IWM advocates educated local stakeholders about the natural water cycle in order to explain the interdependence among suppliers and consumers of watershed services and the environmentally destructive nature of existing production practices. They tried to motivate water users to pay for conservation and restoration efforts by convincing them this was necessary to improve access to quality water. To motivate farmers to change land use practices, IWM advocates presented the formulas used to calculate the opportunity costs of forgoing traditional livestock production and extolled the economic advantages of participating in conservation programs.

While many urban water users resisted the idea of paying more, farmers were the most resistant to the market frame. IWM advocates uniformly expressed surprise and frustration at how farmers rejected their offers, even though their formulas clearly showed that farmers could earn more through the compensation-for-conservation schemes than by raising cattle or growing crops. Many farmers simply did not act like rational economic actors. Interviews with local landowners suggest the market frame failed to motivate them because the frame directly countered strongly held cultural values.

Negotiations between Celica's coalition and one landowner provide a typical example. This farmer made $80 per month selling cheese made from the milk produced by his 10 cows. Under the proposed compensation-for-conservation agreement, he would earn $160 monthly for removing the cattle from part of his land and allowing it to regenerate naturally. In addition to doubling his monthly income, he would no longer have the labor involved with caring for cattle and manufacturing cheese, no small consideration for the aging farmer. He also would have a guaranteed income rather than be subject to the risk of having his cattle stolen or die from thirst (a common occurrence during Celica's dry summer months). As part of the compensation agreement, he also would not pay property taxes, saving him an additional $220 per year.

Despite these economic incentives, the farmer resisted signing the agreement. When asked why, he stressed his need to live off the milk, cheese, and meat provided by the cattle, simply saying "I have to eat my cow."[5] The local IWM advocate responsible for negotiating with Celica's landowners explained this by saying "cattle are a symbol of wealth and prestige for people, and it is very difficult to overcome this cultural norm. . . . There are always landowners that are a little more tied to the land and it is difficult to break this link with the land."[6]

In Tungurahua and Ibarra, where farmers relied on irrigation and indigenous groups were present, resistance to markets for ecosystem services was even greater. In Tungurahua, local NGOs and small-scale farmers utilized both the production/poverty and environmental justice frames to oppose a proposed payment for ecosystem services program, labeling it unjust and anti-poor. They argued the program would place an unreasonable financial burden on farmers that rely on irrigation, which would exacerbate both poverty and the unequal distribution of water resources. Thus, the reforms challenged their goals of reducing poverty through expanded production. Indigenous groups (which represented indigenous smallholder farmers) agreed with these arguments, but also rejected the market frame as violating their cultural values, which prohibit the privatization and commodification of nature.

Rightly or wrongly, many Ecuadorians came to see payment for ecosystem services as commodifying nature and a dangerous step toward water privatization. When concern about water privatization made water management a national issue, the debate over payment for ecosystem services also became national. Equating watershed resources with Pachamama (a sacred deity revered by indigenous people in the Andes), Ecuador's National Confederation of Indigenous Nationalities (CONAIE) and the environmental NGO Acción

---

[5] Interview by author, Celica, Ecuador, March 8, 2010.
[6] Interview by author, Celica, Ecuador, March 11, 2010.

Ecológica mobilized opposition through the slogan "Pachamama is not for sale!" (*La Pachamama no se vende!*).[7] CONAIE and other national indigenous associations directed their local affiliates to reject payment for ecosystem services programs, which they initially did (see chapter 7).

By the mid-2000s, it was clear that employing a market frame was a failed strategy. The term "payment for ecosystem services" was toxic in Ecuador. Even advocates stopped using it. Yet, they didn't give up on basic IWM principles or their policy prescriptions. Rather, they looked for new ways to frame them. The need to find a new framing was acknowledged by international organizations meeting in Quito in April 2006 to discuss the impact and future prospects of market-based instruments in Latin America. The workshop report notes that:

> There appears to be resistance to the term "payment" because some believe this implies automatically a privatization of the services. Experimentation with alternative names and meanings is underway. This project is trying out the term "compensation for environmental services," however, this also creates some negative noise when translated to Spanish (Poats 2007, 9).

Countering with a Conservation Frame

Recognizing the market frame's failure, many IWM coalitions adapted their counter-framing strategy to emphasize an alternative conservation frame. The conservation frame stressed the inherent value of watershed ecosystems, which deserve protection in their own right. In this narrative, environmental problems arose because people individually and societies collectively did not value environmental protection. The solution was for people to better appreciate the value of watershed ecosystems, including the provision of clean water. Watersheds must be restored and protected to ensure the future existence of valuable resources like water, forests, and biodiversity. The frame called on people to consider the need for future access to these resources as an incentive to stop environmentally harmful activities. Watersheds were framed as "water factories" to emphasize their value in sustaining life (see Fig. 6.2). Slogans like "water is life" (*agua es vida*) appealed for people to consider a future without water and bear this in mind when deciding whether to engage in destructive behavior. Slogans like "together for water" (*juntos por el agua*) framed the degradation and

---

[7] Acción Ecológica worked with CONAIE and other indigenous groups to produce a video expressing the arguments behind the slogan "Pachamama is not for sale," available at www.accionecologica.org/component/content/article/313-multimedia/1503-video-la-pachamama-no-se-vende (accessed February 13, 2016).

The forests are our water factories!

The forests are factories of clean and fresh water because they capture rain water and filter it in the subsoil, where we extract the water for our consumption. Because of this, one of the most concerning problems in Zamora is the loss of vegetation. If we don't care for it, Zamora could be converted into a dry territory with extreme weather and without water. Imagine living one day with only one drop of water! We still have time. Together let's conserve the water.

Figure 6.2 Countering with a Conservation Frame. Image source: author's photograph of a campaign poster publicly displayed in Zamora. English translation by author.

contamination of water resources as a collective problem requiring a collective solution. The challenge became delimiting strategic areas for conservation and protecting them from human intervention, or at least from damaging activities related to economic production.

Interestingly, coalitions did not initially adapt their policy proposals to omit market mechanisms (i.e., transfers of payments from water users to landowners). Rather, they found creative ways to de-emphasize the idea of markets and emphasize conservation to protect against future losses. CEDERENA's efforts to create a Pimampiro-style payment for ecosystem services program in Celica are illustrative. While CEDERENA's earlier programs in Pimampiro and El Chaco were labeled payment for ecosystem services programs, Celica's program was renamed Protection of the Quantity and Quality of Water. To emphasize voluntary social cooperation, the money paid by water users was called a "contribution," "collaboration," or "donation," even though CEDERENA proposed making such payments obligatory through municipal ordinances (EcoCiencia 2009). Talk of "payments" to "owners," was replaced by "compensation" and "retribution" to "families" for protecting the forests that provide water for the social good.

Instead of technical descriptions of ecosystem services, Celica's campaign posters talked of "nature offering everything needed for our well-being," including "water for consumption, clean air, [and] medicinal plants." Rather than emphasizing water's economic value, Celica's campaign emphasized water's noneconomic values as the basis for human needs like "food," "health," and "purification" (Cuenca 2008). The main document publicizing Celica's reforms illustrates the coalition's use of a conservation frame:

> Over time human beings have neglected and failed to respect or value water. They believe it is a resource available for their use without any type of restriction, without considering it a recyclable resource. In this process they suffer changes due to the poor use and contamination of water, causing severe damage to people's health. . . . The Program for the Protection of the Quantity and Quality of Water grew out of the need to improve this resource for Celica. (Cuenca 2008, 7)

Conservation frames often utilized highly emotional messages using dramatic imagery and making simple connections between watershed degradation and human suffering. Figure 6.3 shows two typical images that circulated among coalitions. One shows an African boy bathing in cow urine due to water scarcity. The second shows a starving child with the prayer "I promise to do everything possible to not waste water. We pray that this small child will be relieved of his suffering." The implicit message to community members was that they and their children could experience similar suffering unless they mobilized to preserve their water sources.

Unlike the market frame, interview and survey data suggest that the conservation frame did resonate culturally. Surveys conducted by IWM coalitions show that a majority of local populations acknowledged the importance of

Figure 6.3 Campaign Posters Linking Watershed Degradation to Human Suffering.
Image sources: author's photographs of campaign posters publicly displayed in Celica. English translation by author.

conserving watershed resources to ensure future access. The need to conserve water resources resonated strongly in the Sierra region, where water shortages were frequent. Even in the Amazon, where water was abundant, people generally appreciated the value of protecting fragile ecosystems. This was particularly true in communities that bordered national parks that were important community symbols.

Nevertheless, recognizing the value of watershed resources and the need to protect them to ensure future access was not enough to motivate people to change their behavior. This was particularly true for landowners, who resisted limiting their production to support conservation and restoration efforts. While the counter-framing strategy proved useful for agenda setting, and in some cases motivating people to participate in rule-making, it failed to motivate changes in land use practices needed to implement conservation and restoration projects.

One likely problem for the conservation frame is that poverty drives people to discount the future. This would explain why surveys showed a majority of people accepted the idea that "water is life," yet failed to change their behaviors. For many people, agricultural production also represented life. Future water problems, while important, were secondary to the immediate need for economic production. A counter-framing strategy forced people to choose between these two "sources of life," and people typically chose production over conservation.

Frame Displacement Strategy

In all three successful cases, IWM campaigns gained traction after switching to a frame-displacement strategy that redefined the original production/poverty frame to include IWM reform. The redefined production/poverty frame characterized watershed resources as an integral part of the production chain. The destruction of watershed resources led to loss of production and thus income. Managing these resources in an integrated manner was crucial to maintaining, and even improving, production. This made it a poverty-reduction strategy. In contrast to counter-framing strategies, IWM reform (including conservation efforts) were not framed as conflicting with poverty-reduction goals. Rather, they were a strategy for achieving these goals.

The shift to a frame-displacement strategy resulted from negotiation among and learning by local stakeholders, who typically led efforts to craft the new strategy. Chapter 7, for example, describes how local indigenous organizers who joined Tungurahua's IWM coalition developed a strategy to displace the dominant production/poverty frame and include IWM reform: Tungurahua's IWM advocates changed their education campaign to emphasize watershed resources as an integral part of the economic production cycle. Figure 6.4 illustrates the

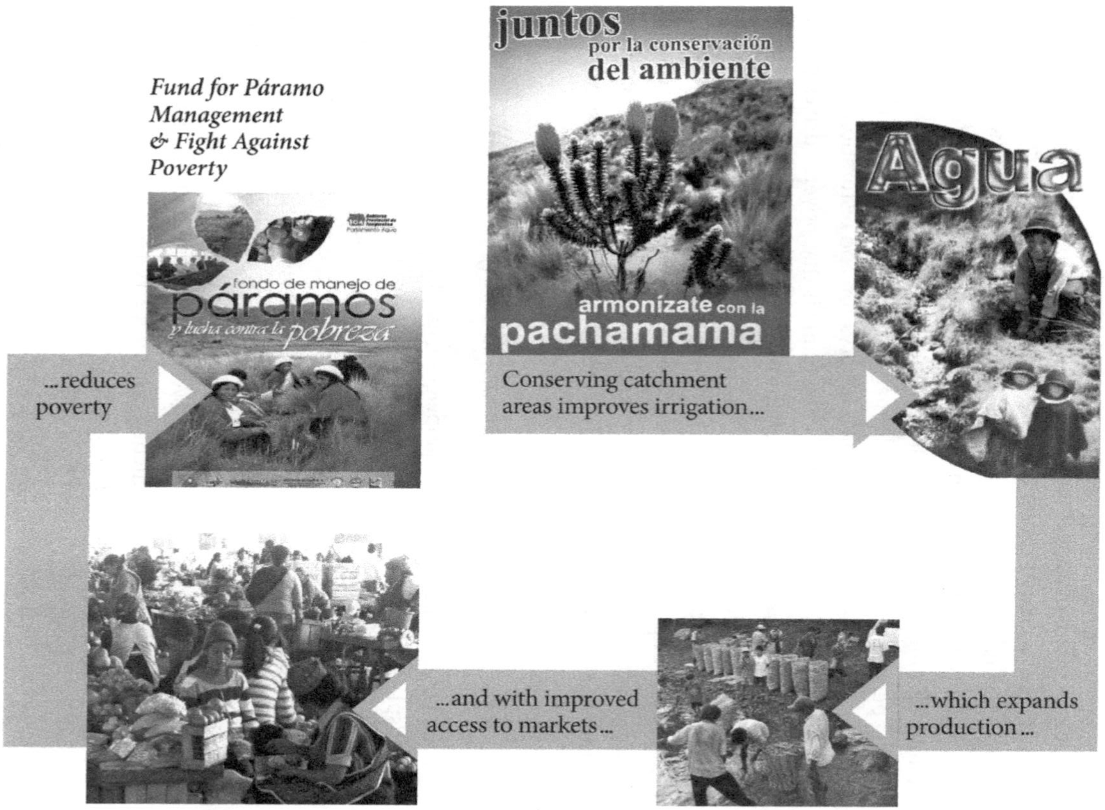
Fund for Páramo Management & Fight Against Poverty
fondo de manejo de
páramos
y lucha contra la pobreza
juntos
por la conservación
del ambiente
armonízate con la
pachamama
Conserving catchment areas improves irrigation...
Agua
...which expands production ...
...and with improved access to markets...
...reduces poverty

Figure 6.4 Displaced Production/Poverty Frame in Tungurahua. Image source: author's photographs of campaign posters publicly displayed in Tungurahua.

logic as presented through images in campaign materials. IWM reform was framed as a strategy for protecting watershed catchment areas to ensure sufficient water for irrigation. Reforms also included strategies for making agricultural production in less ecologically fragile areas more efficient, allowing farmers to increase their overall production. Increasing local farmers' access to markets would further increase their income, lowering poverty levels. In this way, IWM reform, and the conservation of watershed resources, were directly linked to poverty reduction. This link was symbolized in the name given to the financing mechanism at the heart of Tungurahua's IWM reforms—The Fund for Páramo Management *and the Fight Against Poverty* [emphasis added]. The results of this framing strategy are reflected in the words of a local farmer, who said "we have to work to improve the páramos because it is gold; it is what makes the markets function. If there are improvements in my products, I can provide better education for my children. I'll have money to go to the doctor."[8]

The frame displacement strategy was successful not only in Andean watersheds where farmers relied on irrigation. El Chaco's IWM coalition similarly succeeded after framing IWM reform as a strategy for improving economic production and reducing poverty. As I explain later, they did so by framing IWM reform as the best strategy for protecting the flow of rivers and solving the problem of landslides. Slogans like "water, the vital liquid" highlighted the importance of rivers for hydroelectricity and ecotourism, which local politicians and urban residents saw as crucial for economic development. Since both hydroelectricity and ecotourism depended on a healthy ecosystem and strong rivers, IWM reform was viewed as an economic development strategy. For the 80% of El Chaco's residents who raise dairy cattle, landslides represented a serious threat to their production capacity. IWM advocates identified deforestation as the cause of these landslides and presented IWM reform as the best solution. Many farmers subsequently supported the reforms, citing their desire to avoid production losses.

In each case, the frame-displacement strategy was successful because it presented conservation and economic production as complementary, rather than competing, goals. Specifically, the displaced production/poverty frame characterized conservation as necessary to avoid serious losses to production capabilities. These losses included reduced irrigation, soil degradation, and landslides. The displaced frame also stressed economic benefits, including increased efficiency and expanded markets.

Both theory and evidence suggest the frame's loss avoidance component was likely more influential. Prospect theory asserts that people tend to strongly

---

[8] Interview by author, Yatzaputzan, Tungurahua, November 30, 2009.

prefer avoiding losses to acquiring gains (Mercer 2005; Tversky and Kahneman 1981). People therefore make more effort and take more risks to avoid losses than to pursue gains. This would explain why landowners tended to reject IWM advocates' offers of monetary payments to stop producing in ecologically fragile areas, even when they would gain economically. Yet these same landowners agreed to conserve these same areas when they believed not doing so would produce production losses. They were eager to accept compensation in the form of assistance to improve their production capabilities in ways that would protect against losses.

Building Network Capacity

Motivating local stakeholders to join an IWM coalition is one ingredient of success. Another is building an IWM coalition's capacity to concentrate the resources available to diverse stakeholder groups and convert these into pressure for reform. In the three successful cases (Tungurahua, Celica, and El Chaco), IWM advocates devoted substantial time and resources to simultaneously recruiting, training, and organizing members of each major stakeholder group. They created linking institutions to connect diverse stakeholder groups, provide a focal point for concentrating the resources available to each, and convert these into action. Examples include El Chaco's Environmental Management Committee, Tungurahua's Water Parliament, and Celica's Environmental Services Committee. IWM advocates in these cases also created new governance institutions focused on IWM, like municipal environmental management units. This high level of network capacity building produced cohesive, dense, diverse networks of IWM advocates representing all major local stakeholder groups.

Figure 6.5 shows the network ties constructed among watershed stakeholders in Tungurahua and illustrates the kind of dense, inclusive governance networks constructed in successful cases. The size of nodes reflects their degree centrality (i.e., the number of network ties they have), with larger nodes being more central (i.e., having more ties to other nodes). Not surprisingly, GTZ, the German donor agency that first advocated IWM reform through its Watershed Management Project, is among the most central nodes. GTZ's centrality and the density of its network connections with local stakeholder groups reflect its high level of network capacity building. Another indicator is the centrality of linking institutions created by GTZ and other IWM advocates (denoted as circles). Tungurahua's Water Parliament (ParAgua) and watershed management fund (Fondo) have dense ties with local government entities, local landowners, local water users, as well as a variety of external organizations.

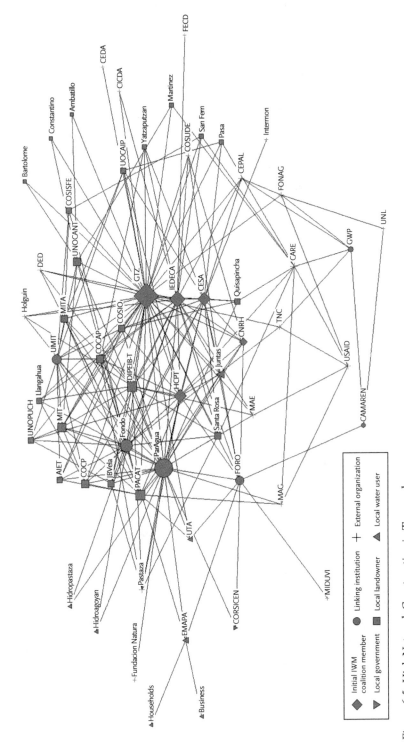

Figure 6.5 High Network Construction in Tungurahua.

In contrast, network capacity building was low and uneven in Ibarra and Pastaza. These coalitions focused on building ties with one or two stakeholder groups seen as particularly instrumental and spent relatively little time and resources constructing ties to other stakeholders. Nor did they create linking institutions. This resulted in narrow coalitions that did not incorporate members from all main stakeholder groups. Network capacity building was most limited in Ibarra. The director of PROFAFOR (the lead organization in Ibarra's IWM coalition) at that time stated that he did not see social mobilization as part of PROFAFOR's role. Rather, he saw PROFAFOR as a technical advisor only; its role was to provide the municipal water company with diagnostic studies of the watershed and design an IWM system.[9]

While Pastaza's coalition recognized the importance of training and organizing advocates among landowner and water user groups, it did not make a sustained effort to do so. When faced with resistance, coalition members focused their limited resources on building support with local government authorities and designing IWM institutions. Figure 6.6 illustrates the sparse ties among stakeholders in Pastaza. There are no linking institutions. Initial coalition members (denoted by diamonds) are tied primarily to local government entities and external organizations. Their ties with most landowners and water users are indirect or nonexistent.

Zamora presents an interesting mixed case in which capacity building was relatively high with landowners and politicians but low with water users. Zamora's IWM coalition was formed by the Ecuadorian conservation NGO Arcoiris, who teamed with The Nature Conservancy, FONAG and others to promote FONAG-style reforms in Zamora as a way to protect Podocarpus National Park. Like other IWM coalitions, Zamora's focused first on mobilizing support among landowners. Arcoiris spent years training and organizing landowners in Zamora's Limón watershed, located in the buffer zone of Podocarpus. The coalition achieved some initial success, thanks to their frame-displacement strategy. In the first year of the campaign (2006–2007), nearly half the watershed's landowners signed compensation-for-conservation agreements. In 2008, politicians approved a draft ordinance creating a local water fund to finance IWM activities.

Despite this initial success, Zamora's IWM reform process collapsed shortly thereafter. Both the municipal ordinance and all but one of the landowner agreements fell through. By 2009, most landowners and politicians refused to work with Zamora's IWM coalition. Conflict surrounding IWM reform became so severe that it caused a breach in the IWM coalition. The Nature Conservancy, Conservation International, and USAID ceased their financial support; Arcoiris

---

[9] Interview by author, Quito, Ecuador, May 19, 2010.

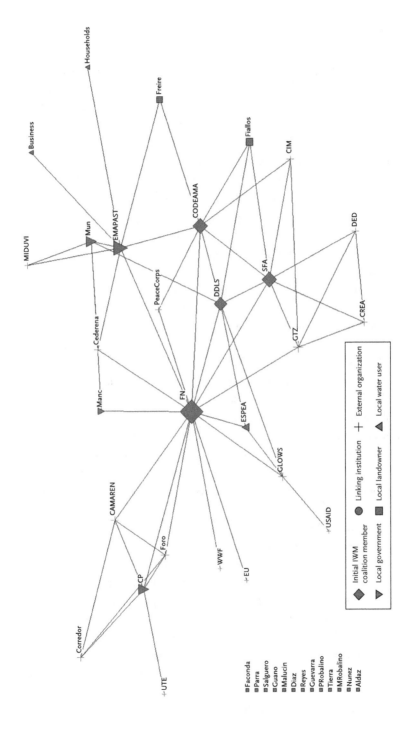

Figure 6.6 Low Network Construction in Pastaza.

left Zamora to pursue projects in other cantons; and the water fund became inactive. What explains this breakdown in the implementation process?

The root of the problem was the coalition's failure to mobilize support among Zamora's water users between 2005 and 2009, when IWM reforms were being designed and implemented. After politicians passed the ordinance establishing a watershed fund, water users strongly rejected the fee on water use meant to finance the compensation agreements made with landowners. Water users pressured the mayor and council members to reject the ordinance, which they did. As a result, the water fund's technical staff were unable to fulfill the terms of the agreements made with landowners. The terms of compensation were changed and compensation was distributed unevenly. This produced jealousy, perceptions of corruption, and distrust of the IWM coalition among landowners. While landowners expressed a desire to pursue IWM techniques, demonstrating a level of norm internalization, they refused to work with Zamora's coalition members. The implementation process stalled and the coalition disbanded.

The breakdown in Zamora illustrates the problem of uneven network activation among local stakeholder groups. Network activation was high among politicians, medium among landowners, but low among water users (see Fig. 6.7). While Zamora's coalition did create a linking organization (Procuencas), it was relatively noninclusive. It linked external IWM advocates with Zamora's municipal government, but lacked representatives of either landowners or water users. The failure to include these stakeholder groups was a crucial difference with linking institutions in the successful cases. Table 6.3 shows this through the index of qualitative variation (IQV) scores for the linking institutions in each case. IQV scores measure the diversity of network ties for a network node on a scale from 0 (a completely homogenous network with only one stakeholder group represented) to 1 (maximum diversity; all stakeholder groups are represented equally) (Agresti and Agresti 1977). Unlike in the successful cases, Zamora's linking institution was quite homogenous, reflecting a relatively low level of network capacity building.

The negative effects of Zamora's uneven network activation highlight how watershed stakeholders are interrelated in a way that makes necessary the simultaneous mobilization of all three stakeholder groups (local government, water users, and landowners). One reason for the uneven network construction in both Pastaza and Zamora was that IWM coalitions responded to stakeholder resistance by switching their focus from social mobilization to another component of the reform process, particularly rule making. By contrast, successful IWM coalitions responded to resistance by increasing their network activation efforts to mobilize pressure from beside.

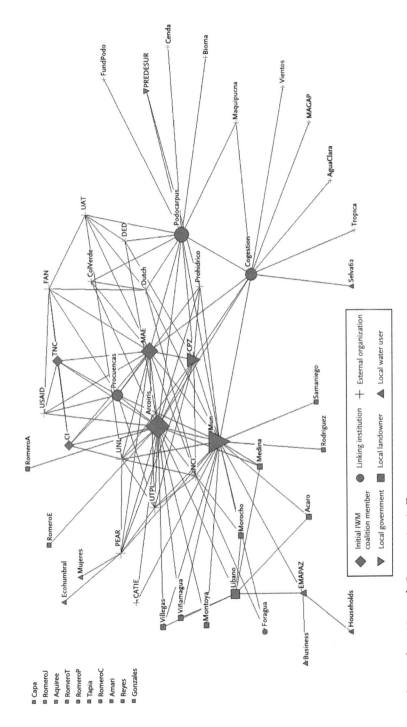

Figure 6.7 Medium Network Construction in Zamora.

Table 6.3 **Network Capacity Building Levels**

	Tungurahua	Celica	El Chaco	Zamora	Ibarra	Pastaza
Reform Success (1–15)	13.5	13	12	8.5	4.5	2.3
Network Capacity Building Level	High	High	High	Mixed; low with water users	Low	Low
IWM Network Cohesion (Avg. Degree)	7.200	6.533	4.963	4.138	1.484	2.571
IWM Network Density	0.122	0.148	0.191	0.072	0.049	0.062
Inclusiveness of Linking Organization (IQV score)	0.837	0.963	0.853	0.263	N/A	N/A
Local Stakeholder Groups Included in Coalition	Politicians, Water Users, Landowners	Politicians, Water Users, Landowners	Politicians, Water Users, Landowners	Politicians, Landowners	Landowners	Politicians

Mobilizing Pressure from Beside in El Chaco

El Chaco's IWM campaign illustrates how successful coalitions simultaneously worked with all stakeholder groups, combining frame-displacement and network capacity-building strategies to mobilize pressure from beside. El Chaco's IWM campaign was spurred by CEDERENA, which selected El Chaco as the site for its first attempt to replicate Pimampiro's payment for ecosystem services program. CEDERENA found a ready ally in the municipal government's Environmental Management Office, which was created during early local network activation (see chapter 5). Together, these organizations formed El Chaco's initial IWM coalition and launched an IWM campaign in early 2004.

A key component of CEDERENA's strategy was forming a working group comprised of all major stakeholder groups. CEDERENA's initial education campaign motivated enough local support to form a working group of 20 people representing each of the canton's parishes and various governmental and private organizations. Members represented the fire department, the Civil Defense Corps, neighborhood associations, school associations, park guards from the Condor Bioreserve, local farmers, municipal government experts, and others. This marked the first time residents of El Chaco had organized around environmental issues.[10]

One purpose of the working group was to expand El Chaco's pool of local environmental experts (local knowledge communities). To this end, CEDERENA conducted training workshops to strengthen the group's technical capacity. CEDERENA also used the working group as a tool for further network activation. The group's members did much of the legwork involved with building popular support for the reform process and recruiting other landowners and civil society members into the IWM coalition. Workshops convened by the working group served as the space where community members, municipal experts, and CEDERENA staff designed El Chaco's IWM reform proposal (Yaguache et al. 2005, 43).[11] In this way, the working group constituted a linking institution that facilitated local network activation.

Importantly, El Chaco's IWM coalition engaged in network activation with all three stakeholder groups simultaneously (Yaguache et al. 2005, 41). Local park guards responsible for monitoring the Condor Bioreserve facilitated coalition members' access to landowners since their work provided frequent interaction with farmers living in the watershed. With their help, CEDERENA, municipal experts, and the work team repeatedly met with landowners to discuss

[10] Working group member, interview by author, El Chaco, Ecuador, April 7, 2010; CEDERENA expert working in El Chaco, interview by author, Ibarra, Ecuador, March 11, 2010.

[11] Interviews by author with multiple working group members, El Chaco, Ecuador, April 7–8, 2010.

the possibility of IWM reform. Community-based participatory research was a key strategy for mobilizing landowners. Coalition leaders organized fieldtrips with landowners to carry out diagnostic studies and jointly analyze the relationship between livestock farming and water quality. After months of intense negotiations and training, members of the municipal government, landowners, CEDERENA, and the working group agreed to jointly create a management plan for the San Marcos watershed through a participatory process.

At the same time, CEDERENA worked to train and organize El Chaco's urban population (the main water users). Working group members held informal meetings and organized people through neighborhood associations and schools. Once again, participatory research was an important strategy. IWM advocates led trips into the watershed to learn which areas were most fragile, to analyze how ecological conditions above affect water access below, and to discuss possible measures for protecting water-related resources. These trips also provided opportunities for discussions and negotiations between water users and landowners. Simultaneously, coalition members negotiated the support of politicians and bureaucrats within the municipal government. As with landowners and water users, this occurred through regular meetings, workshops, and participatory research projects. CEDERENA even brought a delegation from El Chaco to Pimampiro to study its watershed management program.

This intense, simultaneous network activation paid off. In August 2004, the municipal government approved the ordinance establishing El Chaco's IWM reforms, modeled on Pimampiro's payment for ecosystem services program. The ordinance required the creation of a fund within the municipal government to pay for protecting water-related ecosystem services, to be financed through a tax on water use. The ordinance also set the criteria for negotiating compensation-for-conservation agreements with landowners.[12] Moreover, the ordinance called for the creation of an Environmental Services Committee, representing all three stakeholder groups. The committee was charged with overseeing the fund, providing a participatory planning process to guide the program's actions, monitoring and evaluating projects, and negotiating compensation agreements with landowners.

As in Pastaza and Zamora, designing new IWM systems proved much easier than implementing them. In 2005, CEDERENA left and the process lost momentum. Landowners rejected IWM advocates' proposals, claiming the cash payments were not sufficient. Using formulas from CEDERENA's valuation studies, IMW advocates explained that landowners would earn more through

---

[12] Based on valuation studies of ecosystem services and the opportunity costs associated with lost production, the program offered landowners $5 per month per hectare of forest conserved and $3 per month per hectare of pasture allowed to regenerate naturally. The municipality agreed to provide landowners the materials needed to fence off protected areas and reforest.

the compensation agreement than what they currently earned by raising cattle. As in Pastaza, these technical explanations were ineffective. IWM advocates became frustrated when landowners clung to traditional production practices despite their inferior earning potential. It was also difficult to sustain social mobilization. Citizen participation in the Environmental Services Committee declined and it soon disbanded.

Fortunately, another Ecuadorian environmental NGO, EcoCiencia, provided continuity to the reform process. As a conduit for The Nature Conservancy's IWM advocacy efforts, EcoCiencia decided to support El Chaco's fledgling IWM reform process. Like CEDERENA, EcoCiencia focused on simultaneous network activation with all three stakeholder groups (López 2008, 57). EcoCiencia began in 2006 by training a group of citizen "environmental managers" representing each parish and stakeholder group. After a year of training, 18 environmental managers formed a new Environmental Management Committee as the main space for linking watershed stakeholders and coordinating IWM reform efforts (López et al. 2007, 22).

As newly trained committee members began experimenting with local IWM projects in their parishes, municipal IWM advocates continued to negotiate compensation-for-conservation agreements with landowners, with little success. By 2008, however, things were turning around due to the coalition's renewed efforts to mobilize water users. Thanks to a change in framing strategy and learning from local experimentation, the coalition's education campaign, conducted 2007–2008, began to have a multiplier effect. Water users mobilized to exert pressure from beside on politicians and landowners, who in turn began to pressure each other. This set in motion a virtuous cycle of pressure from beside.

In addition to gathering information, training and organizing citizens, and designing and implementing watershed management projects, El Chaco's Environmental Management Committee challenged and pressured politicians and citizens who deviated from environmental practices required by municipal ordinances. As Committee President Edgar Silva explained,

> We have even begun to question the municipal government. For example, when they construct new roads they often do not have an environmental impact study even though they are required to, and we challenge them on this. Expanding the agricultural frontier is a serious problem— deforestation of the forests, damage of fauna and flora. We have questioned landowners and the municipal government about this and told them they need to do these studies and comply. . . . The Environmental Management Committee exists to coordinate these types of actions.[13]

[13] Interview by author, El Chaco, Ecuador, April 7, 2010.

El Chaco's IWM coalition also worked to mobilize broader social pressure through an education campaign that linked IWM reform to the global problem of climate change. Watershed conservation and restoration efforts were framed as a way to "reduce the social and environmental vulnerability associated with climate change."[14] The coalition's education campaign advanced this idea through community workshops, organizing within schools, and public displays of art and protest. This message resonated broadly with residents, who were used to seeing news reports of natural disasters attributed to climate change and equated these with local disasters caused by frequent landslides.[15]

Local IWM advocates recognized that landslides were an effective symbol for mobilizing support. They crafted a frame-displacement strategy that framed IWM reform as the best strategy for solving the problem of landslides. Consequently, IWM reform became a strategy for improving economic production and reducing poverty. Eighty percent of El Chaco's residents raise cattle, and for them landslides represent a serious threat to their production capacity. In the years before and during the IWM campaign, El Chaco experienced repeated natural disasters that destroyed farmers' homes, livestock, crops, and equipment, wiping out their livelihood. By identifying deforestation as the cause of these landslides and IWM reforms as the best solution, IWM advocates gave farmers a short-term economic incentive to support the reforms.

The following explanation by one farmer is representative of those given by landowners for why they began supporting IWM reform:

> One day, out of nothing came a phenomenal storm and five people died. People have begun to say that these changes are because we are not caring for the environment properly. I tell them they are right. So we are now starting to see interest in doing something. . . . Here in El Chaco we have had a large number of landslides. These have cut off roads and communication and have even threatened our production and source of livelihood. The bamboo and trees that used to be along the rivers served as a buffer to regulate the water flow . . . and served as a natural barrier. But since we have cut all these down, the landslides extend very far and hurt us.[16]

Another farmer who lost his house, belongings, and livestock in a landslide concluded, "I am paying for what I did," referring to his deforestation of the area. "So

[14] PowerPoint presentation used by EcoCiencia in El Chaco training workshops.

[15] Interviews by author with various landowners, water users, and government officials, El Chaco, Ecuador, April 7, 14, 15, 2010.

[16] Interview by author, El Chaco, Ecuador, April 15, 2010.

now I too am interested in restoring the watershed, and am planting different species of trees."[17]

The municipal government cited pressure from water users as a main factor motivating its renewed effort to implement the stalled IWM program. According to one government report:

> the constant landslides that destroyed the canton's potable water systems propelled civil society to protest, demanding that the municipal government find a solution. So at the request of the community of water users . . . [the canton's] various actors began to meet to implement the [IWM reform] proposal that is of vital importance for the community. (Zarria 2009, 2)

The frame-displacement strategy of linking watershed protection to economic production also contributed to the government's motivation. Slogans like "water, the vital liquid" highlighted the importance of rivers for hydroelectricity and ecotourism, which local politicians and many urban residents saw as key to economic development. Since both hydroelectricity and ecotourism depended on healthy ecosystems and strong rivers, IWM reforms were viewed as an economic development strategy. At a 2008 forum on IWM, El Chaco's mayor explained,

> For us, in El Chaco, water is a blessing; it permits us to hold world rafting championships, and is permitting us to have the Coca Codo Sinclair hydroelectric project. But water is not something that is increasing, but rather is progressively decreasing. For this reason I congratulate EcoCiencia for coming to work in a sustainable manner, and El Chaco's Environmental Management Committee for taking the responsibility of defending future generations. (EcoCiencia 2009, 2)

By 2008, IWM advocates in the Municipal Environmental Management Unit were enjoying greater success in negotiating compensation for conservation agreements with landowners. This was partly due to pressure from beside. For years, negotiations with landowners failed due to disagreement over compensation levels. Motivated by pressure from civil society, municipal government representatives in turn pressured landowners to lower their expectations and negotiate agreements by threatening to expropriate the land at market value.[18]

---

[17] Interview by author, El Chaco, Ecuador, April 14, 2010.

[18] Director, El Chaco's Environmental Management Unit, interview by author, El Chaco, Ecuador, April 20, 2010.

This tactic was not unique to El Chaco; municipal IWM advocates also employed it in other cases. Trotsky Riera, coordinator of Nature and Culture International (NCI) in Zamora, explained the dynamics behind this form of pressure from beside:

> landowners think NGOs have lots of money and ask exorbitant prices for their land. For NCI, the way it generally works is you need to get the mayor to talk seriously about expropriating the land for public use, which is legal under the constitution. There is a line that says the needs of the many should be put over the needs of the few. Because the local government has legal limits on how much it can spend, it is generally way below the price that NCI will offer. So NCI pressures the local governments to threaten expropriation and scare the landowners into negotiating a fairer price with NCI. But this depends on the will of the mayor and interest in conservation.[19]

A key adaptation to the IWM program, resulting from experimentation by local IWM advocates, also contributed to increased success with landowners. In 2008, coalition members proposed a new compensation system based on local experiments with "integrated farms" conducted by local farmers trained by CEDERENA and EcoCiencia. Under the new system, landowners who signed conservation agreements did not receive cash payments. Rather, they received training and equipment to develop an integrated farm that would increase the efficiency of production, allowing farmers to increase their production and income while using less land. This enabled farmers to conserve and restore land in strategic catchment areas while still enjoying higher profits, which provided an incentive to continue participating in the system. The training and equipment to create the integrated farming system was provided up front, and the value of the equipment was amortized over the life of the conservation agreement. This compensation scheme was financed through the payment for ecosystem services fund.

According to municipal personnel, this adaptation came from the experimental measures pursued by local farmers who were members of CEDERENA's working group or EcoCiencia's Environmental Management Committee. Several of these farmers were also trained in IWM through local technical universities, particularly the Ecological Polytechnic School of the Amazon (ESPEA). The indirect effects of these efforts to create local knowledge communities again illustrate the power of nodal governance.

[19] Interview by author, Zamora, Ecuador, February 11, 2010.

One of the first to experiment with integrated farming was Milton Hugo, a farmer who owns much of the Linares watershed's catchment area. Hugo credits his training as a member of CEDERENA's initial working group, his studies at ESPEA, and his discussions with municipal experts with generating his ideas for how to improve his production while restoring the watershed. According to Hugo, other landowners initially ridiculed him.

> The first time we were building the stable for raising cattle and small animals, people would stop in the road and ask me what I was doing, because in this time the land was very ugly from the construction. I told him I was building a house where cows and small animals would live. They laughed and told me I was crazy. But we continued on.[20]

Over time, the new system allowed Hugo to greatly expand his milk production while reducing the number of cattle. This allowed him to reforest stream banks and estuaries with native bamboo, which retains water and prevents soil erosion. His compensation-for-conservation agreement also gave him a mulcher, which he used to mulch bamboo and other native plants to feed his cattle. This had the dual advantage of restoring the watershed's ecological integrity while improving his cattle's nutrition, which in turn increased his milk production. Hugo recycled organic trash and used it to feed worms, which he used to feed his ducks. These and other innovations made Hugo one of the most successful landowners at implementing IWM reform. His integrated farm became an agro-tourism attraction; visitors come from across Ecuador and even from other countries to learn about integrated farming.

According to Hugo, his experience had a strong impact on other landowners.

> Now, those that were laughing before are copying me. They are now starting to see the value, and are getting the materials [from the payment for ecosystem services program]. Initially, they only built some small structures for pigs. But now they understand they can do much more with the bamboo. Before, we all cut down everything to grow tomatoes and oranges, and fumigated too much, killing both good and bad species. But now, this is being transformed with the bamboo, with the idea of protecting the watershed. They [other landowners in the canton] are beginning to understand this is good. They have invited me to talk with them about these issues. . . . Since I'm in Linares with some innovative ideas, the others trust me a lot, and they have asked

---

[20] Interview by author, El Chaco, Ecuador, April 7, 2010.

me to represent them. They want to organize themselves and form an association.[21]

Hugo is describing another kind of pressure from beside—the ability of respected community members to attract support among fellow stakeholders and co-opt opponents by providing a positive example. It is hard to measure the individual impact of this soft pressure relative to the more coercive pressure exerted by protesting water users and municipal threats to expropriate land, not to mention the frame-displacement strategy. No doubt all contributed to the increased landowner support for IWM reform seen after 2008. By 2010, IWM advocates had contracts with 80 of El Chaco's roughly 600 landowners and were working with all of them.[22]

El Chaco is now considered one of the more successful cases of IWM reform in Ecuador. At the time of writing, the financing and participatory decision-making mechanisms designed through the IWM reform process were functioning and producing tangible results. As planned, the environmental tax increased over five years to 6.8%, where it remains. This money is collected and capitalizes the payment for ecosystem services fund, which finances the conservation, restoration, and monitoring of the canton's five principal watersheds, as outlined in their respective integrated management plans. A continuous environmental education campaign sustains the support of El Chaco's residents. Perhaps most important, a corps of trained, local organizers uses local IWM institutions to drive the reform process forward.

Conclusion

This chapter employed frame and social network analysis to show how different combinations of framing and network capacity-building strategies produce different outcomes during phase 2 of grassroots global governance. When IWM coalitions combined frame-displacement with high levels of network capacity building, reform processes endured long enough for local experiments with IWM to be implemented. That is because this combination of strategies produced diverse IWM coalitions—representing each local stakeholder group—with the motivation and capacity to mobilize the pressure from beside needed to propel the reform process forward. To show how this occurs, the chapter traced El Chaco's IWM campaign.

[21] Interview by author, El Chaco, Ecuador, April 7, 2010.
[22] Director, Department of Production, Municipal Government of El Chaco, interview by author, El Chaco, Ecuador, April 23, 2010.

The chapter also showed how other combinations of framing and capacity-building strategies led IWM campaigns to break down at various stages of phase 2. Counter-framing strategies combined with low network capacity building produced breakdown either during agenda setting with politicians (e.g., Ibarra) or social mobilization (e.g., Pastaza). A counter-framing strategy combined with low capacity building produced breakdown during the implementation stage (e.g., Zamora). High capacity building combined with a counter-framing strategy produced breakdown during the rule-making stage (e.g., Tungurahua; see chapter 7).

This chapter's case comparisons also highlighted the benefits of participatory research as a network activation strategy and the importance of mobilizing local stakeholder groups simultaneously rather than sequentially. Rather than persisting in the face of resistance, Pastaza's coalition retreated to work with other stakeholders, hoping to mobilize pressure from beside. This was one reason for their technical approach to rule-making. Unable to mobilize pressure among landowners and water users, IWM advocates were left to design IWM institutions with a relatively small group of government experts. Ultimately, this strategy proved ineffective. Given the pushback by many local stakeholders and the absence of local pressure for reform, politicians saw IWM reform as politically risky and ignored the program. By contrast, El Chaco's IWM coalition took a highly participatory approach to information gathering and rule making, seeing these as sociopolitical processes rather than purely technical ones. This approach led the coalition to mobilize support among all stakeholder groups simultaneously, rather than sequentially. This, in turn, allowed a virtuous cycle of mutual pressure from beside to emerge.

7

Local Experimentation
in Tungurahua

Tungurahua is not only the most successful of the six cases, but the only one in which an initial reform attempt failed yet a subsequent effort succeeded. It therefore provides an excellent opportunity to analyze the interaction effects of different network activation strategies over time. This chapter traces Tungurahua's IWM reform process to show how different combinations of strategies produce different outcomes during phase 2 of grassroots global governance.

The chapter's first section describes how early local network activation facilitated the rise of a local IWM coalition and created fertile conditions for pursing IWM reform. IWM advocates initially spent a great deal of time training and organizing local knowledge communities, many of whom became influential local brokers during phase 2. The second section shows how, despite high levels of capacity building, two strategic choices led IWM reform efforts to break down during the rule-making stage. First, outside IWM advocates adopted a technical approach to rule making, hiring outside experts to design proposed IWM institutions. They also employed counter-framing strategies to motivate local stakeholders to support the proposal. This combination of strategies initially incorporated many local stakeholder groups into the reform process, but led them to reject proposed IWM institutions, causing reform efforts to break down at the rule-making stage. The remainder of the chapter analyzes how IWM advocates spent years reactivating stakeholder networks and achieved success after making two changes in strategy: adopting a participatory approach to rule making and employing a frame-displacement strategy.

The third and fourth sections examine how outside IWM advocates used a participatory approach to rule making to recruit representatives of those stakeholder groups that had sabotaged the first IWM proposal: irrigation councils, campesino farmer associations, and indigenous movements. Many of these representatives were community organizers originally trained during early local network activation, illustrating the lasting effects of phase 1 on phase 2 of grassroots global governance. These community organizers became key brokers and influential members of Tungurahua's IWM coalition due to their ability to mobilize support among water councils, indigenous movements, and communities of landowners. To illustrate this influence, the chapter's fifth section shows how local brokers crafted frame-displacement strategies that succeeded in motivating indigenous and campesino groups to participate in IWM reform efforts.

Together, the chapter's sections highlight a second benefit of tracing a single reform process. It reveals how transnational governance networks govern indirectly through network activation. Outside IWM advocates responded to resistance by local stakeholders by training and organizing respected members of resistant stakeholder groups to serve as local brokers between these groups and the transnational IWM network. These local brokers played a crucial role in adapting the coalitions' network activation strategies to mobilize local support. By tracing the rise of local brokers in Tungurahua's IWM coalition, the chapter shows how influence within transnational governance networks shifts from outside actors to local actors during phase 2.

A third purpose of tracing the Tungurahua case is to show how local advocates used their power to contest, translate, and adapt IWM principles to fit local realities. The chapter's final section examines how local stakeholders altered the design of IWM institutions to fit local norms and the interests of local stakeholder groups. Through negotiation, experimentation, and learning, local IWM advocates crafted a unique set of IWM institutions that coupled core global IWM principles with local indigenous norms and practices. Tungurahua's "New Governance Model" (as locals dubbed it) was widely heralded as an innovative and successful way to sustainably manage natural resources. By showing how ordinary farmers, community organizers, and indigenous activists guided the way global IWM principles were applied locally and consequently evolved, the chapter demonstrates how grassroots actors become global governors.

Early Local Network Activation

The origins of Tungurahua's watershed management reforms can be traced to the 1980s, when international development organizations introduced several programs to combat soil erosion caused by the expansion of the agricultural frontier into the páramos. Leading examples include CARE International's Project for the Sustainable Use of Andean Lands (PROMUSTA) and the Soil Conservation and Agroforestry in the Andean Region program established by the German Organization for Technical Cooperation, GTZ. These programs complemented the work of national Ecuadorian NGOs like CESA (Ecuadorian

Center for Agricultural Services) and IEDECA (Institute of Ecology and Development of Andean Communities).

These projects had three important impacts. First, they collected information that quantified reductions in water flow noticed by local communities, raising awareness of the problem. Second, the focus on combating soil erosion provided a conceptual link between conservation and agricultural production that was innovative at the time. The programs encouraged farmers to maintain sustainable practices by mixing technical improvements in production (e.g., through better irrigation) with complementary programs that demonstrated short-term benefits of conservation (Winters et al. 1998).

Third, the programs trained and organized communities around the issue of sustainable natural resource management and constructed networks of local "farmer organizers" dedicated to promoting more sustainable agricultural production. The programs also provided an organizational basis for them to pursue this goal. One example is FUNDIAT (Foundation for the Holistic Development of Tungurahuan Farmers)—a linking institution created by local organizers trained by PROMUSTA. Among other things, FUNDIAT provided community courses on sustainable agriculture and conservation. As I will show, several local organizers trained by PROMUSTA became leading members of Tungurahua's IWM reform coalition.

Network Activation through Water Councils

During the 1990s several factors contributed to severe water conflicts in Tungurahua, with ethnic undertones. Poor indigenous farmers expanded the agricultural frontier further into the páramos, causing its degradation. This exacerbated water deficits and reduced the quality and quantity of water available to downstream users, including wealthier mestizo farmers employing irrigation, urban consumers in Ambato, and hydroelectric companies. Historically, wealthier mestizos living in lower areas controlled the water councils and canals channeling water for irrigation and consumption, while poorer indigenous farmers living in the watershed's upper zone were marginalized from decision making. This resulted in unequal distribution of water.

In response to requests for help from water councils, CESA and IEDECA developed programs to address these issues. At first, CESA and IEDECA focused on technical improvements for irrigation canals, but this strategy changed in the late 1990s. As chapter 4 explained, Ecuadorian development experts were influenced by the writings on IWM coming out of ECLAC, the UN's economic commission in Latin America that served as the regional committee for the Global Water Partnership. Exposure to IWM concepts prompted CESA and IEDECA to change their focus from technical infrastructure to social organization.[1] They began working to change the way water councils were managed, arguing that organizational issues were key to resolving water conflicts; infrastructure was only a medium.

The German development agency GTZ provided general support and integrated these efforts through its Watershed Management Project, PROMACH.[2] Launched in 1998, PROMACH's mission was to unite the efforts of various organizations working on watershed management and to institutionalize the integrated management of the Ambato River watershed through both a participatory decision-making body and a watershed management fund (Metais and Cruz 2003). Beginning in 1999 the leading "governors" on water resource issues in Tungurahua—GTZ, CESA, IEDECA, and the local branch of Ecuador's National Council for Water Resources (CNRH)—began to meet informally to discuss strategies for moving forward. IWM experts from GTZ stressed the need to address watershed resources as a whole and to integrate stakeholders from throughout the watershed in the management process. They argued that improvements in the efficiency of canals would not matter if the decline in water flow were not addressed. Sustainably managing the sources of water in the páramos was therefore crucial. This required collaboration among mestizos living below and indigenous living above.

Water councils became an early space where these IWM advocates built ties between landowners living in the catchment areas (i.e., indigenous farmers in the páramos) and water users living below (e.g., mestizo ranchers and farmers). Water councils were marked by power inequalities, with wealthier mestizo farmers holding leadership positions and controlling access to water, often to the detriment of poorer indigenous farmers. Beginning in the late 1990s, CESA, IEDECA, and GTZ worked with indigenous and mestizo council members to raise awareness of indigenous sources of power, including the ability to cut off water access. Sometimes indigenous groups used this power in extreme ways, cutting off the flow of water to downstream users and even sabotaging irrigation canals.

IWM advocates helped channel this pressure from beside to foster a sense of balance of power and interdependence, while also strengthening and restructuring water councils. By training council members and mediating conflicts, advocates from CESA, IEDECA, and GTZ helped increase the equality of decision

---

[1] CESA representative, interview by author, Ibarra, Ecuador, June 15, 2010; IEDECA representative, interview by author, Ambato, Ecuador, October 19, 2009.

[2] Chapter 4 described GTZ's link to the IWM network based around the Global Water Partnership and ECLAC, as well as PROMACH's creation and role in promoting IWM norms.

making and strengthen councils' capacity to manage water more effectively. This was not an easy process. It required convincing all stakeholders that they were dependent on each other to achieve a mutual goal—stable access to quality water.

It also required pressure from beside. Noting that the indigenous could cut off water sources, mediators persuaded mestizos to include marginalized groups in leadership positions and to make decision making more equitable. In exchange, mediators convinced indigenous groups living in the páramos to provide additional water to those below and to protect the páramos. IWM advocates also worked with water councils to formalize processes for managing water more efficiently and equitably. Much of this work took place through training programs on IWM designed by CAMAREN, the national consortium of Ecuadorian organizations dedicated to improving natural resource management (see chapter 4). In several cases these efforts created organizational links among stakeholders that previously were separated by power disparities, geography, class, and race.[3]

Network Activation among Landowners

While working with water councils, CESA and IEDECA also worked with indigenous communities living in the páramos to change their land-use practices. They trained community organizers and worked with them to gather information on the watershed ecosystem (Fig. 7.1 shows one such training). This, along with workshops on páramo conservation, changed community perceptions regarding the link between the expansion of the agricultural frontier into the páramos and decreased water flow. As a result, many local community organizers embraced IWM principles and helped institutionalize changes through community accords (Actas de Acuerdo) and páramo management plans.

The number of accords and páramo management plans spread rapidly among indigenous communities in the late 1990s to early 2000s. The agreements produced significant changes, including the relocation of families and animals to lower areas and an agreement to not expand the agricultural frontier. In exchange, these communities demanded financial and technical assistance from the provincial government and water users below, both for protecting the páramos and for improving their production capacity outside the páramos. They expressed these demands in marches and protests, as well as threats to cut off water. As the IWM reform process advanced during the 2000s, CESA, IEDECA, and GTZ

[3] Increased connections among stakeholders and more equitable management of water councils were produced for various major canals, including Cunucyacu-Chimborazo, Chiquicahua, Toallo Comunidades, and Toallo Alobamba.

Figure 7.1 Training Local Knowledge Communities in the Páramos of Yatzaputzán.
Photograph by Rodrigo Chontasi, IEDECA-Tungurahua, reproduced with permission.

encouraged these demands as a way to build support and pressure from beside for a watershed management financing mechanism.

Network Activation among Local Politicians

Pressure by water users and indigenous communities was key to placing IWM reform on the local political agenda and incorporating local politicians into the IWM coalition. Efforts to involve the provincial government proved fruitless until 2000, when Fernando Naranjo was elected prefect. Naranjo held a series of assemblies for municipal governments and community groups to identify their development needs and priorities. Based on the importance citizens gave to water, Naranjo embraced the issue as a priority and asked GTZ to be his strategic advisor in addressing it.[4] Provincial government leaders said pressure by water councils and indigenous communities drove the government's new focus on watershed management in the early 2000s.[5] This effectively placed

---

[4] Provincial government official, interview by author, Ambato, Ecuador, January 6, 2010.

[5] Provincial government official, interview by author, Ambato, Ecuador, October 12, 2009; environmental management specialist, IEDECA, interview by author, Ambato, Ecuador, October 19, 2009.

IWM reform on the political agenda. Responding to popular demands for a formal commitment, the provincial government signed a contract with CESA, IEDECA, GTZ-PROMACH, and CNRH to coordinate resources and strategies with the purpose of creating a new IWM program. Tungurahua's IWM coalition was born.

Tungurahua's Failed IWM Campaign (Breakdown during Rule Making)

GTZ coordinated the coalition's efforts through PROMACH. In line with dominant international norms, GTZ advocated a market for ecosystem services to shape the incentives of water resource users and to finance watershed conservation and improvements to canals. In 2001, with provincial government support, GTZ hired a Costa Rican team to design a payment for ecosystem services program based on recently established programs in Costa Rica and the Ecuadorian canton Pimampiro (Comisión Ejecutiva Provincial 2002). This technical team included Doris Cordero, a Costa Rican forestry expert involved in one of the world's first payment for ecosystem services programs in Heredia, Costa Rica. Cordero subsequently worked for GTZ in Tungurahua and later helped design Ibarra's IWM reform proposal (see chapter 5).

High Network Capacity Building

From the beginning, Tungurahua's IWM coalition engaged in a high level of network capacity building. Efforts to create a new linking institution that would unite the watershed's stakeholders around IWM reform came to fruition in 2001, when Tungurahua's Provincial Water Resources Forum was created. Chapter 4 described how in 2000 the consortium CAMAREN founded Ecuador's national Water Resources Forum. In July 2001, CAMAREN approached CESA and GTZ about creating a provincial forum to prepare Tungurahuans for participating in the national Forum's first meeting. Tungurahua's coalition members agreed and named GTZ's Aline Aroyo the forum's regional coordinator.[6] She and other IWM advocates spent the next several months mobilizing Tungurahuan stakeholders to participate in the province's first water resources forum, held on January 22, 2002.

Tungurahua's provincial forum was attended by a diverse array of stakeholder groups, including 41 representatives of public and private institutions and NGOs

---

[6] CESA later became the coordinator of Tungurahua's Provincial Water Resources Forum.

as well as 72 directors of irrigation and potable water councils. Participants put forth several proposals for addressing identified needs, decentralizing watershed management, and creating a participatory mechanism that would allow stakeholders to discuss issues and make agreements at the watershed level (Mesa de Trabajo Provincial 2002). Participants at the forum also announced plans to create a participatory body charged with developing an integrated watershed management plan.

The provincial government and GTZ used the forum to announce their plans for IWM reform, including the creation of a local financing mechanism. In his keynote speech, Prefect Fernando Naranjo announced plans to create a watershed management fund financed by a payment for ecosystem services scheme (Foro Provincial de los Recursos Hídricos en Tungurahua 2002, 2, 9). Carlos Sánchez, the government's director of water resources announced the provincial government would make an initial capital investment, but that the fund would subsequently be financed through a tax on water use.

The provincial government and GTZ were confident the proposal would receive widespread social support. Noting people's increased understanding of watershed management issues, Sánchez asserted that "many [people] are prepared to cooperate and pay the [Provincial] Council taxes to be reinvested. If the Provincial Council makes an investment of around $100,000 over the next two or three months, they will be willing to invest with their taxes for at least thirty years" (Foro Provincial de los Recursos Hídricos en Tungurahua 2002, 19).

Counter-Framing with a Market Frame

The imagery and language surrounding the IWM reform proposal reflected the market frame Tungurahua's coalition used to counter the dominant production/poverty frame. Reform proposals, promotional materials, and public speeches consistently identified problems in the supply and demand for water and blamed them on the failure to place an economic value on ecosystem services (Comisión Ejecutiva Provincial 2002; Foro Provincial de los Recursos Hídricos en Tungurahua 2002; Maldonado and Kosmus 2003; Metais and Cruz 2003). The coalition's reform proposal argued that, because natural resources constitute a form of "capital . . . it is necessary to identify and value environmental goods and services as one element of the economic system" (Comisión Ejecutiva Provincial 2002, 4). "Consumers" of environmental goods and services must make "payments" to "owners" of the land in the watershed in exchange for dedicating this land to "producing" these goods and services. These payments represent the "opportunity cost of forgoing potential income that the land could generate through alternative economic activities" (Comisión Ejecutiva Provincial 2002, 3, 15).

GTZ and the provincial government unveiled the proposal developed by the Costa Rican team at a public assembly in February 2002. The plan called for a tax of two cents per cubic meter of water, which would be invested in a fund used to finance conservation, restoration, and development efforts (Comisión Ejecutiva Provincial 2002, 34). Given previous social support for watershed management reform generally, GTZ and the provincial government were shocked when the proposal met with fierce resistance. The response by watershed stakeholders illustrates the ineffectiveness of a market-based counter-framing strategy.

Members of farmer associations, irrigation councils, and development NGOs utilized production/poverty and environmental justice frames to oppose the proposal, labeling them unjust and anti-poor. They noted that 70% of the funds would come from the agricultural sector, while hydroelectric companies would provide 25%, and domestic, commercial, and industrial consumption combined would account for only 5%. They complained the plan would finance the program on the backs of poor farmers least able to afford it, which would exacerbate poverty and the unequal distribution of water resources.

Indigenous groups (which represented indigenous smallholder farmers) agreed with these arguments, but they also rejected the market frame as violating their cultural values, which prohibit the privatization and commodification of nature. Since concern about water privatization had made water management a national issue (see chapter 4), Ecuador's National Confederation of Indigenous Nationalities, CONAIE, intervened to oppose Tungurahua's IWM reform proposal. Chapter 6 described how CONAIE and Tungurahua's indigenous movements utilized cultural symbols to challenge the payment for ecosystem services concept. Equating watershed resources with Pachamama, a sacred deity revered by Andean indigenous people, CONAIE mobilized opposition through the slogan "Pachamama is not for sale!" CONAIE and other national indigenous associations directed their affiliates in Tungurahua to reject the payment for ecosystem services program, which they did.[7] The severity of the backlash startled the provincial government, and Prefect Naranjo later declared he would never accept a payment for ecosystem services system.[8] The phrase "payment for ecosystem services" became toxic, and no organization (including GTZ and the provincial government) publicly supported such a program.

---

[7] Former president, Indigenous Movement of Tungurahua-Atocha (MITA), interview by author, Ambato, Ecuador, November 18, 2009; indigenous organizer, Unity and Development of the Indigenous Movements of Tungurahua, interview by author, Ambato, Ecuador, November 18, 2009; indigenous community organizer, interview by author, Ambato, Ecuador, October 26, 2009.

[8] Provincial government official, interview by author, Ambato, Ecuador, January 6, 2010.

Tungurahua's experience illustrates the breakdown of grassroots global governance during the rule-making stage of phase 2. Even when an IWM coalition succeeds in placing IWM reform on the agenda of local authorities and mobilizes social support, the proposed rules may be rejected, particularly when they are insensitive to local cultural conditions and developed without local stakeholder involvement. The negative response strained relationships among coalition members. CESA and IEDECA, which had strong ties to local farmers and indigenous communities, criticized GTZ for "imposing" the proposal. Tungurahua's IWM coalition members stopped meeting and collaborating. Such rejection could easily have ended the reform campaign. However, IWM advocates regrouped and began rebuilding relationships through network activation, particularly with those stakeholders that resisted the first IWM proposal. Tungurahua's coalition eventually achieved success after making two changes in strategy: adopting a participatory approach to rule making and employing a frame-displacement strategy.

Rebuilding the Coalition through Participatory Rule Making

After the debacle surrounding payment for ecosystem services, Prefect Naranjo went to GTZ-PROMACH's lead technician and said, "You got me into this, now how do I get out of it?"[9] This time, GTZ advocated a more participatory approach to constructing watershed management institutions. The new recommendation stemmed from lessons GTZ learned from its role helping to create a new participatory IWM system in the neighboring Pachanlica watershed.[10] Naranjo was impressed with the participatory watershed management institutions GTZ-PROMACH helped create in Pachanlica, and he asked GTZ to help carry out a similar process at the provincial level. This process produced what Naranjo called a "New Governance Model" (*Nuevo Modelo de Gestión*) to promote development in the province.

From late 2002 to early 2003 the provincial government and GTZ sponsored community-level workshops to identify communities' needs and priorities. After compiling this information, in April 2003, 355 representatives of various public and private organizations attended a provincial assembly to agree on a development agenda. The participants proposed constructing a "New Tungurahuan

[9] GTZ technical staffer, interview by author, Ambato, Ecuador, October 21, 2009.

[10] For a description of the South-Western Association (*Frente Sur-Occidental*) and related reforms in Pachanlica, see Pérez De Mora (2009).

Provincial Government" that would be "participatory, in which all actors would combine forces to achieve development in the province [and] improve the population's living conditions" (Gobierno Provincial de Tungurahua 2009, 7–8).

Tungurahua's New Provincial Government (*Nuevo Gobierno Provincial*) was constituted one year later through the creation of three participatory institutions related to the three issue areas identified as pillars of development: water, people, and work. These three *espacios de concertación* (spaces for negotiating social contracts) allowed any actor to participate in working groups tasked with developing policy related to each issue area. Civil society organizations soon demanded these spaces be given legal powers on par with the Provincial Council, and they were subsequently reconstituted as "parliaments" within the provincial government.

Tungurahua's Water Parliament became a powerful new governing and linking institution in the IWM network. It linked local stakeholders and provided a forum for them to contest and negotiate ideas for how to manage watershed resources. These negotiations occurred through four working groups dealing with the páramos, irrigation, potable water, and sanitation.[11] Not coincidentally, the technical secretary of the Water Parliament, Luís Cuji, was a community organizer trained by CARE's PROMUSTA program in the 1990s. In fact, many working group members were former community organizers or water council members trained and organized in the 1990s by IWM advocates like GTZ, CESA, and IEDECA. Their leadership in Tungurahua's Water Parliament reflects the indirect governance that occurs through network activation.

As the Water Parliament was forming, the IWM coalition continued to gather information needed to create IWM plans. One task was to inventory the watershed's resources. The failed 2002 proposal taught GTZ the importance of treating rule making as a social process, and GTZ saw the inventory as an opportunity to switch strategies. In one inventory report, GTZ stated,

> a first lesson [is that] it would be a mistake . . . to start the inventory without first rooting this action in a local political agenda . . . that had the commitment of various actors. A second lesson, derived from the first [is that] the inventory is above all a political and social decision, and only later becomes a technical decision. (Crespo 2004, 8)

As a result, IWM advocates conducted the watershed inventory according to the principles of community based participatory research (Wallerstein and Duran 2003). A technical team formed by coalition partners collaborated with

---

[11] For details, see Gobierno Provincial de Tungurahua (2006).

community members in all aspects of the information-gathering process. In each community, local farmers and water council members guided the technical team through the watershed, identifying key areas and describing problems. Once information was collected, the technical team and community members jointly analyzed and interpreted the results and determined how these should be used for action.

This latter step resulted in the Master Plan for Tungurahua's Water Resources, which presented recommendations for integrated watershed management. This plan was also created in a highly participatory process—a series of public forums and technical meetings attended by 498 people representing 227 community organizations and 227,447 water users (Honorable Consejo Provincial de Tungurahua 2006, 6). According to several participants, this process not only provided baseline information necessary for decision making, but also raised the awareness, motivation, and technical capacity of community members to participate in watershed management activities. In addition, it strengthened ties between IWM advocates and community members and provided a sense of local ownership over the process.

This social approach to rule making helped maintain a high level of citizen participation in the Water Parliament. In its first year, representatives of 187 public and private organizations participated in the Water Parliament (Honorable Consejo Provincial de Tungurahua 2006, 2). Over the next several years, the number of participating organizations steadily increased. By 2009 there were 597 participants.[12] The Water Parliament became an important linking institution connecting stakeholders and serving as a focal point for mobilizing the material, informational, and social resources needed to advance IWM reform.

Activating Indigenous Networks

Noticeably absent from the Water Parliament were the province's three powerful indigenous movements—Indigenous Movement of Tungurahua (MIT), Indigenous Movement of Tungurahua-Atocha (MITA), and Association of Evangelical Indigenous of Tungurahua (AIET). Their absence was worrisome to GTZ, given indigenous groups' role in undermining the 2002 proposal. Recognizing that indigenous support would be crucial for future success, in 2003 GTZ technician Waldemar Wirsig convened a meeting of the province's indigenous movements to explain the governance changes and appeal for indigenous participation.

[12] Water Parliament's membership database, obtained from the Water Parliament's Coordinator.

Wirsig knew that Tungurahua's three indigenous movements were divided by religious and political differences.[13] While all represented Kichwa peoples, they affiliated with different national indigenous movements, competed as rivals in elections, and often differed on policy. Each represented a different set of Kichwa communities and secondary organizations in the watershed, creating an obstacle to collective action. Wirsig proposed that the movements unify to strengthen their influence in the new participatory institutions. Indigenous leaders were skeptical, but Wirsig continued to press, noting that their absence could isolate them from decisions on issues important to them, including páramo and water management. Wirsig offered to provide the training and resources to create a unified entity that would represent the three movements.[14]

A few members of MITA and AIET—community organizers previously trained during early local network activation—were sympathetic to Wirsig's argument and attended meetings of the Water Parliament. Seeing that real decisions were being made without their input, they lobbied movement leaders to join. MITA and AIET decided to participate in the New Governance Model, but MIT refused, accusing them of "selling the páramos" and privatizing water.[15] GTZ-PROMACH trained two indigenous technical experts (one from AIET and another from MITA) to oversee indigenous participation. After AIET and MITA took concrete actions, MIT also joined, and PROMACH trained one of its members to join the indigenous technical team.

On February 15, 2004, the three indigenous movements contracted GTZ to provide "institutional strengthening" and facilitate collaboration on natural resource management (Moreta et al. 2004). GTZ held workshops, but participation by movement members was initially low. To raise awareness and participation, the three indigenous experts trained by GTZ conducted an education campaign in all indigenous communities, facilitated by work teams formed in each of the 22 indigenous secondary organizations. This process was difficult, but the technical team was persistent. According to one indigenous organizer,

> The people were amazed and saw that this was the only process that united the three [indigenous] movements. Some saw this as good, but others saw it as bad because they saw their own political interests at

[13] MIT broke off from MITA soon after its founding in the 1970s amid leadership struggles. AIET formed separately to advocate for evangelical indigenous communities.

[14] Indigenous leader and organizer, Unity and Development of the Indigenous Movements of Tungurahua, interview by author, Ambato, Ecuador, November 18, 2009; Former president, Indigenous Movement of Tungurahua-Atocha (MITA), interview by author, Ambato, Ecuador, November 18, 2009.

[15] Indigenous leader and organizer, Unity and Development of the Indigenous Movements of Tungurahua, interview by author, Ambato, Ecuador, November 18, 2009.

risk. . . . In any case, we continued struggling in this process. We tried to educate the people. . . . We told them that if the business organizations and universities were participating . . . we also wanted to be kept in mind. With this ideal we had to educate all the communities.[16]

Given the negative reaction to a market frame, Tungurahua's IWM advocates recognized the need to switch their framing strategy. Hoping to draw on concerns over water scarcity, IWM advocates switched to a counter-framing strategy based on a conservation frame that called for protecting watershed resources to ensure future access to water.[17] This idea was captured through slogans like "There where water originates, grows life" (*Allí donde nace el agua crece la vida*) and "Life depends on water; does water depend on life?" (*La vida depende del agua. ¿El agua depende de la vida?*). Through workshops, training sessions, and publicity materials, Tungurahua's IWM coalition promoted the idea that the páramo had an inherent value apart from its use for agriculture and therefore should be conserved and restored, for example by removing agriculture and planting trees. Despite the new framing strategy and high level of capacity building, indigenous and campesino participation in reform efforts remained low. A turning point came when local advocates developed a frame-displacement strategy to redefine both the existing environmental justice and production/poverty frames to include IWM reform.

Switching to a Frame-Displacement Strategy

Recognizing that it lacked credibility with indigenous and campesino communities, GTZ hired an indigenous organizer, Washington Chapalbay, as an adviser and broker between GTZ and indigenous communities. Chapalbay had extensive experience as a community organizer for agro-ecological projects, having been trained by CARE's PROMUSTA program in the 1990s. The following sections describe how local brokers like Chapalbay and GTZ-trained indigenous experts gained influence in Tungurahua's IWM coalition due to their ability to activate indigenous and campesino networks. They used this influence to

---

[16] Interview with author, Ambato, Ecuador, November 18, 2009.

[17] Documents from the coalition's inventories of natural resources in the Ambato Watershed and their program Conservation of Natural Resources and Rural Irrigation in the Upper Ambato River Watershed (CORICAM) consistently stress the hydrological importance of natural resources and the need to protect these to ensure future access to quality water (Crespo 2004; Honorable Consejo Provincial de Tungurahua et al. 2004; Arias et al. 2005; IEDECA 2006a). To the extent production and poverty are discussed, they are described as problems exacerbating pressures on natural resources. The focus is on changing production practices to allow for effective conservation.

adapt both the coalition's network activation strategies and its proposed IWM institutions.

One example of local IWM advocates' influence is the way they crafted new frame-displacement strategies to mobilize indigenous and campesino support. Indigenous advocates knew they needed to contest CONAIE's use of Pachamama to mobilize opposition to IWM reform. In workshops, training sessions, and publicity materials, they drew upon CONAIE's linking of the páramos with the Andean deity Pachamama, and framed páramo conservation (and thus IWM reform) as "protecting" and "living in harmony with Pachamama" (see Fig. 7.2). Their language regarding IWM reform frequently characterized indigenous communities as the "owners of the páramo." While this was not always legally true, it referenced indigenous groups' struggle for access to land and water and the páramo's cultural symbolism. In this way, indigenous IWM advocates displaced the environmental justice frame to include IWM reform.

The real turning point came when indigenous IWM advocates framed IWM reform as a strategy for improving agricultural production and reducing poverty. This strategy resulted from learning that occurred through repeated negotiations with community members. Recognizing the priority local communities gave to agricultural production and poverty reduction, indigenous IWM advocates and their allies in GTZ held new workshops allowing communities to develop IWM

Image
Tungurahua's *páramo*

Slogan
Together for environmental conservation... put yourself in harmony with *Pachamama*

Figure 7.2 Displaced Environmental Justice Frame. Image source: author's photograph of a campaign poster publicly displayed in Tungurahua. English translation by author.

reform proposals based around agro-ecological production and expanded access to markets.

The focus on agricultural production and marketing attracted greater interest and participation by community members. Indigenous organizers channeled this interest into community-level workshops to develop action plans. As the process gained support, community members identified other priorities and agreed they should pursue related action plans within the new provincial government structure. In 2005, the three indigenous movements, with the support of their communities, formed a common front in pursuit of five action items: agro-ecological production, páramo management, education, health, and organizational strengthening (Gobierno Provincial de Tungurahua 2006, 32). They called this common front *Mushuk Yuyay* (Kichwa for "new ideas"). The concept mushuk yuyay explicitly linked "the protection of natural resources, and specifically the páramos," with "agro-ecological production oriented toward food security for rural families and the sale of surplus production" (Gobierno Provincial de Tungurahua 2006, 33).

The process of creating Mushuk Yuyay produced agreement among the three indigenous movements and their constituent communities regarding a strategy for watershed management. The strategy incorporated some ideas that had long been advocated by NGOs like CESA and IEDECA. These included voluntary community agreements to limit the expansion of the agricultural frontier and páramo management plans designed to restore key water catchment areas. However, community members argued that water users living below should compensate them for restoring the catchment areas. Specifically, they demanded resources to enhance agricultural production in lower areas to offset their lost opportunities in the páramo. Thus, the indigenous strategy was based on compensation through improved agricultural production in lower areas in exchange for conserving and restoring the páramo above.

To better pursue this agenda in Tungurahua's Water Parliament, the three indigenous movements formed a new linking institution—United Indigenous and Campesino Movements of Tungurahua (*Unidad de los Movimientos Indígenas y Campesinos de Tungurahua*). The organization's then-coordinator explained the logic behind framing IWM reform as an agricultural production strategy:

> You cannot just go to people and tell them they cannot produce any more because this is páramo, because these people need to find economic income to support their families. ... So I proposed to [CESA and IEDECA] the creation of a fund that would permit us to invest in the local economic initiatives of the people living in the páramo. This would be more effective than an ordinance that simply says you cannot produce above this line, or to simply tell people to plant trees to protect

water. Instead of saying this, we should say, here we have a budget—and so that we do not continue to destroy the páramo with new pasture and crops, let's promote alternative production and provide support so that people can have more efficient production and don't need to use a lot of land. So that if you raise cattle, provide support to improve pastures and supplement this with raising small animals so that you can produce more milk with fewer cows. And doing all this in lower [less fragile] areas. These are the kinds of things the people will like, and they will work more than putting prohibitions on the people.[18]

This indigenous activist was essentially saying that the previous conservation frame failed to mobilize community support because it placed IWM reform in opposition to peoples' goal of reducing poverty through expanded production. The implicit message was that mobilizing people required tapping into the dominant production/poverty frame.

Interestingly, the indigenous proposal for a páramo management fund had similar features to GTZ's original payment-for-ecosystem-services proposal. Those who consume water pay into a fund used to provide incentives for those living in the watershed to conserve and restore catchment areas. But rather than a payment for an ecosystem service, the indigenous framed their proposal in terms of providing "compensation" or "retribution" for sacrifices communities made for the benefit of all watershed stakeholders. This use of an environmental justice frame opened the way for IWM reform where the market frame had not.

Tungurahua's IWM coalition quickly seized this opportunity and shifted to a frame-displacement strategy that redefined the dominant production/poverty frame to include IWM reform. IWM advocates changed their education campaign to emphasize IWM reform as an integral part of the economic production cycle. Chapter 6 detailed the strategy's logic; it framed IWM reform as a strategy for ensuring sufficient water for irrigation, and thus expanded production, which in turn would reduce poverty through improved marketing and sales (see Fig. 6.4). In this way, IWM reform, including the conservation of watershed resources, was directly linked to poverty reduction. This link was symbolized in the name given to the financing mechanism at the heart of Tungurahua's IWM reforms—The Fund for Páramo Management and the Fight Against Poverty.

IWM promotional materials following the creation of Mushuk Yuyay illustrate this new, displaced production/poverty frame. One characterizes the proposed páramo management fund as "a mechanism for generating socio-productive options for the indigenous and rural population, in this way contributing to the

---

[18] Interview by author, Ambato, Ecuador, November 18, 2009.

reduction of poverty and the conservation of the páramos" (Gobierno Provincial de Tungurahua 2006, 34). The report similarly describes how Tungurahua's Water Parliament facilitates

> the appropriate management of the páramos, which makes possible its protection and the fight against poverty among the population. Initiatives being implemented include improvements to water distribution infrastructure and the equality of its allocation, technical improvements to production and irrigation, the associated commercialization, and more just prices for agricultural products. (Gobierno Provincial de Tungurahua 2006, 17)

This image of IWM reform as a strategy for expanding production and reducing poverty contrasts starkly with the previous counter-framing strategies, which prompted local actors to view IWM reform as being opposed to these goals.

An IWM advocate with GTZ explained that the decision to switch to a displaced production/poverty frame was "a conscious strategy. It was a response to the context that we found ourselves in. . . . For us [the initial resistance to IWM reform] was a resistance to the semantics and not to the concept."[19] This motivated GTZ to search for a frame that would resonate better. The GTZ staffer described the rationale behind the change in strategy this way:

> Politically, the resistance to environmental services comes from the perception that there is a commodification of environmental services. Among the extreme environmentalists there is a resistance to marketization or valuation . . . these are prohibited words for these extremists. . . . What is interesting about Tungurahua is that, despite this resistance to the semantics of environmental services, the concept is accepted. That is, the concept that ecosystems provide services for human beings . . . is accepted. And that people should be compensated for caring for these ecosystems to ensure the services continue. So really, we do not understand where the problem comes from. But we have maintained a policy of continuing to move forward, supporting mechanisms that locally have changed their focus. In the Fund [for Páramo Management] there originally was a payment for environmental services mechanism. Now the mechanism is a form of compensation for efforts made by people who are changing their behavior. Another interesting thing is the second part of the name–Fight Against Poverty. Politically, this is

---

[19] Interview by author, Quito, Ecuador, May 31, 2011.

what is sold in the province, rather than caring for the páramo. Because people tend to think of the páramo, and ecosystems in general, as productive spaces. If you do not produce vegetables or animals, they are not productive. In regard to the problem of poverty, the view is that the páramo has to solve the structural problem of poverty. This is the rationale behind their views. We believe that the conservation of these ecosystems is intimately related to improving the quality of life for the people that live in these ecosystems. For this reason, we really pushed . . . to ensure that these funds are really invested in effective conservation of these ecosystems, improving the quality of life for the people.

The influence of this change in framing strategy is shown through images drawn by community members living in the páramos. One member of Tungurahua's IWM coalition, the development NGO IEDECA, conducted an exercise to evaluate the effectiveness of their strategy linking IWM reform to improved agricultural production. At the start of their educational campaign IEDECA asked community members to draw a picture of the páramos. In later workshops, these same community members were asked to draw the páramos again to see if there was any change in their conception of watershed resources. This exercise was carried out with hundreds of community members. Figure 7.3 depicts a set of drawings by one individual that are representative. As expected, the first picture depicts the páramos as a productive space devoid of trees, where local farmers burn páramo to plant crops and raise cows, pigs, and horses. No water exists in the drawing. The second drawing is very different. Here, the upper area (where water collects) is heavily vegetated and includes an ecological reserve. Native llamas, whose padded feet do not damage páramo vegetation, replace cows, pigs, and horses, whose cloven hoofs destroy páramo vegetation. These nonnative livestock are relocated to stables in less fragile areas below. The stables separate livestock from water, which flows down from the páramos to fields farmed in lower, less-fragile areas.

These pictures admittedly provide only indirect and anecdotal evidence of the effectiveness of IWM advocates' frame-displacement strategy. But they are consistent with the change in language and symbolism used by IWM advocates. They are also consistent with the fact that it was only after IWM reform was framed as a strategy for improving production and reducing poverty that Tungurahua's stakeholders mobilized to create the local financing mechanism at the heart of the new watershed governance system. Interestingly, national indigenous organizations like CONAIE remained opposed to these reforms and encouraged local indigenous movements to boycott Tungurahua's IWM institutions, yet Tungurahua's indigenous communities resisted this pressure and became leading advocates of IWM reform.

Figure 7.3 Results of IEDECA's Frame Displacement Campaign in Tungurahua. Photographs by author.

Experimenting with Institutional Adaptations

Once unified and mobilized, indigenous groups greatly increased their influence in the Water Parliament and other participatory institutions in Tungurahua's New Governance Model. By 2006, indigenous peoples comprised 65% of participants in the three parliaments and held 50% of the parliaments' leadership positions.[20] They used this influence to negotiate with traditionally powerful stakeholder groups, including irrigation and water councils and hydroelectric companies. As early as 2006, the Water Parliament became a forum for channeling mutual pressure from beside, allowing community members to debate ideas for getting different water users to contribute to a common fund to finance local economic initiatives. This provided an opening for IWM advocates to renew their efforts to create a local financing mechanism for watershed management.

In 2006 GTZ worked with The Nature Conservancy-Ecuador to develop a proposal modeled on FONAG, Quito's pioneering water trust fund (described in chapter 4). Indigenous groups refused to sign this proposal, again citing concerns about the commodification and privatization of nature. GTZ responded by asking the indigenous movements to develop their own proposal and offered technical support. The first indigenous proposal called for NGOs to provide all the funding, which was rejected by CESA and IEDECA, among other organizations. For two years, GTZ, CESA, and IEDECA negotiated with indigenous movements and other watershed stakeholder groups, including water councils, Ambato's municipal water company, and hydroelectric companies. In 2008, this contestation produced a highly innovative watershed financing mechanism—Tungurahua's Fund for Páramo Management and Fight Against Poverty.

The fund's unique institutional features reflect how contestation and experimentation led local stakeholders to combine global IWM principles with elements of local norms and practices. Tungurahua's indigenous movements proposed the fund's final design, which was structured to fit with indigenous norms for living in harmony with nature (sumak kawsay in Kichwa or buen vivir in Spanish) and their concerns about the commodification and privatization of natural resources. Two institutional adaptations were crucial to overcoming indigenous concerns: voluntary contributions and no individual compensation. Tungurahua's fund is capitalized with annual voluntary contributions from its eight partners (identified later), who serve on the board of directors. This differentiates it from most other watershed financing mechanisms, in which payments are made obligatory by market contracts, government ordinances, or

---

[20] Coordinator, Tungurahua's Water Parliament, interview by author, Ambato, Ecuador, October 20, 2009.

fees levied on water use. Unlike a strict payment for ecosystem services scheme, Tungurahua's fund does not directly compensate individual landowners. Rather, it finances a range of activities at the watershed or community level designed to benefit the whole ecosystem, including the communities living within.[21]

According to indigenous leaders, these two institutional adaptations were crucial for overcoming concerns about the commodification and privatization of natural resources. Since financial contributions are voluntary and individuals do not receive compensation, the financing mechanism lacks the characteristics of a market transaction. By designing projects at the watershed or community level, Tungurahua's trust fund reinforces the notion of watershed resources being public goods and promotes a sense of community responsibility. According to indigenous leaders and farmers, this distinction is crucial because it emphasizes the public nature of natural resources and the focus on human well-being in harmony with nature.

Because the fund's institutional structure facilitates voluntary, multi-stakeholder collaboration to implement community-level projects, it has cultural resonance. It is consistent with the indigenous tradition of *mingas*. Minga means "collective work" in Kichwa, and refers to the centuries-old indigenous tradition of family labor exchange. It is an important concept throughout Ecuador, particularly among popular and poor sectors, both indigenous and mestizo. Mingas use norms of exchange and reciprocity to motivate community members to participate in voluntary, unpaid projects that benefit community members. Traditionally, mingas are used mostly in farming and building houses. But Tungurahua's IWM institutions organize community mingas to implement watershed management projects financed by the fund.

Importantly, Tungurahua's paramo management fund includes representatives from all major stakeholder groups: local politicians (i.e., Tungurahua's provincial government), water user groups (the municipal water company for Ambato and two hydroelectric companies), and the province's three indigenous movements, which represent landowners living in the watershed. In October 2011, the Ambato regional electric company also joined.

Since 2008, these organizations' voluntary contributions have totaled $460,000 annually. Sixty percent is invested to grow the fiduciary fund, while 40% goes toward financing projects defined in annual operating plans (Rojas 2012). Projects are also financed by interest from the trust's investments and special donations from external organizations. Working groups in the Water Parliament submit project proposals to the fund's technical secretariat, which

---

[21] Kauffman (2014) provides a detailed description of Tungurahua's páramo management fund and the projects it funds.

approves and prioritizes the projects. Priority is given to financing páramo management plans created at the community level and coordinated by the province's three indigenous movements. By 2012, roughly 85% of expenses went toward financing 10 such plans, addressing portions of the páramo controlled by 10 different communities (Rojas 2012).

As a result, 17,635 hectares of páramo were being conserved and restored for the first time through community agreements. Anecdotal evidence suggests some improvement in vegetation and water quality. In the páramos of Yanahurco, for example, natural vegetation is returning in roughly 80% of the territory. Tests also showed improved water quality.[22] In terms of socioeconomic effects, by 2012 more than 2,000 community members were trained in conservation, sustainable agriculture and irrigation, and water and páramo management. Nearly 2,200 families benefited from economic and production assistance (Rojas 2012). Perhaps the biggest changes were the improved social capacity and commitment to sustainable watershed management, demonstrated by the community development and implementation of páramo management plans, water users' continued contribution to the páramo management fund, and stakeholder participation in the Water Parliament. For all these reasons, Tungurahua is often characterized in Ecuadorian development circles as a highly innovative, successful example of IWM reform.

Conclusion

The Tungurahua case illustrates the various mechanisms at work in phase 2 of grassroots global governance. Transnational IWM networks expanded to Tungurahua by training local knowledge communities and organizing them through linking institutions. This facilitated the formation of a local IWM coalition and its subsequent expansion among landowners, water users, and local government representatives. Tungurahua's IWM coalition adapted its framing and capacity-building strategies over time as it learned from its interaction with local stakeholders. Indeed, the incorporation of local stakeholders into the coalition facilitated changes in strategy. For example, indigenous organizers trained by GTZ played a key role in crafting the frame-displacement strategy that ultimately motivated the indigenous communities—the watershed's main landowners—to participate in the IWM reform process.

---

[22] The Tungurahua fund's technical secretariat performed tests using the Water Quality Index (WQI), which showed an increase in water quality from 0.60 to 0.71. The fund's technical secretary provided the results to the author.

As in other cases, Tungurahua's experience shows the importance of treating rule making as a social, rather than purely technical, exercise, as well as creating institutions through which multiple stakeholders can collaborate in this process. Linking institutions such as the Water Parliament and Tungurahua's Provincial Water Resources Forum channeled pressure from beside, served as focal points for mobilizing material and social resources, provided structures for maintaining the participation of stakeholders, and constituted spaces where local actors could tweak reform models to be more appropriate to local conditions.

The result was a highly innovative institutional adaptation of a global idea based on local norms. Tungurahuans accepted the global principle that water users and other stakeholders should pay to protect watershed ecosystem services. However, they rejected the idea of creating a market, which would require privatizing watershed resources. Bucking conventional wisdom, they created a mechanism that provides a stable source of local revenue for financing watershed management activities, but that does not privatize watershed resources or involve a market transaction.

The next chapter shows that Tungurahua's páramo management fund was but one of many innovations in watershed management associated with Tungurahua's New Governance Model. Importantly, these innovations stemmed from efforts to adapt global ideas regarding IWM to fit local, indigenous norms that challenge Western notions of sustainable development. Tungurahua's IWM reform process provided local stakeholders an opportunity to experiment with institutionalizing an alternative model of sustainable development rooted in indigenous norms. The perceived success of this experimentation raised the profile of Tungurahua's New Governance Model in indigenous and development circles across Ecuador. Local and foreign activists opposed to the dominant global vision of sustainable development pointed to Tungurahua as evidence that an alternative approach was viable and as an example of what it might look like. Chapter 8 shows how Tungurahua's experiment with IWM reform influenced Ecuador's national development strategy and consequently pushed global discussion toward an alternative model of sustainable development. In so doing, it illustrates the connection between phase 2 and phase 3 of grassroots global governance.

8

Phase 3

Global Impacts of Local Experiments

Chapter 7 described how indigenous and campesino farmers in Tungurahua resisted efforts by international advocates to implement an IWM system based on markets for ecosystem services. However, these farmers recognized that a new IWM system might dovetail with their long-standing struggle for greater control over land and water resources. They negotiated with outside IWM advocates to experiment with an alternative program rooted in indigenous norms that challenged the dominant international model of sustainable development. Their approach sought to realize the Kichwa concept sumak kawsay (buen vivir in Spanish), which refers to living in harmony with nature rather than dominating nature or removing human presence through conservation. When Tungurahua's indigenous movements united, they became a dominant force in the province's new Water Parliament. This gave them significant influence over the province's IWM reform process, allowing them to infuse indigenous norms into IWM institutions, policies, and practices. The resulting governance system marked the first time the ideal of sumak kawsay was institutionalized within formal government structures.

Since then, the term sumak kawsay and its Spanish translation buen vivir have infiltrated international discourse surrounding sustainable development, moving global discussion toward a search for new ways to live in harmony with nature, including by granting rights to nature. This chapter traces the process by which Tungurahua's experiment with IWM reform helped spark this change in order to examine phase 3 of grassroots global governance. I first define sumak kawsay, contrast this with the traditional, Western notion of development, and then describe how Tungurahua's IWM reform efforts produced the first experiment with institutionalizing sumak kawsay. The chapter's second part shows how Tungurahua's experiment was scaled up nationally through network activation, resulting in Ecuador's National Plan for Buen Vivir. This plan guides Ecuador's national development strategy, which has become part of a greater international campaign for the rights of nature and alternative paths of sustainable development—a global movement for buen vivir.

The chapter then shows how Ecuador's experiment with buen vivir has influenced the global discourse on sustainable development. In particular, Ecuador's experience catalyzed international organizing and action around a new global idea—the rights of nature—both at the international level and domestically in countries around the world. Ecuador is held up as a concrete example of an alternative to the dominant approach pursued through the Rio+20 UN Conference on Sustainable Development. Consequently, the Tungurahua case illuminates how local populations working with competing interpretations from international agendas experiment with innovative local governance regimes and how the scaling up of these regimes carries local norms, principles, and practices to the global level, where they challenge traditional thinking.

By tracing the influence of Tungurahua's IWM reforms on global sustainable development discourse and organizing around the rights of nature, the chapter illustrates how governance networks that form around local experiments expand upward through the mechanisms of network activation. Members engage in strategic framing, share information and technology, train new knowledge communities, and organize them through linking institutions. They also create or alter international governance institutions to concentrate and direct resources toward implementing new policies and practices.

This chapter also highlights a key characteristic of bottom-up network activation. As governance networks expand nationally and internationally, and contestation over principles and practices shifts to national and international arenas, organizations with more influence in these arenas take on leading roles in transnational governance networks. National governments play a particularly important role in international policymaking circles, while international NGOs and IGOs have a global impact via their international programming and activism. These organizations use their influence to manage how principles and practices that are scaled up from local experiments are defined internationally, shaping the evolution of global ideas.

For example, Ecuador's government and international NGOs are influencing the way sumak kawsay/buen vivir are defined in international policy arenas, and thus are shaping what it means to live in harmony with nature. By infusing these indigenous concepts with new meaning, based on organizational interests, they are driving the evolution of these concepts at the international level, just as grassroots actors altered the meaning of global ideas when applying them in local arenas. As a result, international discourse surrounding sumak kawsay/buen vivir differs from the way grassroots indigenous organizations in Tungurahua discuss the terms. While these concepts evolved when scaled up, they retained elements of local norms and consequently are altering international organizing and discourse about how to conceptualize and practice sustainable development. Consequently, the scaling up of buen vivir illustrates not only how network activation from the grassroots to the global level alters international discourse and organizing around global ideas, but also how the evolution of global ideas is impacted by the shift in power within transnational networks that accompanies shifts in policy arenas.

The following case study shows how the packaging of local experiments' principles and practices into new meta-concepts—ideas for tackling global problems—facilitates international mobilization. Meta-concepts like buen vivir set goals with broad appeal, like human well-being, sustainable development, and climate change mitigation. Over time, principles and practices from multiple local experiments are incorporated into meta-concepts. This gives them a level of generality that facilitates international collaboration among organizations with distinct interests. While national governments and international organizations invariably add their own interpretations, meta-concepts nevertheless provide a platform for diffusing local norms, principles, and practices to the international level. Sometimes, they challenge existing global ideas, as in the case of buen vivir. The local ideas contained in meta-concepts drive the evolution of global discourse, the policies of international organizations, and international structures for tackling global problems. In short, they drive the evolution of global ideas.

Buen Vivir as an Alternative Development Model

Ecuador's national indigenous uprising in the 1990s was spurred in part by opposition to development policies based on neoliberal economic theory. Indigenous leaders have since advocated an alternative development approach consistent with the ancient indigenous concept sumak kawsay. Sumak kawsay (a Kichwa term) is translated in Spanish as buen vivir, and could loosely be translated in English as the "good life," "well-being," or "living well." As Rieckmann et al. (2011, 443) note, key elements of sumak kawsay include:

harmony, dialogue, and equity among human beings as well as between humankind and nature; the sustainable use of natural resources (the planet is seen as "Pachamama"—"Mother Earth"); the maintenance of ecological systems and cycles; equity, solidarity, and dignity; respect for diversity; ethics of responsibility; and harmonious life instead of linear development.

The idea behind sumak kawsay (buen vivir) is to live "well," in the sense of "living in harmony and equilibrium" with nature and other people (Oviedo 2014, 271). The goal is not to live "better," in the sense of striving for perpetual material improvement or competing to live better than others (Lalander 2014). The concept therefore breaks with the globally dominant notion of development as accumulation through economic growth. Proponents see it as an alternative to conventional sustainable development that overcomes a false dilemma posed by Western ideals (Chuji 2014; Fatheurer 2011).

The dominant international concept of development derives from the Western ideals of individualism, progress as the linear unfolding of history, and the separation of humankind from nature. Western thought has long presented individuals as lords or lawmakers of nature, while viewing development as increasing consumption and production (Fatheurer 2011). Nature is framed as a quantity of natural resources to be manipulated by individuals to pursue development.

In the 1980s, concern with the environmental consequences of rapid development gave rise to the internationally dominant concept of sustainable development, which seeks both ecological sustainability and economic growth (Brundtland 1987). Despite disagreement over the best strategy, most approaches to sustainable development start from the premise that human intervention in nature is problematic. Particularly before the 1990s, most international environmental organizations viewed economic growth as the cause of environmental problems, such as the incursion of pristine areas by extractive processes. They advocated a pure conservation approach of delineating natural areas to be conserved and protected from human intervention, for example through the creation of national parks (Zimmerer 2011). Since the 1992 UN Conference on Environment and Development, it has been widely accepted that poverty spurs environmental degradation and economic growth is the solution. Despite this shift, international discourse has remained centered on the dilemma of how to protect the environment given humanity's right to exploit nature for economic growth.

To reconcile the problems of poverty and conservation, many Northern NGOs and donor agencies promote integrated conservation and development projects in low-income countries, including through the IWM reforms discussed in this book. As previous chapters described, IWM projects proposed by international advocates typically combine macroeconomic poverty eradication measures with protection of fragile ecosystems from encroachment by poor people (Hughes and Flintan 2001). The poverty reduction component typically focuses on integrating local production into export markets. On the conservation side, market mechanisms are advocated to give local communities incentives to engage in conservation. Assuming local actors will conserve and restore designated natural areas if adequately compensated, markets for ecosystem services are promoted as a way to change the incentives of local actors to engage in less ecologically destructive behaviors (Pagiola 2006; Wunder 2005).

Buen vivir (sumak kawsay) rejects conventional notions of development based on Western ideals of individualism, a dualism between humankind and nature, and linear progress through material growth. Buen vivir sidesteps the Western sustainable development dilemma by seeking neither to dominate nature nor to conserve and protect it from human intervention. Rather than a linear progression of accumulation, development is understood as the attainment and reproduction of the equilibrium state of buen vivir, or living in harmony with nature.

Mónica Chuji, an Amazonian Kichwa leader and spokesperson for Ecuador's indigenous movement CONAIE, interprets buen vivir and its relationship to development this way:

> In the indigenous world, Sumak Kawsay (living in harmony or Buen Vivir) signifies having healthy and fertile land and territory. It implies cultivating what is necessary [for food security] with a diversity of crops. Further, it implies preserving, caring for, and keeping the rivers, forests, the air, the mountains, etc., clean. It means collectively managing land; education based on our own values; and constant communication. It also means governing based on an ethical code and the recognition and respect for the rights of others. . . . Sumak Kawsay (living in harmony or Buen Vivir) advocates that nature no longer be seen as a factor of production or as a productive force, but rather an inherent part of the social being. . . . Sumak Kawsay questions theories of development that in the past proposed the existence of "developed" and "under-developed" (or "developing") countries, and that even recommended prescriptions for overcoming this state of under-development. The core of the prescription was to extend the exploitation of nature, decrease rights and to commercialize the labor force. . . . Sumak Kawsay (Buen Vivir) is distinct from this concept of "development." (Chuji 2014, 231–33)

Buen vivir is difficult to define because it is not meant to be a preformulated route to sustainable development. Fundamental to the concept is the recognition of rights of a diversity of peoples, deliberation, and respect for many ideas. It involves a dialogue within and among communities to determine the best pathways of sustainable development. Therefore, buen vivir will manifest itself differently in various social and environmental contexts. Tungurahua's New Governance Model and watershed management regime provide one concrete example.

Tungurahua's Experiment with Buen Vivir

When it became clear that a new watershed governance system was being constructed with or without their participation, Tungurahua's divided indigenous movements and communities agreed in 2005 to form a common front to ensure the process reflected indigenous norms and priorities (see chapter 7). Indigenous leaders named this common front Mushuk Yuyay (Kichwa for "new ideas") to contrast their approach to governance and development with that traditionally taken by the Ecuadorian state, international NGOs, and donor agencies.[1]

Rather than a focus on individualism, economic growth, and protecting nature from human intervention, Mushuk Yuyay's agenda reflected norms associated with buen vivir. It advocated a governance process based on dialogue and "interculturality" (respect for diverse ideas and cultural traditions) to "improve the quality of life" through a development strategy based on "economic solidarity," "communal interest," "collective rights," and the "sustainable management of resources, education and health" (Gobierno Provincial de Tungurahua 2008, 26–27). Mushuk Yuyay understood sustainable development as achieving and maintaining well-being through a strategy that integrated the restoration of páramo ecosystems, food security, and education to create healthy communities. This was reflected in the five pillars of the movement's agenda: páramo management, food production, health, education, and organizational strengthening (Gobierno Provincial de Tungurahua 2006, 32).

A central objective of Mushuk Yuyay was restoring and caring for the páramo ecosystem, which is not only an important water source but also a cultural and religious symbol for Ecuador's Andean indigenous groups. In accordance with buen vivir, their restoration strategy sought to improve the well-being of the páramo ecosystem by helping communities living within it to improve their well-being while maintaining a balance with nature. Community plant nurseries were created to support the reforestation of degraded areas with native species, including those with medicinal qualities. Consequently, reforestation was integrated into a new health program that combined Western and indigenous knowledge.

Mushuk Yuyay also combined páramo restoration with agricultural programs to promote food security and reduce poverty. Members created the Association of Agro-ecological Producers of Tungurahua (PACAT) to train farmers in ecological practices that produce healthier foods (ecologically and nutritionally). Rather than monoculture for export markets, PACAT emphasized a return to

---

[1] Mushuk Yuyay was the formal name given to this association of indigenous movements to advance their common agenda.

traditional crops that were ecologically friendly and provided a healthier diet. PACAT also facilitated collective projects to expand local markets in Ambato (Tungurahua's capital city) and to increase the efficiency of water canals and agricultural output. Cattle and pigs, whose cloven hooves destroy páramo vegetation, were removed from water catchment areas and replaced with native species, including guinea pigs and alpaca, whose padded feet do not damage páramo vegetation. New species compatible with restoration (e.g., trout farms) were introduced to provide additional protein. The organization *Wuaylla Ñan* (Green Path) was created to collect and process waste and supply organic fertilizer to PACAT. To build human capacity and maintain indigenous culture, Mushuk Yuyay launched a literacy campaign that promoted bilingual education, considered the fourth pillar of development.

The fifth pillar was strengthening indigenous organizations' ability to better press their agenda within Tungurahua's New Governance Model. The three indigenous movements formalized their association through the linking institution, United Indigenous and Campesino Movements of Tungurahua (*Unidad de los Movimientos Indígenas y Campesinos de Tungurahua*). Organizational strengthening allowed the indigenous movements to dominate the Water Parliament and other local participatory decision-making bodies. By 2006, they comprised 65% of participants in provincial government parliaments, and they held 50% of leadership positions.[2] Chapter 7 described how indigenous groups used this influence to adapt initial proposals for a local IWM financing mechanism to meet the principles of buen vivir. The result was an innovative watershed trust fund that did not create a market for ecosystem services, but instead relied on voluntary contributions and collaborative projects at the community and watershed levels.

Network Activation to Scale Up
Buen Vivir Nationally

By 2007, the watershed management system created through Tungurahua's New Governance Model gained national attention as a successful example of participatory governance based on the principles of buen vivir—a model for ecologically sustainable development with an emphasis on interculturality and human well-being. This attention partly resulted from the publicity provided by donor agencies and NGOs working in Tungurahua. But Tungurahua's experience also diffused up through the corporatist structure of Ecuador's national indigenous

---

[2] Technical director, Tungurahua's Water Parliament, interview by author, Ambato, October 20, 2009.

movements, which had long advocated buen vivir as an alternative to neoliberal development strategies. Communities in several other Andean provinces (e.g., Chimborazo, Cañar, Azuay) also had mobilized under the banner of Mushuk Yuyay to express new ideas for development.[3] While this idea was percolating among indigenous communities across Ecuador, those in Tungurahua went furthest in institutionalizing a development strategy reflecting sumak kawsay principles. Tungurahua's experiment with IWM reform showed for the first time what an alternative to neoliberalism might look like in practice. As I show here, this demonstration had both national and international consequences.

Importantly, Tungurahua's New Governance Model took form just as Ecuador began a process of state restructuring. In April 2007, Ecuadorians overwhelmingly approved a referendum to convene an assembly charged with writing a new constitution. Indigenous groups viewed the referendum as a rejection of the neoliberal economic model, which they argued undermined the well-being of the majority of Ecuadorians by shifting the country's wealth to elite corporate interests. This, along with neoliberalism's embrace of development through increased consumerism, led indigenous groups to frame buen vivir in opposition to neoliberalism. They viewed the constituent assembly as a long-awaited political opening to pursue an alternative development path based on indigenous goals and values (Cholango 2007).

Believing they would be most influential by working with the government of newly elected President Correa, many indigenous activists joined Correa's movement, contributing to Correa's majority in the assembly (Becker 2011a, 49). These included representatives of Ecuador's national indigenous movements (e.g., Mónica Chuji of the National Confederation of the Association of Indigenous Peoples of Ecuador, CONAIE, and Pedro de la Cruz of the National Confederation of Peasant, Indigenous, and Black Organizations, FENOCIN), but also Vicente Masaquiza, a representative of Tungurahua's united indigenous movements. These indigenous leaders and their allies succeeded in placing buen vivir at the center of Ecuador's new constitution.

Ecuador's 2008 constitution preamble states, "We decide to construct a new form of civil society, in diversity and harmony with nature to achieve buen vivir, sumak kawsay" (Republic of Ecuador 2008, 3). According to Alberto Acosta (2010), the president of Ecuador's Constitutional Assembly, the significance of incorporating buen vivir into the constitution lies in its reorientation of the country's development model. Title VII stipulates that buen vivir must be the foundation of a new development model "that is environmentally balanced and respectful

---

[3] See http://mushukyuyay.blogspot.com (accessed June 20, 2016) and http://mushukyuyay.weebly.com (accessed June 20, 2016).

of cultural diversity, conserves biodiversity and the natural regeneration capacity of ecosystems."

Title II identifies the principles of buen vivir that are to guide this new development model. It presents buen vivir as a set of rights. Not coincidentally, these reflect the pillars of Mushuk Yuyay's agenda in Tungurahua. Articles 12 and 13, for example, recognize the principle of food sovereignty and establish Ecuadorians' right to water and "sufficient nutritional food, preferably produced locally and in keeping with [communities'] various identities and cultural traditions." Article 14 recognizes "the right of the population to live in a healthy and ecologically balanced environment that guarantees sustainability and good living (sumak kawsay)," achieved through "the protection of ecosystems, biodiversity and the integrity of the country's genetic assets, the prevention of environmental damage, and the recovery of degraded natural spaces" (Republic of Ecuador 2008, Article 14). Other rights include intercultural and inclusive access to communication, education, housing, and health.

Buen vivir is not simply third-generation human rights. Ecuador's Constitution is the world's first to grant nature formal rights, treating nature as a subject rather than an object. For example, Title II Chapter 7 grants nature the right to exist, maintain its integrity as an ecosystem, and regenerate "its life cycles, structure, functions and evolutionary processes" (Republic of Ecuador 2008, Articles 71–73). Nature also has the right to be restored if injured, independent of human claims for compensation. Moreover, the Constitution empowers any person to enforce these rights in court. Granting rights to nature was meant to give nature more importance, prevent environmental damage, create environmental awareness, and thus create the basis for a harmonic coexistence between people and nature, the essence of sumak kawsay (Acosta 2009). By integrating human rights and the rights of nature, buen vivir "requires that individuals, communities, peoples and nations . . . exercise their responsibilities in the context of interculturalism, respect for diversity and of harmonious coexistence with nature" (Republic of Ecuador 2008, Article 275).

After Ecuador's Constitution was approved, the Ministry of Planning and Development was charged with creating a five-year development plan for realizing buen vivir. Technocrats in Quito understandably had difficulty envisioning how to operationalize buen vivir. According to a senior ministry official in charge of Planning and Development, Tungurahua's experience provided an important model for national bureaucrats designing the plan.[4] This was due in no small part to the promotional efforts of the German Organization for Technical Cooperation (GTZ), which was a leading member of Tungurahua's IWM reform coalition as well as a close advisor to the Ministry of Planning and Development (see chapter 4).

---

[4] Interview by author, Quito, Ecuador, May 20, 2011.

The influence of Tungurahua's experimental IWM system is reflected in the similarities between its institutions and approach and those of Ecuador's national government, as seen in the Constitution and national development plan. Correa's government also has sought to create a New Governance Model based on citizen participation as a foundation for a more democratic, deliberative, and intercultural approach to development. Explicitly rejecting neoliberalism, Ecuador's Constitution and development plan envision a form of development rooted in respect for local wisdom, cultural values and practices; equitable access to natural resources like land and water; agricultural production for local markets to achieve food security; education; health; and environmental rights.

Implementation of buen vivir through Ecuador's new governance model is far from perfect. Critics accuse Correa's government of manipulating the institutions of citizen participation to circumvent his opposition while promoting large-scale resource extraction in violation of buen vivir principles. Indeed, some indigenous and environmental activists argue that the Ecuadorian government's treatment of buen vivir is inconsistent with sumak kawsay. They accuse government leaders of coopting and twisting the concept's meaning to justify a traditional Western development model rooted in resource extraction and increased consumption (e.g., Cholango 2010; Oviedo 2014; Simbaña 2011).

Nevertheless, Ecuador's codification of buen vivir has had important international effects. Ecuador's Constitution and National Plan for Buen Vivir provide one of the clearest articulations of a new development model based on buen vivir. Despite controversies over government actions like increased mining concessions, many buen vivir principles, like the rights of nature, are gradually being put into practice by the national government, subnational governments, and communities (Kauffman and Martin 2016). In doing so, Ecuadorians are demonstrating the viability of buen vivir as an alternative to conventional development. This has spurred an international movement for buen vivir that is altering the global debate over how to conceptualize sustainable development.

Network Activation to Promote
Buen Vivir Globally

When Ecuador became the world's first country to grant nature constitutional rights (under the label of buen vivir), it garnered international attention and became a model for various organizations advocating a more ecocentric approach to sustainable development. Other features of Ecuador's new development approach similarly inspired organizations with different concerns. Some emphasized the recognition and respect for indigenous rights, knowledge, and customs. Others were drawn by the fierce attacks on neoliberal economic policies.

As the first internationally recognized, tangible example of buen vivir, Ecuador's political project established buen vivir as a global meta-concept and strongly influenced its initial content. Three elements of Ecuador's political project were particularly influential on the construction of buen vivir in international discourse. First, it equated buen vivir with the Kichwa concept sumak kawsay and described this in English as "living in harmony with nature." Second, it operationalized buen vivir as a set of constitutional rights that integrated human rights with the rights of nature. Third, it framed buen vivir in opposition to neoliberal economic policies. These ingredients established buen vivir as a global meta-concept able to connect various actors around the world, from indigenous movements to rights of nature activists to left-leaning academics, social activists, and policymakers opposed to neoliberalism. While these organizations had different interests, buen vivir provided a platform for organizing around a common goal—challenging the dominant international approach to sustainable development.

Indigenous Mobilization around Buen Vivir

Indigenous groups across the Andes have concepts comparable to sumak kawsay. These too came to be translated as buen vivir and incorporated into the meta-concept.[5] Inspired by Ecuador's new Constitution, indigenous and campesino movements across the Andes used buen vivir to frame their efforts to restructure state–society relations around a new development model that respects indigenous rights, promotes indigenous political participation, and is rooted in indigenous norms for living in harmony with nature and people. In 2010, for example, Mario Palacios, then-president of Peru's national indigenous confederation CONACAMI, described his movement's goal as constructing

---

[5] Examples include suma kamana (Bolivia-Quechua language), allin kawsay (Peru-Quechua language), suma qamaña (Bolivia and Peru-Aymara language), and ñande reko (Bolivia and Paraguay-Guaraní language) (Albó 2009; Altmann 2013; Thomson 2011). Despite similarities, there are different opinions on how to interpret these various concepts. Buen vivir therefore represents a variety of indigenous discursive and practice-related "platforms" (Gudynas 2011) for considering and practicing alternative visions of development. A large literature has arisen problematizing different interpretations of buen vivir and sumak kawsay, including the view that these are distinct concepts (e.g., Acosta and Martínez 2009; Hidalgo-Capitán et al. 2014; Lalander 2014). Describing these different interpretations is beyond the scope of this book. While acknowledging the differences, I use the terms as they are typically used in relation to Ecuador's political project of institutionalizing buen vivir and in international discourse. I therefore use sumak kawsay and buen vivir interchangeably.

a political proposal that is also a proposal for life, a project of life—el buen vivir. This project, which translates in Quechua as allin kawsay or in Aymara as sumah qamana, . . . encompasses a new vision, a new way of seeing, that is different from Western developmentalism in that we call for harmony with, and respect for, Mother Earth [Pachamama]. (quoted in Poole 2010)

After Ecuador, Bolivia's indigenous and campesino movements were most successful in institutionalizing buen vivir nationally. In 2010, the government of indigenous president Evo Morales adopted the Law of the Rights of Mother Earth (*Ley de Derechos de Madre Tierra*). The law grants nature various rights, including to maintain the integrity of its systems and processes, to regenerate, to maintain biodiversity without genetic modification or structural alteration, to pure water and clean air, to maintain its equilibrium, and to be free of pollution. Like Ecuador's Constitution, Bolivia's law empowers people to initiate court action against other parties in order to protect nature's rights. The law was upgraded in 2012 to the Framework Law of Mother Earth and Integral Development to Live Well (*Ley Marco de la Madre Tierra y Desarrollo Integral para Vivir Bien*). The framework status allows the law to supersede other laws, including those on mining, hydrocarbons, and water. The reference to "living well" alludes to the call for public policy to be guided by the indigenous concept of suma quamaña, or vivir bien, and to approach development in a way that integrates human needs and rights with those of nature.[6]

Constructing a Global Alliance for the Rights of Nature

Ecuador's example also inspired a new level of international organizing and pressure by rights of nature activists. Seeking to build on the momentum provided by Ecuador's constitutional changes, rights of nature activists from around the world gathered in Ecuador in 2010 for their first international conference. At the meeting, participants founded the Global Alliance for the Rights of Nature, a linking institution that connects indigenous, environmental rights, human rights, community development, and governmental organizations around the world. Their objective is to "encourage the recognition and effective implementation of Rights of Nature through the creation of a world network of individuals and organizations that, through active cooperation, collective action and legal tools, based on Rights of Nature as an idea whose time has come, can change the

---

[6] While Bolivian discourse refers to the concepts of vivir bien (Spanish) and suma quamaña (Aymara), these are generally understood to be equivalent with the Ecuadorian terms buen vivir and sumak kawsay, which are more frequently used in international discourse.

direction humanity is taking our planet."[7] In other words, the Global Alliance seeks to change global environmental policy through nodal governance.

The alliance's web page reveals its strategy for promoting rights of nature internationally through nodal governance. By "driving Rights of Nature into law like Ecuador did in its 2008 National Constitution," the alliance seeks "to reproduce this concept virally through the world, invading systems of thought and juridical systems." To realize this goal, alliance members formed four working groups—new governing nodes in the transnational rights of nature network. The legislative assistance working group works with organizations, communities, and local and national governments to implement legal provisions protecting the rights of nature. The international advocacy working group works to strengthen and expand the rights of nature network by facilitating connections. It also organizes campaigns to promote the incorporation of rights of nature into global policy forums, including the United Nations Framework Convention on Climate Change (UNFCCC) and conferences on sustainable development. The communications and learning working group supports these efforts with outreach, education, and social networking programs. The indigenous peoples-ancestral knowledge working group works to ensure that efforts to implement rights of nature are guided by indigenous knowledge and customs.

Incorporating Buen Vivir into the UN System

When it comes to promoting buen vivir within international policy forums, states play a leading role in the transnational governance network due to their privileged position in this arena. The Ecuadorian and Bolivian governments have led efforts to incorporate buen vivir principles—including rights for nature—into the UN system in order to alter international discourse and policy regarding the environment and development. This is not surprising given the strength of the domestic buen vivir networks in these countries and the framing of buen vivir in opposition to neoliberalism.

As early as 2008, Ecuador's government argued in UN forums that the UN's development approach, and specifically the Millennium Development Goals, should be redefined to reflect the principles of buen vivir, which it defined in English as "well-being" and "living in harmony with nature" (Ecuador Permanent Mission to the United Nations 2008). There were several parts to Ecuador's strategy for displacing the dominant development frame. One was to frame the right to live within a healthy environment as a human right,

---

[7] "Founding the Global Alliance." International Gathering for Rights of Nature in Patate, Ecuador, September 2010, http://therightsofnature.org/founding-meeting (accessed February 17, 2016).

making the rights of nature "a prerequisite to recognizing human rights" and buen vivir a strategy for improving human rights.[8] A second component was to link human rights and development by arguing that both sought to improve people's well-being (buen vivir). These arguments presented buen vivir as an effective way to incorporate human rights into national development strategies, which would, in turn, help governments achieve the Millennium Development Goals. In 2010, this framing led the UN Human Rights Office to help Ecuador's government develop and distribute a manual for replicating internationally Ecuador's plan for buen vivir as a model alternative development path (UN High Commissioner on Human Rights 2010). The manual was piloted in the water and sanitation sector—fitting, given the defining role IWM reform played in Ecuador's buen vivir project.

Transnational organizing around buen vivir and the rights of nature quickly became intertwined with climate change. In 2010, reacting to failed climate change efforts in Copenhagen, over 35,000 people from 140 nations attended a World People's Conference on Climate Change and Rights of Mother Earth in Cochabamba, Bolivia. Attendees adopted the Universal Declaration of the Rights of Mother Earth, which mirror the rights of nature granted in Ecuador's Constitution and later in Bolivian law. The Declaration's description of Mother Earth reflects the Andean indigenous worldview of nature as Pachamama (Mother Earth), the "source of life" and "well-being."[9] The Declaration also expresses the principles of buen vivir and the requirements for living in "harmony with Mother Earth." Echoing the arguments of Ecuador's government, the preamble affirms that defending the rights of nature is necessary to guarantee human rights, "and that there are existing cultures, practices and laws that do so" (a thinly veiled call to follow Ecuador's and Bolivia's lead). Failing to do so puts "life as we know it today at risk through phenomena like climate change." Bolivian President Evo Morales strongly advocated this idea in international climate change negotiations. At the 2010 UN climate change conference in Cancun, Mexico, he called for the UN to adopt a universal declaration of rights of nature, saying:

> In past decades, the United Nations approved human rights, then civil rights, economic and political rights, and finally a few years ago indigenous rights. In this new century, it is time to debate and discuss rights of Mother Earth.[10]

[8] This idea is contained in Ecuador's Constitution and is frequently raised by Ecuadorian diplomats in international forums (e.g., United Nations 2013b).

[9] http://therightsofnature.org/universal-declaration/ (accessed June 20, 2016).

[10] "President Morales speaking at COP16 in Cancun" World People's Conference on Climate Change and the Rights of Mother Earth, website, https://pwccc.wordpress.com/2010/12/09/president-morales-speaking-at-the-un/ (accessed March 18, 2016).

While the UN has yet to adopt a universal declaration of the rights of nature, the transnational buen vivir network did establish a platform within the UN General Assembly for advancing buen vivir. In 2009, the Ecuadorian and Bolivian governments initiated intergovernmental negotiations on the principles of "Harmony with Nature." This led to several resolutions requiring the UN Secretary General to issue annual reports on Harmony with Nature and establishing annual Interactive Dialogues of the General Assembly on Harmony with Nature. The dialogues are held on April 22, traditionally known as Earth Day. In 2009, the General Assembly proclaimed this International Mother Earth Day, acknowledging the Andean indigenous norms guiding the principles of Harmony with Nature. At the dialogues, governments discuss strategies for realizing "sustainable development in harmony with nature" and sharing national experiences on criteria and indicators for measuring sustainable development in harmony with nature. Each year, Ecuador's National Plan for Buen Vivir has been presented as a roadmap for participants (Ecuadorian Permanent Mission to the UN 2012). To share information and promote the idea, the UN established a website dedicated to "Harmony with Nature."[11]

Seeking to build on the momentum provided by these events, proponents of buen vivir mobilized at the 2012 UN Conference on Sustainable Development in Rio de Janeiro (Rio+20), where they advocated making buen vivir and rights of nature "the foundation of sustainability." Sympathetic governments, led by Ecuador and Bolivia, pushed to incorporate buen vivir and rights of nature into the discussion at the Rio+20 summit. Ecuador had laid the groundwork the previous February, when Environment Ministers from the Community of Latin American and Caribbean States (CELAC) met in Quito to develop a common platform in advance of the summit. At Ecuador's urging, CELAC members committed "to discussing [at the Rio+20 summit] a universal declaration of the rights of nature as an instrument for achieving buen vivir" (CELAC 2012). At the summit, Ecuador, Bolivia, Costa Rica, and Paraguay together called for the UN to include the rights of nature in the final agreement. While this did not occur, Ecuadorian delegates did place buen vivir within the agreed upon outcomes by insisting on the inclusion of Article 39 in the final document. Articles 39–40 state,

> We recognize that the planet Earth and its ecosystems are our home and that Mother Earth is a common expression in a number of countries and regions and we note that some countries recognize the rights of nature in the context of the promotion of sustainable development.

[11] http://harmonywithnatureun.org (accessed March 19, 2016).

We are convinced that in order to achieve a just balance among the economic, social and environment needs of present and future generations, it is necessary to promote harmony with nature. We call for holistic and integrated approaches to sustainable development which will guide humanity to live in harmony with nature and lead to efforts to restore the health and integrity of the Earth's ecosystem. (United Nations 2012)

While governments negotiated at the official summit, civil society groups organized a parallel People's Summit Rio+20. Among other things, the People's Summit was used to expand the rights of nature network and plan campaigns to promote buen vivir and rights of nature as an alternative to neoliberal development policies. Dissatisfied with the outcome of the formal summit, members of the People's Summit issued their own report, *Another Future is Possible*.[12] The report articulates an alternative vision of sustainable development rooted in buen vivir. The following passage is representative of the language used, and illustrates the influence of buen vivir on the development approach advocated:

The urgent, yet feasible and necessary, task of searching for a new civilization path at the dawn of the twenty-first century is that of building a system capable of transitioning from a patriarchal order that enslaves nature and is founded on a reductionist and separatist vision of the relationships between nature and human beings to a system capable of reestablishing complex and harmonious relationships between the two, integrating them into the extensive cycle of Mother Earth. . . . [T]he new economic and regulatory systems . . . must be capable of strengthening the rights and respect of all beings comprising Mother Earth, whatever their own cultures, traditions and customs may be. Therefore, dealing with the measure and articulation of human wellbeing in economic systems means dealing inseparably with the wellbeing of Mother Earth, now and for future generations. It is for this reason that we propose the re-appreciation of the knowledge, wisdom and ancestral practices of indigenous peoples, affirmed in the experience of a wellbeing rooted in the concept of "Living Well," to the peoples of the world. (*Another Future is Possible*, 29–30)

One effect of transnational mobilization around buen vivir is that the language of buen vivir now permeates the UN system. In addition to climate change and sustainable development conference documents, buen vivir language pervades the

---

[12] Available online at https://commonsblog.files.wordpress.com/2012/06/another-future-is-possible_english_web.pdf (accessed March 13, 2016).

strategic plan for implementing the Convention on Biological Diversity, issued at the 2010 Conference of Parties. This plan is entitled "Living in Harmony with Nature" and envisions "a world living in harmony with nature" where "by 2050, biodiversity is valued, conserved, restored and wisely used, maintaining eco-system services, sustaining a healthy planet and delivering benefits essential for all people."[13] The resolution adopted at the 2013 UN Forum on Forests similarly calls for policies that "guide humanity towards living in harmony with nature."[14] Buen vivir principles also inform the conceptual framework guiding the work program for the UN Intergovernmental Science-Policy Platform for Biodiversity and Ecosystem Services, adopted in 2013 (UNEP 2013). Similar language per-vades UN General Assembly and Secretary General reports (described in the next section).

Changing Policies

It is tempting to dismiss international discourse as cheap talk that has little effect on policy. However, the international mobilization around buen vivir and the rights of nature is influencing policy decisions made by organizations and governments at all levels. A growing number of governments are joining Ecuador and Bolivia in adopting rights of nature legal provisions. In 2012, India's Supreme Court recognized under the Constitution that "human interest[s] do not take automatic precedence [over the environment] and humans have obligations to nonhumans independently of human interest."[15] New Zealand's government has recognized the Whanganui River and its tributaries as a legal entity, with rights to exist and flourish as an integrated, living whole.[16] Mexico's 2013 Environmental Law for the Protection of the Earth similarly recognizes the Earth's rights to exist, to maintain an equilibrium in its natural cycles and processes, and to regenerate if damaged.[17] In the United States, more than three dozen municipalities, including Pittsburgh, Pennsylvania, have adopted local

---

[13] Article 11. Available online at https://www.cbd.int/decision/cop/?id=12268 (accessed March 16, 2016).

[14] Article 18d. Available online at http://www.un.org/esa/forests/pdf/session_documents/unff10/ResolutionWG2UNFF10.pdf (accessed March 18, 2016).

[15] India's Supreme Court decision and legal documents pertaining to rights of nature provisions in other countries are available at http://harmonywithnatureun.org/rightsofnature.html (accessed February 14, 2016).

[16] Agreement Entitles Whanganui River To Legal Identity, nzherald.co.nz, August 30, 2012, http://www.nzherald.co.nz/nz/news/article.cfm?c_id=1&objectid=10830586 (accessed March 16, 2016).

[17] http://harmonywithnatureun.org/content/documents/290Mexico-%20Environmental%20law_protection%20of%20the%20Earth_.pdf (accessed March 16, 2016).

laws recognizing the rights of nature. Many of these are used to prohibit hydraulic fracking. Similar local laws are being created in Brazil.[18]

The global spread of rights of nature legal provisions demonstrates the concrete effects of international programming by members of the Global Alliance for the Rights of Nature. NGOs like the Community Environmental Legal Defense Fund, Earth Law Center, Global Exchange, Earth Laws Network, The Pachamama Alliance, and the Environmental Law Alliance Worldwide spurred and helped draft many of the laws mentioned above. Yet, as happens with nodal governance, efforts to promote rights of nature have moved beyond the Global Alliance. Even mainstream global environmental organizations now place the rights of nature at the center of their programming. For example, in 2012, the International Union for Conservation of Nature (IUCN)—"the world's oldest and largest global environmental organization"—made the rights of nature "the fundamental and absolute key element for planning, action and assessment at all levels and in all areas of intervention including in all decisions taken with regard to IUCN's plans, programmes and projects."[19] As part of this resolution, IUCN members also called for a new program to advocate the rights of nature globally. It and other organizations are part of a new global governance network dedicated to implementing a new global idea—the rights of nature—as a means for living in harmony with nature.

To facilitate their efforts, rights of nature advocates created a new international governing institution—The International Tribunal for the Rights of Nature. This "people's tribunal" investigates, tries, and decides cases involving alleged violations of the 2010 Universal Declaration of the Rights of Mother Earth (discussed earlier). Domestic rights of nature laws are also considered when violations occur in jurisdictions covered by these laws. The tribunal was proposed by Alberto Acosta, president of the Constituent Assembly that drafted Ecuador's pioneering Constitution (again illustrating the global effects of Ecuador's experiment with buen vivir). The idea was inspired by the International War Crimes Tribunal and the Permanent Peoples' Tribunal, established by citizens to identify, investigate, and publicize human rights violations.[20] Just as these tribunals provided social pressure to create and strengthen international human rights law,

---

[18] For information on local rights of nature ordinances in the U.S. and Brazil, see http://www. harmonywithnatureun.org/rightsofnature.html (accessed March 16, 2016).

[19] IUCN 2012, 147–148. IUCN's website states that its members include "more than 1,200 government and NGO Members and almost 11,000 volunteer experts in some 160 countries," http://www.iucn.org/about/ (accessed March 18, 2016).

[20] Nobel Prize winner Bertrand Russell created the International War Crimes Tribunal in 1966 to investigate human rights abuses committed against Vietnamese peoples resulting from U.S. military intervention in Vietnam (Duffett 1968). Inspired by the Russell Tribunal, law experts and rights activists established The Permanent Peoples' Tribunal to investigate and provide judgments on violations of human rights around the world (Blaser 1992).

the rights of nature tribunal is meant to foster international rights of nature law. While the tribunal's decisions do not carry the force of formal law, they serve several purposes, articulated in Article 2 of the tribunal's constitution:

[1] to further develop Earth jurisprudence by writing and disseminating judgments that interpret the Earth Rights Declaration and apply the rights and obligations in it to the specific facts of the cases which it hears; [2] to promote both the universal acceptance among the peoples of the world that they have a duty to respect the intrinsic rights of all natural beings, and universal observance of the rights and duties contained in the Earth Rights Declaration; and [3] to demonstrate how the application of the rights and duties of the Earth Rights Declaration promote the harmonious co-existence of humans and other beings in a manner that enhances the integrity, health and functioning of the whole Earth community.[21]

The first hearing of the International Tribunal for the Rights of Nature was held in Quito, Ecuador, on January 17, 2014. Renowned scholar and environmental activist Dr. Vandana Shiva presided over the hearing, along with nine other prominent thinkers, lawyers, and activists from seven countries and five continents. The tribunal considered nine alleged violations of the Universal Declaration of the Rights of Mother Earth and, for Ecuadorian cases, of the Ecuadorian Constitution. Cases involved the BP Deepwater Horizon oil spill, destruction of Australia's Great Barrier Reef, hydraulic fracking in the United States, and open-pit mining in Ecuador, among other violations. The tribunal has since met twice more, most recently in parallel to the 2015 UN Framework Convention on Climate Change. The timing was meant to highlight the inadequacy of traditional approaches to addressing climate change—the quintessential global problem—and to raise awareness of alternatives rooted in buen vivir principles.

As the 2015 deadline for the Millennium Development Goals approaches, the above actions are shaping debates over how sustainable development should be conceptualized in a post-2015 development agenda. A significant number of governmental, intergovernmental, and nongovernmental organizations now insist that the dominant anthropocentric development paradigm be replaced with a new, more ecocentric development paradigm based on living in harmony with nature. UN Secretary General Ban Ki-moon is among those leading the charge. The secretary general regularly highlights the deficiencies of perpetual economic growth and urges a new paradigm "for living in harmony with nature"

---

[21] Available online at http://therightsofnature.org/peoples-convention-tribunal/ (accessed March 16, 2016).

based on ecological economics. A 2013 report by Ban Ki-moon is illustrative. In it, he writes that constructing this new paradigm requires

> the redefinition of humankind's needs and the recognition of the need to move beyond the unsustainable pursuit of ever-increasing economic growth without concern for social development and nature. Harmony with nature implies that people do not assume that they have unlimited resources or means. . . . Harmony with nature also calls for a rehabilitation of the human spirit, the concept of holism, and for its relevance as a factor in the pursuit of a lifestyle that respects the rights of nature. . . . This means adopting a new paradigm that includes harmonious relationships with nature. . . . A paradigm for a new economics must go beyond neoclassical and environmental economics and learn instead from the concepts of deep ecology, the rights of nature and systems theory. . . . In the discussions leading up to the formulation of the post-2015 development agenda, nature must be placed at the core of sustainable development. (United Nations 2013a, 12, 16)

In response to the secretary general's call, the UN General Assembly dedicated its 2014 Interactive Dialogue on Harmony with Nature to examining "key characteristics of a new, non-anthropocentric paradigm [for sustainable development] and further [identifying] strategies on how the society subsequently would need to function consistent with this paradigm."[22] The General Assembly's 2016 dialogue is focused on strategies for promoting "Earth Jurisprudence" (i.e., rights of nature laws) worldwide.[23]

Conclusion

Buen vivir is still a weak international norm that is highly contested within domestic and international policy arenas. Arguments for buen vivir and the rights of nature remain a counter-discourse. The point of this chapter was not to argue that buen vivir has become the dominant development paradigm. The anthropocentric development paradigm remains dominant and is unlikely to

[22] UN General Assembly, Interactive Dialogue on Harmony with Nature, April 22, 2014, http://www.harmonywithnatureun.org/index.php?page=view&type=12&nr=40 (accessed January 18, 2015).

[23] UN General Assembly, "Sustainable Development: Harmony with Nature." Report of the Second Committee, December 14, 2015, https://static1.squarespace.com/static/55914fd1e4b01fb0b851a814/t/567a0263a12f445fc5bd9823/1450836579863/HwN+Resolution+14+Dec+2015.pdf (accessed March 16, 2016).

disappear any time soon. Rather, the point of this chapter was to show how the rise of a new global idea—buen vivir—is spurring real contestation over international norms and policies regarding sustainable development and humans' relationship to nature.

While the anthropocentric paradigm remains dominant, it arguably faces its most significant challenge in modern history. Implementing rights of nature as a means for living in harmony with nature is no longer a fringe idea. The range of organizations advocating a new development approach based on this global idea has grown far beyond radical environmental groups and a few leftist Latin American governments. At the 2014 Summit of G77 states and China, heads of state and government collectively expressed their conviction that

> to achieve a just balance among the economic, social and environmental needs of present and future generations, it is necessary to promote harmony with nature and the Earth. . . . We understand that sustainable development involves a change in the order of priorities from the generation of material wealth to the satisfaction of human needs in harmony with nature. The excessive orientation towards profit neither respects Mother Earth nor takes into account human needs. . . . We call for a holistic, integrated approach to sustainable development . . . to guide humanity to live in harmony with nature and lead to efforts to restore the health and integrity of the Earth's ecosystems. (G77 2014)

Mainstream NGOs, governments, and intergovernmental organizations increasingly invoke this new global idea to challenge traditional approaches to addressing global problems like poverty and climate change. While difficult to measure, the spread of rights of nature laws and advocacy by prominent world leaders suggest this counter-norm is gaining international legitimacy.

Pope Francis's comments to the UN General Assembly illustrate the normative contestation that now exists and the degree to which buen vivir principles are gaining international legitimacy. The pope spoke on September 25, 2015—the opening day of the World Summit to adopt the 2030 Agenda for Sustainable Development. Pope Francis invoked buen vivir principles to critique the dominant, anthropocentric, economic development approach and to advocate rights of nature as an urgent and necessary solution to poverty and climate change. Criticizing the "oppressive lending systems" of international financial agencies and the "selfish and boundless thirst for power and material prosperity," the pope stated that

> today's world presents us with . . . broad sectors which are vulnerable, victims of power badly exercised: for example, the natural environment

and the vast ranks of the excluded. These sectors are closely interconnected and made increasingly fragile by dominant political and economic relationships. That is why their rights must be forcefully affirmed,
by working to protect the environment and by putting an end to exclusion. First, it must be stated that a true "right of the environment" does
exist, for two reasons. First, because we human beings are part of the
environment. We live in communion with it, since the environment itself entails ethical limits which human activity must acknowledge and
respect. . . . Second, because every creature, particularly a living creature, has an intrinsic value, in its existence, its life, its beauty and its interdependence with other creatures.[24]

Of course, neither the rights of nature nor sumak kawsay (the Andean indigenous concept translated in Spanish as buen vivir) are new ideas. Both have
existed for generations. What is new is the political project of institutionalizing
principles and practices associated with buen vivir at the national and international levels. This chapter showed that this political project grew out of local
experiments by grassroots actors who used Tungurahua's IWM reform process
as an opportunity to institutionalize a new development model rooted in the
principles of sumak kawsay. The fact that international mobilization behind
buen vivir and rights of nature emerged out of Ecuador's experiment is not lost
on international actors. Ban Ki-moon's call for a new development paradigm
and the IUCN's declaration to make rights of nature the basis of its policymaking both cite Ecuador's institutionalization of buen vivir as an inspiration for
their decisions. Despite its many imperfections, Ecuador's experiment with
buen vivir continues to be recognized by advocates within the UN and the
Global Alliance for the Rights of Nature.

The power of local experiments like that in Tungurahua is that outsiders who
are dissatisfied with existing strategies for tackling global problems point to
them as "proof of concept" that an alternative is viable (Ansell 2011). They activate their own networks to scale up local experiments internationally. To facilitate international organizing, they package local principles and practices under
new meta-concepts with broad appeal. Drawing on local norms and practices,
these new global ideas challenge existing thinking about global best practices.

A key lesson of the buen vivir case is that the norms, principles, and practices
that inform international debates and strategies for tackling global problems are
often forged at the grassroots level. Grassroots actors like campesino farmers,

indigenous activists, community organizers, and municipal bureaucrats do not participate personally in international debates or global governance structures. However, they influence both in two ways. First, they guide and implement local experiments, based on local principles and practices, which provide meaning to new global ideas around which new global governance structures form. Second, they initiate the network activation processes that ultimately make these new global ideas salient internationally. This indirect influence is the essence of nodal governance. Through nodal governance, grassroots actors participate in the construction of new global governance systems. While their influence is rarely acknowledged, they too are global governors.

Conclusion

Rethinking Global Governance

It is now axiomatic to say that global governance has evolved beyond the conventional notion of multilateral agreements negotiated by states. New forms of global governance have emerged in the wake of states' failure to adequately address many pressing problems. Yet, these global governance structures are poorly understood, fueling calls for new frameworks that explain: (1) the different ways global authority is structured and exercised; (2) how power is distributed and exercised within these structures; (3) how national and local systems intersect with and push against these structures; (4) how interests are articulated and pursued; (5) how global governance systems change; and (6) the causes and drivers of change (Weiss and Wilkinson 2014). This book answered this call by providing a framework for understanding a global governance structure that commonly forms around local-cumulative problems like deforestation, poverty, disease, and climate change. I call this *grassroots global governance*.

Structuring and Exercising Authority

Global governance scholars have long recognized that, in addition to states and IGOs, transnational networks of activists and experts play an important role. The Ecuadorian cases of IWM reform show that transnational advocacy networks include an even broader selection of actors. In particular, they highlight the agency of local politicians, bureaucrats, and citizens in rural areas of less-developed countries. These grassroots actors work with international NGOs and donor agencies to create policies and practices that combine global principles with local norms and leadership. Although rural, subnational actors are under-emphasized in the international relations literature, their agency is taken for granted by development scholars and practitioners. It is almost cliché to note that international development projects must be locally owned and embedded to be successful (Brinkerhoff and Brinkerhoff 2010; Michel 1997; Morrison 2010). The contribution of this book is not to demonstrate the importance of local agency but to illuminate the interactive processes by which local actors influence norm and policy adoption among stakeholders at the local, national and international levels.

Through a process Acharya (2009) calls "constitutive localization," local actors in the book's case studies adapted global norms to suit their local context. But they did much more than this. They influenced the governance process more generally by participating in all stages of the policy process, from problem identification and coalition building, to agenda setting, rule making, and implementation. Local politicians, government experts, landowners, water-user groups, and civil society organizations drew on a variety of sources of power to pressure one another to either adopt or resist proposed IWM reforms. The outcome of this contest determined whether reforms succeeded or failed. Moreover, these community members pressured international NGOs, IGOs, donor agencies, national governments, and others to change their policies and their strategies for pursuing them. This produced an evolution in the conservation mechanisms advocated by these global governors, not just in Ecuador, but internationally. In this way, Ecuador's local IWM reform processes illuminate the multidirectional influence that occurs within transnational networks comprised of actors operating at the local, national, and international levels.

The diversity of actors involved and their multidirectional influence necessitates a more complex view of transnational advocacy networks than conventionally portrayed. The relationships in Ecuador's IWM networks crosscut the traditional categories of actor type (e.g., public or private) and scale (international, national, and subnational). These networks include members of local and national governments (e.g., municipal environmental departments and state donor agencies), intergovernmental organizations (e.g., UN Food and Agriculture Organization and Global Water Partnership), private companies (e.g., hydroelectric plants and water companies), epistemic communities (e.g., water experts within universities and development organizations), and civic organizations (e.g., irrigation councils and indigenous groups). All of these actors are potential governors capable of steering society toward new forms of watershed management.

The problem of scale is not simply that network relationships regularly crosscut conceptual levels. More important, it is often difficult to determine whether network members are "transnational," "international," "national," or "local." International NGOs (e.g., The Nature Conservancy and Nature and Culture International), donor agencies (e.g., GIZ and USAID), and even intergovernmental organizations (e.g., UN Food and Agriculture Organization and Global Water Partnership) are typically represented by local Ecuadorians. Rather than their institutional position, they often rely on their personal relationships with local stakeholders to pursue their policy objectives. The same is true for Ecuador's Environment Ministry. To the extent the Ministry was present in the Ecuadorian cases, it was through local community members hired to manage protected areas. Forest guards regularly admitted they played down their Ministry affiliation to do their job, particularly when confronting violators. They relied instead on personal relationships and their status as community members to pressure violators to comply.

Focusing on organizational names leaves the impression of foreign nationals swooping down on local communities to share their wisdom and expertise. The individuals representing these organizations reveal a far more complex and blurry image of scale and direction of influence. GTZ's representative to Tungurahua's indigenous communities, Washington Chapalbay, is a local indigenous community organizer (see chapter 7). He does not fit the usual profile of a "rooted cosmopolitan" (Tarrow 2005), much less a "transnational actor." Yet his is the face of GTZ for many indigenous communities in Tungurahua. Paulo Bustamante similarly put a local face on Nature and Culture International in Celica (see chapter 5). Native to the communities where they work, local brokers like Bustamante and Chabalpay rely on their community relationships to pursue their agendas. Similarly, The Nature Conservancy's role in creating Quito's water trust fund, FONAG, was due to the fact that Juan Black, the Ecuadorian conservationist who developed the idea, constituted The Nature Conservancy's Latin American division, based in Quito. Black's ties to other members of Ecuador's environmental movement, including Quito's then-mayor Roque Sevilla, arguably contributed more to the program's success than any support from The Nature Conservancy's Washington, District of Columbia, office.

These individuals—Chapalbay, Bustamante, and Black—illustrate why the boundary between local and international is blurry. They are local actors, born and raised in the communities where they work. But they are also transnational, not because they are cosmopolitans who frequently travel abroad to conferences, but because their organizational affiliations link them to transnational networks pursuing a global policy agenda. They show that "transnational actors" are not necessarily foreign to the localities where they work.

It would be equally erroneous to assume that all representatives of local, grassroots NGOs are local community members. The German forestry expert Martin Schroeder was a founder and president of Pastaza's local environmental NGO CODEAMA. Another German, Steven Gatter, worked for the local NGO Servicio Forestal Amazónico (SFA). CODEAMA and SFA were founding members of Pastaza's local IWM coalition. U.S. environmental activist Curtis Hofmann was a leader of the local NGO Colinas Verdes, which was a founding member of the Podocarpus Program in Zamora. These foreign members did not undermine these NGOs' status or credibility as local organizations since most of the NGOs' members were local Ecuadorians. But they did provide important ties to transnational governance networks. These examples show that, through the diversity of their individual representatives, organizations in transnational networks can simultaneously carry local and international identities, and therefore represent multiple scales. This makes them influential nodes in global governance networks.

Just as organizations have members representing different scales, individuals in transnational networks may wear multiple hats and represent organizations traditionally understood to exist at different scales. For example, Pablo Lloret is a municipal water expert by profession (i.e., a local government bureaucrat) and was the first technical secretary of Quito's water trust fund, FONAG (a local, public–private hybrid). However, he is also a university professor, a leading member of CAMAREN (the national consortium of Ecuadorian organizations dedicated to improving natural resource management), and a representative of the Global Water Partnership (a global organization founded by the World Bank, UN Development Programme, and Swedish International Development Cooperation Agency). For a time, Lloret was the president of the Global Water Partnership's South American division.

Is Lloret a local, national, or international actor? In truth, he is all three. Many of the Ecuadorian protagonists in my case studies were at one time or another representatives of local community organizations, local NGOs, local government departments, and either international NGOs, donor agencies and/ or inter-governmental organizations. They often held more than one of these affiliations simultaneously. They also moved regularly between public and private entities. These individuals were leading protagonists precisely because their multiple affiliations made them key brokers connecting different stakeholder groups.

These brokers illustrate the danger of creating artificial conceptual divisions between international, transnational, and local actors when thinking about the subnational effects of global governance processes. One danger is the tendency to characterize the process as a contest between transnational actors (assumed to be foreign nationals) and local actors. By contrast, Ecuador's coalitions of IWM advocates included both locals and foreigners; this is precisely what made these coalitions transnational. The reform processes consisted of attempts by coalition members—both local and foreign— to pressure non-coalition members to adopt policies that, while originating at the global level, were shaped by local actors drawing on local knowledge and values. When local actors joined with national and international allies to implement the global policy agenda known as IWM, they became part of the global governance process.

Since scale and actor type do not ensure discreet categories of network members, nodal governance theory becomes a useful framework for analyzing how authority is exercised in global governance. Nodal governance theory views organizations as nodes in a network. Nodes are not distinguished by their organizational type (e.g., state or nonstate) or scale (e.g., global, national, or local), but rather their network ties and ability to influence other nodes. Each node's influence is determined by the resources at its disposal, its methods for exerting influence, and the way it thinks about the issue it seeks to govern. Organizations may directly govern the people who are subject to their influence, or they may govern indirectly by influencing other nodes that are accessible to them through networks and which in turn have the power to influence others.

One implication is that organizations often exercise authority indirectly. They expand the scope of their influence through network activation—pressuring and/or persuading other individuals and organizations to support a new policy. They, in turn, use the resources and methods at their disposal to promote the new policy among their network contacts. In this way, the initial governing nodes expand the reach of their influence. For example, external members of Ecuador's local IWM coalitions recruited supportive members of the three targeted stakeholder groups (landowners, water users, and local government) to join their coalition and relied on them to pressure resistant stakeholders. Of course, influence in nodal governance does not always flow from the global to the local level. Individuals and organizations that operate at the local level can similarly exercise indirect authority globally. As I show here and in chapter 8, they do so by activating networks of organizations operating nationally and internationally to promote policies and practices developed locally.

Distributing and Exercising Power

One insight of grassroots global governance theory is that the organization at the center of a governance network—the one with the most power—shifts depending on the arena where ideas and policies are being contested. This varies across the three phases of grassroots global governance. By explaining progression through these phases, grassroots global governance theory explains why leadership within transnational governance networks changes over time.

In grassroots global governance, international policymakers' goal is to change behaviors on the ground by implementing global ideas, like integrated watershed management, sustainable livestock, or participatory budgeting. This requires contesting global ideas in domestic arenas, from legislatures and government bureaucracies to the media and streets. This process is full of political struggle. There is inevitably pushback at both the national and local levels. Social movements, business interests, politicians, and others mobilize to oppose the proposed global idea. When they effectively challenge global governance networks in one arena, network members must shift to another arena where they may have more leverage. To do so, network members must expand their network to include domestic actors able to navigate national and local structures and guide the struggle. As a result, domestic actors become increasingly influential in grassroots global governance as the process moves through phases 1 and 2.

In phase 1, the struggle over global ideas moves from international arenas to domestic arenas. To shape practices on the ground, global governance networks must expand their influence to the local level. There are different pathways for influencing local policies and practices. Network members might work through national political systems or try to influence local governments and citizens directly. Both paths require navigating the national context—the existing rules, practices, political institutions, sociopolitical alliances, and cultural norms.

Each national context is unique and presents its own specific set of challenges. In Ecuador during the 1990s, powerful social movements arose at a time of extreme political and economic instability, making them relatively strong vis-à-vis the state. In this context, activists, national bureaucrats, and national politicians obstructed various efforts to implement IWM reform through the national policy process. As a result, IWM advocates shifted contestation to social arenas and activated social networks to promote IWM reform through informal processes.

Ecuador's experience is typical of grassroots global governance not because social movements must always be the gatekeepers of global ideas, or because global ideas always diffuse to the local level through informal processes. Rather, the generalizable lesson for phase 1 is that national context will always create obstacles that empower some domestic actors to serve as gatekeepers. By shaping the pattern of network expansion, such gatekeepers influence how global ideas are defined and operationalized domestically.

This is equally true in national contexts where state institutions are strong and national governments work to implement global ideas through national policy. For example, Brazilian national government policy sought to operationalize integrated water resources management principles, including through the creation of river basin committees. Rebecca Neaera Abers and Margaret Keck (2013) explain how these efforts were undermined by Brazil's complex configuration of organizations and rules, a phenomenon they call "institutional entanglement." This feature of Brazilian national context provided ample opportunity for domestic gatekeepers—bureaucrats, politicians, corporate interests, and others—to block the implementation of river basin committees. Yet, while many efforts failed, some succeeded due to the ability of domestic brokers working inside and outside of government to navigate Brazil's national context, including by activating informal networks to conduct local experiments.

Stephanie McNulty's (2011) comparison of successful and failed attempts to implement decentralized participatory governance arrangements in Peru provides another example from a different global idea. During the 1990s, multilateral banks and international donor agencies promoted decentralization across the developing world as a way to enhance democracy through local participation (e.g., Selee and Tulchin 2004; Crook and Manor 1998). McNulty shows how national politicians opposed giving more power to civil society and blocked implementation of many Regional Coordination Councils—decentralized participatory institutions called for under Peru's 2002 constitution and subsequent implementing legislation. Nevertheless, experiments with other local participatory institutions succeeded in some regions due to the efforts of supportive regional presidents working with a well-organized civil society.

These and other examples demonstrate that while each national context is unique, each contains roadblocks for transnational governance networks seeking to implement global ideas locally. Governance networks need influential domestic actors to guide them through national contexts. This gives such actors significant power in phase 1.

Rethinking Bilateral Activists

Who are these domestic brokers? Sometimes, they fit Paul Steinberg's description of "bilateral activists." For Steinberg (2001), such people are "bilateral" because they are equally at home in both international and national policy circles. These are highly educated, cosmopolitan, urban professionals with strong ties to international organizations. They engage with global ideas through their travels and because of their worldly outlook. Their technical, financial, and/or scientific expertise makes them influential in domestic policy circles within developing countries. Since Steinberg wants to explain national environmental policy, he emphasizes their ability to navigate and exert influence within national government. Bilateral activists, he notes, "are likely to have the Rockefeller Foundation on one phone line and a presidential advisor on the other" (Steinberg 2001, 10). Their domestic political expertise and influence is valuable to foreigners, since it is difficult for them to acquire.

Ecuador's experience with IWM reform shows, however, that global governance networks often also need bilateral activists able to navigate and exert influence within social arenas. These people may not be political insiders. Rather, they are bilateral in that they have strong ties with both international policy advocates and domestic social movements and civil society organizations. A good example is Pablo Lloret, the Spanish educated water resources engineer who became the Global Water Partnerships' Ecuadorian representative. Lloret was well known within agricultural, development, and environmental networks for creating the country's first participatory watershed council. He contributed greatly to the spread of IWM, but not by influencing national politicians or bureaucrats. Rather, he expanded IWM networks' influence by training local IWM know-ledge communities and creating national linking institutions like CAMAREN and the National Water Resources Forum. These linking institutions provided platforms for connecting domestic and foreign IWM advocates; building ties with Ecuador's local governments and campesino, indigenous, and conserva-tion movements; and negotiating collaborative projects. In other words, Lloret helped expand transnational IWM networks to the grassroots level by activating domestic social networks.

Whether they operate in national policy or social arenas, bilateral activists' ability to navigate national context gives them considerable power within global governance networks during phase 1. They use this power to pursue their own agenda. They are, after all, bilateral *activists* and not mere go-betweens. In shep-herding global ideas through domestic social networks, bilateral activists influ-ence how global ideas are defined and operationalized domestically. They mold global ideas to fit the values and priorities of politically influential domestic in-terest groups. In Ecuador, this meant designing IWM programs that reflected the values and priorities of Ecuador's campesino, indigenous, and environmental movements. Lloret described this as adopting "a more Ecuadorian way" of doing IWM.[1] As a result, Ecuador's IWM programs prioritize watershed conservation over infrastructure development, equitable access over efficiency, and participa-tory decision-making over control by technical experts.

Bilateral activists are equally important during phase 2 of grassroots global governance, when it comes to putting global ideas into practice. Local systems intersect with and push back against global governance networks. Foreign net-work members are much further removed from local politics than national politics. It is even harder for them to acquire local expertise, navigate local con-texts, and exert influence directly. Grassroots actors like smallholder farmers, heads of household, and municipal bureaucrats are less vulnerable than national politicians to pressure by foreign governments and international organizations. Global governance networks must therefore rely on grassroots actors to provide this expertise, navigate local contexts, and exert pressure.

Like Steinberg's bilateral activists, these grassroots actors live in two worlds, but a different two worlds than their national counterparts. Often, they work for

[1] Interview with author, Quito, Ecuador, April 18, 2011.

organizations with a transnational presence. As members of transnational governance networks, they are conversant with global ideas and interact with foreign network members. However, their second world is that of rural communities in the Global South. It is the world of smallholder farmers, neighborhood associations, grassroots indigenous organizations, local irrigation councils, and bureaucrats from small, rural municipalities. Many of these grassroots bilateral activists look nothing like Steinberg's protagonists. They are not highly educated, urban cosmopolitans. They do not frequent international conferences or travel abroad extensively. Most do not speak English. Their outlook is decidedly local. But they are influential members of their communities. This makes them powerful members of their global governance networks.

Grassroots bilateral activists look like Miguel Tisalema. Tisalema is an indigenous activist from Chibuleo, a small parish in the upper part of Tungurahua's Ambato watershed. He came of age during the late 1970s when the Tungurahua Indigenous Movement (*Movimiento Indígena de Tungurahua*, MIT) formed around the struggle for land and water access. Tisalema became a leader in the movement and was a local representative to Ecuador's national indigenous movement, CONAIE. He also worked with NGOs like CARE and the Swedish and German bilateral cooperation agencies working in Tungurahua. During the 2000s, Tisalema served several terms on his parish council. In 2004, he was one of three indigenous leaders trained by GTZ to mobilize indigenous participation in Tungurahua's IWM reform process (see chapter 7). When Tungurahua's three indigenous movements formed a linking institution to facilitate collaboration, he was chosen to co-manage this organization and provide technical support to indigenous communities experimenting with IWM. Tisalema's various ties made him a key broker between outside IWM advocates, local community organizations, indigenous movements, and local government. He pushed Tungurahua's IWM reform process forward by mobilizing indigenous and community involvement and providing local expertise. His power to do so came from his local legitimacy, rooted in a lifetime of community activism.

Pressure from Beside

The main protagonists in phase 2 of grassroots global governance are grassroots bilateral activists like Miguel Tisalema and Washington Chapalbay (from Tungurahua), Esteban Zarria (from El Chaco), Paulo Bustamante (from Celica), and Trotsky Riera (in Zamora). They and others like them led IWM reform efforts on the ground. They were at the center of local IWM coalitions. While many worked for international organizations, their influence did not come from organizational prestige or an ability to attract outside resources. Rather, their power came from their ability to influence local stakeholders whose behaviors IWM advocates sought to change.

Grassroots bilateral activists influenced local stakeholders in part by changing peoples' perceptions of their interests. They did so by sharing information, strategically framing IWM reform to resonate with local values, providing training, and leading by example. Local stakeholders-turned-IWM activists were the first to experiment with IWM reforms, as El Chaco's Milton Hugo did with his integrated farm (see chapter 6). Successful experiments granted legitimacy to reform efforts, and local activists used this to attract additional support.

Grassroots bilateral activists were also uniquely positioned to exert stronger forms of pressure. They used their influence with landowners and water users to organize public demonstrations, marches, and petitions to pressure local politicians. They used similar methods to pressure landowners and water users. In extreme cases, pressure was quite coercive, as when Tungurahuan indigenous landowners sabotaged water canals to pressure downstream water users. IWM advocates also used the coercive power of municipal governments to pressure resistant water users and landowners. When negotiations with landowners were hampered by disagreements over land values, municipal IWM advocates threatened to expropriate land if they could not negotiate an alternative arrangement. Thus, grassroots bilateral activists pushed the IWM reform process forward by wielding both "soft" and "hard" pressure from beside.

Grassroots Drivers of System Change

Phase 2 of grassroots global governance is arguably the most important phase. What happens in phase 2 determines whether or not action is taken on the ground to address global problems. But it can also change the way global problems are framed in international discourse, the solutions advocated, and the institutions created to implement these solutions globally. This is because the local struggle over global ideas that occurs during phase 2 is a creative process. Grassroots communities are where global ideas often get road tested. These tests are not controlled and do not occur in a vacuum. They are shaped by local context and contestation among local, national, and international actors. Advocates have to adapt to unique and often fluid conditions. They are designing new local governance arrangements from scratch, based on new policies and practices. Templates proposed from outside are soon recognized as flawed and discarded or adapted. Advocates are forced to improvise and experiment.

Grassroots activists are generally the ones improvising and experimenting. They use their power during phase 2 to adapt global ideas like IWM and sustainable development to fit local conditions. They do this in part through strategic framing. It was local IWM advocates who framed IWM reform as a strategy for improving production and reducing poverty, recognizing this was the best strategy for mobilizing stakeholder support. Grassroots activists also experiment with innovative local governance arrangements that combine elements of global principles and policies with local norms and practices. The mixing of global and local elements produces slippage between the way a global idea is conventionally understood internationally and the way it is operationalized locally. The global idea therefore evolves by taking on new meaning through the creative process of experimentation at the local level. In Ecuador, for example, the concepts of IWM and sustainable development evolved when local actors incorporated indigenous norms and practices associated with sumak kawsay (buen vivir).

When local experiments are perceived to offer viable, effective, and innovative solutions to longstanding problems, they quickly gain a successful reputation. This attracts the attention of outsiders opposed to conventional approaches to tackling global problems like deforestation, poverty, or climate change. Successful local experiments demonstrate that an alternative's approach is both viable and promising. Thus, successful experiments provide legitimacy both to these opponents' cause and to the new way of conceptualizing a global idea.

Whether or not local experiments drive the evolution of a global idea internationally depends on whether transnational networks form to advocate the new version in international arenas. Here too, grassroots bilateral activists play an influential role. They use their relationship with members of broader transnational networks to activate these networks behind the goal of scaling up local experiments. For example, the Ecuadorians that created Quito's pioneering watershed trust fund, FONAG, used their ties with The Nature Conservancy to activate a transnational network that now promotes similar watershed trust funds internationally. Since 2000, at least 15 watershed trust funds have been created or are under development across Latin America.[2]

This phenomenon is not unique to IWM. Participatory budgeting is another global idea that emerged from a local experiment through bottom-up network activation by grassroots activists. Participatory budgeting was first implemented in Porto Alegre in 1989 following the election of the leftist Workers Party.[3] High rates of citizen participation and studies showing improved government performance gave the experiment a successful reputation. Brian Wampler (2010) describes how local actors involved with Porto Alegre's experiment used

[2] "Creating Water Funds for People and Nature." The Nature Conservancy (website), www.nature.org/ourinitiatives/regions/latinamerica/water-funds-of-south-america.xml (accessed April 2, 2016). See also Kauffman (2014).

[3] For details of the program and the conditions leading to its creation, see Abers (2000); Avritzer (2002); Baiocchi (2005).

bottom-up network activation to scale up the experiment nationally and internationally (see also Sintomer et al. 2010). As a result, participatory budgeting
is now a global "best practice," promoted by international organizations, donor
agencies, and NGOs as a strategy for achieving "good governance."

Participatory budgeting initially diffused nationally through Brazil's Workers
Party and its network of affiliated civil society organizations. Local facilitators
from Porto Alegre and other early experiments were hired to train knowledge
communities and organize programs in other cities. Participatory budgeting
began to diffuse internationally after Brazilian advocates tapped into a network
centered around the UN-HABITAT's Urban Management Program (PGU).
PGU is a transnational network spanning 140 cities in 58 countries that works
to "promote innovative urban management practices, establish and strengthen
municipal networks, and influence local and national urban policies."[4] UN-
HABITAT raised participatory budgeting to international prominence by nam-
ing it one of the best 40 practices at its 1996 conference. Beginning in 1997,
PGU's Program for Latin America and the Caribbean actively promoted Porto
Alegre-style participatory budgeting programs across Latin America. As a result,
there were roughly 920 participatory budgeting programs in Latin America by
2010 (Sintomer et al. 2010, 9).

The World Social Forum was a linking institution that played a key role in
establishing participatory budgeting as a truly global idea. The first World Social
Forum was held in Porto Alegre in 2001. Twelve thousand activists, academics,
and policymakers came from around the world to discuss how to create more
just societies in the face of globalization and to organize efforts to do so. The
forum was co-sponsored by Porto Alegre's government, which touted its participatory budgeting model as a way to make governance more equitable, just,
and democratic. Porto Alegre's program received widespread attention, and the
annual meetings of the World Social Forum became an important site for organizing efforts to replicate it globally. Four of the first five meetings of the World
Social Forum were held in Porto Alegre, reflecting its power to inspire transnational organizing around governance reform. Network activation through the
World Social Forum brought participatory budgeting from the Global South
to the Global North and established it as a truly global idea. Inspired by Porto
Alegre, leftist social movements and local governments from Europe attended
the World Social Forum and subsequently adopted participatory budgeting in
their municipalities.

---

[4] UN-HABITAT is the United Nations Human Settlements Program; http://ww2.unhabitat.
org/programmes/ump/ (accessed March 16, 2016).

While participatory budgeting networks were initially highly politicized, due to their origin in radical social movements and political parties, the UN-HABITAT network helped depoliticize the idea by framing it in terms of "good" (i.e., efficient and transparent) governance, rather than social justice. This provided a more neutral and technocratic legitimacy. The good governance framing facilitated cooperation between radical local governments and international organizations associated with neoliberalism. Indeed, the World Bank is now a leading provider of information and resources to participatory budgeting programs in Latin America, including in Porto Alegre. In Eastern Europe, Asia, and Africa, participatory budgeting is now promoted mainly from outside by organizations commonly associated with global governance. International organizations like the World Bank, donor agencies like USAID and GIZ, and NGOs like CARE promote participatory budgeting through their governance programs. Participatory budgeting is now a global policy prescription for tackling global problems like poverty and poor governance.

The cases of participatory budgeting and buen vivir both illustrate how leadership in transnational governance networks shifts during Phase 3 of grassroots global governance. As contestation over global ideas shifts back to national and international policy arenas, leadership shifts back to the actors with the power to exert influence in these arenas. National bilateral activists once again become important brokers, helping to scale up local experiments nationally and internationally. For example, leaders of Brazil's national Workers Party activated transnational networks of leftist politicians and social movements to replicate participatory budgeting globally. Leaders of Ecuador's national indigenous movements similarly organized pressure on the Ecuadorian state to incorporate the values of buen vivir into Ecuador's constitution. The activation of Ecuador's state gave indigenous activists and other buen vivir advocates a pathway for influencing discussions of sustainable development in international policy circles. Once local experiments transform into global ideas, organizations we normally think of as global governors—national governments, IGOs, and international NGOs—once again become leading players. At this point, the cycle of grassroots global governance begins again, with transnational governance networks forming to promote the new global idea internationally.

To summarize, three lessons from grassroots global governance theory explain why grassroots actors and processes affect change in global ideas and governance structures. First, power shifts among members of transnational governance networks as the arenas where global ideas are contested shift from the international to the local level and back. Second, when local experiments endure long enough to produce innovative, unique institutional adaptations of global ideas, they are often perceived as successful and scaled up internationally. This is one way that global ideas emerge and evolve. Third, this process is guided and directed by grassroots actors not usually associated with global governance.

Policy Implications

In addition to the network capacity-building and framing strategies described in previous chapters, the Ecuadorian cases suggest several lessons for practitioners and scholars. One general lesson is that changes in local governance systems, much like changes in national regimes, come through nonlinear processes comprised of incremental steps. Successful IWM campaigns were built on a foundation created by previous environmental programs, many of which might be considered failures when measured by their short-term goals.

Zamora's IWM reform process is illustrative. IWM reform first came to Zamora in 1997 through the Podocarpus Program. The program was established by the Dutch government in collaboration with Ecuador's forestry institute and local NGOs to support the conservation of Podocarpus National Park. Few tangible projects or increased protections for Podocarpus National Park resulted from the program. However, the Podocarpus Program raised awareness of water issues for the first time, changed peoples' expectations regarding natural resource management, transformed relationships, and produced new institutions like Zamora's municipal environmental management unit. On this new foundation a second reform process emerged, based around Procuencas (a water trust fund modeled on Quito's FONAG). This attempt progressed further, producing more tangible results and a greater level of institutionalization. While there are indications that Procuencas may not be sustainable, it appears to have provided the basis for a third initiative for institutionalizing IWM in Zamora. In 2011, Zamoran officials were negotiating with Nature and Culture International to join the regional water trust fund Foragua.

A similar progression occurred in the other cases. Short-term projects in the 1980s and 1990s—including PROMUSTA and PROCOSA in Tungurahua, the Dry Forest Project in Celica, and various programs to protect ecological reserves in and around El Chaco—laid the foundation for subsequent, more successful, IWM reform efforts.[5] The democratization literature provides an appropriate analogy that helps explain why efforts to implement global ideas like IWM may succeed even where many facilitating conditions are absent, a situation common in less-developed countries (Abers 2007). Sheri Berman (2007)

---

[5] PROMUSTA is the Project for the Sustainable Use of Andean Lands (*Proyecto Manejo del Uso Sostenible de Tierras Andinas*); PROCOSA is the Soil Conservation and Agroforestry in the Andean Region Program (*Programa Conservación de Suelos y Agroforestería en la Región Andina*).

notes that where conditions are not ripe, democratization is not likely to last. However, each experience with democracy changes people's expectations and leaves institutional legacies that provide a new foundation on which the next democratization effort can be built. In this way, the process inches forward over time. Similarly, individual environmental programs often end without achieving many of their goals. Yet they too change expectations and relationships and leave institutional legacies that may contribute to a longer-term process of local environmental governance reform.

One policy implication is that early investments in creating knowledge communities can produce long-term, unintended benefits. This book's case comparisons suggest this was among the most important legacies of environmental management programs in the 1990s (i.e., during phase 1 of grassroots global governance). For reasons described above, municipal experts and community organizers were crucial for advancing the reform process. A related legacy was the creation of environmental management units within local governments.

These local knowledge communities often took a decade or more to form. They typically emerged from programs not directly related to IWM. Rather, they originated through programs focused on issues like biodiversity conservation, soil degradation, community forestry, and agro-ecological production. Years after these projects ended, local experts and organizers trained through these programs joined the IWM campaigns and drew on their network connections to pursue this new policy agenda. In this way, mobilization for IWM reform built on previous mobilization around other aspects of environmental management. This phenomenon is reminiscent of Albert Hirschman's Principle of Conservation and Mutation of Social Energy. In his study of grassroots collective action in rural Latin America, Hirschman (1984, 43) observed that local actors seeking social change did not abandon this aspiration even though the programs and "movements in which they had participated may have aborted or petered out." These participants learned from their failure, stored their "social energy," and drew on it later to participate in new programs or movements. This explains why IWM coalitions had greater success mobilizing local stakeholders in areas where locals had previously participated in other types of environmental programs.

A second, related lesson is that foreign NGOs may come and go but local reform processes can continue. NGOs can facilitate lasting changes in local development even if their projects are relatively short-term and they leave after several years. In virtually each successful case of IWM reform, the process survived changes in foreign NGO sponsors, as well as political administrations. What appears to be important is that the local and international advocates who initiate the reform process build enough of a foundation (through local institutions and social networks) that future actors (including local governments, grassroots organizations, and NGOs) have an incentive and the capacity to build on this foundation before it degrades and is lost. This lesson in no way undermines the criticisms of NGOs' short time horizons and other negative consequences of decisions being driven by funding concerns (e.g., Cooley and Ron 2002). Local environmental management projects will do better where there is continuity of effort. Rather, the lesson is that NGOs can mitigate these negative consequences by investing in local knowledge communities and designing projects to build on those of previous NGOs working in a locality.

A third lesson is the importance of treating the institutionalization of global ideas as primarily a social, rather than technical, exercise. Even when IWM coalitions succeeded in placing IWM reform on the agenda of local authorities and social groups, the proposed rules ran the risk of being rejected, particularly when they were developed without the involvement of local communities and were insensitive to local cultural conditions. This was a problem in less-successful cases where the rule-making phase was viewed as a technical exercise involving the transfer of knowledge from experts to community members. Rules were presented to social groups for approval once drafted; this was a common understanding of community participation. Community members were most often included in the process of gathering information and identifying needs and less frequently in the process of designing ordinances, financing mechanisms, and participatory institutions. In the more-successful cases, social spaces were created to allow multiple stakeholders to collaborate in the rule-making phase. These spaces served as a focal point for mobilizing material and social resources, a structure for maintaining the participation of stakeholders, and a space where local actors could adapt reform designs to be more appropriate to local circumstances.

An important policy implication is that advocates of IWM and other global ideas do not have to get the reform model perfect from the beginning, provided there is a process allowing local actors to tweak proposals. Currently, meetings of local and international NGOs, donor agencies, and water experts often focus on debating what model of IWM reform they should promote in a locality. This book's findings suggest that the most important factor determining success is not the initial model diffused to an area. It is more important that local and outside advocates construct spaces where local actors can meet to design a model that suits local conditions. While proposing models and options is an important role for NGOs, more important roles include building local capacity (training locals with expertise in these issues) and creating linking organizations (providing a space) that allow local actors to adapt models to suit the local reality. While this idea is commonly found in development rhetoric, it is not often practiced.

Despite the need for flexibility in institutional design, the cases described here suggest that certain features may help sustain the IWM reform process.

Designing IWM institutions (i.e., the participatory decision-making and financing mechanisms) with difficult exit rules for local governments can help mitigate clientelistic tendencies that frequently undermine development projects. New mayors often try to abolish and discredit programs of the previous mayor, which can undermine longer-term development efforts. A common feature of Ecuador's water trust funds is that local governments can only withdraw after mayors convene all stakeholders and publicly justify their decision. In at least two cases (Celica and Quito), new mayors announced their intention to withdraw from their respective water trust funds (Foragua and FONAG) soon after being elected. However, they reversed their decisions after learning the exit rules. It is impossible to know the reason for their reversals. But it is reasonable to presume their decisions were influenced by the prospect of public shaming for undermining popular norms of sustainable natural resource management for personal political gain.

Rethinking Global Governors

This book calls for an expanded understanding of how global governance is constructed and who is involved. Global governance is not just about foreign experts from the World Bank and international NGOs parachuting in to tell locals what to do. Grassroots actors in Ecuador and elsewhere neither accept nor reject global principles and practices as initially presented. Rather, they negotiate with outsiders on whether and how to adapt them to fit with local realities. Sometimes this results in experimentation, learning, and the creation of innovative local governance arrangements—unique institutional applications of global ideas. Savvy international actors learn from these experiences and consequently change their discourse and strategies for tackling global problems. The grassroots level is therefore not an object of global governance but a terrain where global governance is created. This is where global strategies for tackling problems like poverty, tuberculosis, deforestation, and climate change are tried out and adapted. As a result, global governance is in part constituted locally through the struggle, negotiation, experimentation, and learning that take place among various international, national, and grassroots actors, including many that are absent in most studies of global governance.

An important implication is that global governance is not the sole province of international elites, national politicians, and globetrotting cosmopolitans. A variety of individuals from rural communities in less-developed countries are influential members of global governance networks. Local Ecuadorians—from municipal experts to social movement activists to community organizers—are influential members of transnational IWM networks despite never having left Ecuador. Many rarely leave their province. In fact, it is their rootedness in their communities that gives them power within the network. By guiding the way global ideas are applied at the local level and consequently evolve, grassroots actors in turn reshape international actors' thinking, discourse, and the strategies they pursue globally. In this way, grassroots actors play a central role in the global governance process. They too are global governors.

METHODOLOGICAL APPENDIX

Data for the case comparisons presented in chapters 3 through 8 was collected during 34 months of fieldwork in Ecuador, conducted in four trips between 2006 and 2015. For seven months during 2006 and 2008, I collected data on local government natural resource reforms (including IWM reform) across Ecuador. I used this information to identify the universe of cases and select the six case studies, as described in chapter 1. I then spent two years (2009–2011) conducting the research for the case comparisons. On average, I spent roughly four months in each of the six cantons, interviewing key stakeholders; observing meetings, watershed conditions, and watershed management activities; and collecting primary documents. I also spent several months in Quito interviewing and collecting documents from national government agencies and transnational organizations working in Ecuador. In 2015 I spent another three months in Ecuador updating the status of local IWM reforms, studying the application of buen vivir and rights of nature, and analyzing attempts by Ecuador's government and other organizations to promote buen vivir and rights of nature internationally.

In total, I conducted more than 250 in-depth, semi-structured interviews with representatives of parish, municipal, provincial, and national governments; local and international NGOs and donor agencies working in each area; private companies (e.g., hydroelectric and municipal water companies); indigenous groups; community organizations (e.g., irrigation councils and neighborhood associations); individual landowners; and academics. For each case study, I selected the initial group of interviewees based on social maps of the stakeholders in each watershed produced by development NGOs working in the area. I verified these social maps and expanded the list of stakeholders to interview using snowball sampling, which is useful for identifying less-obvious relationships (Hanneman and Riddle 2005; Neuman 2007). The diverse array of stakeholders interviewed and broad spectrum of viewpoints expressed provided a detailed and balanced picture of the reform process.

I also collected hundreds of primary documents related to IWM reform efforts in the six cases. These documents came from members of local IWM coalitions, their allies in transnational IWM networks, local and national governments, and various stakeholder groups in each watershed. Documents collected included project proposals and evaluations, diagnostic studies, campaign promotional materials, contracts, municipal ordinances, meeting minutes, and correspondence. These documents provided a chronology of the reform process as well as valuable information on the strategies, intentions, and relationships among various actors, and how these changed over time. The documents gave me a baseline against which to situate the interview data. Comparing the information from these documents with interview data allowed me to triangulate, increasing the credibility and validity of the research results.

I used the collected data to employ three methodological techniques. First, I used process tracing in each case study to identify "the intervening causal process—the causal chain and causal mechanism—between" possible explanatory variables and the outcome of IWM reform (George and Bennett 2005, 206). I did this by reconstructing from the evidence "theoretically explicit narratives that carefully trace and compare the sequences of events constituting the process" of IWM reform (Aminzade 1993, 108). Comparing these sequences across cases made it possible to identify the causal mechanisms that connected causes and effects, and thus test my proposed theoretical model (Falleti 2006; George and Bennett 2005).

Second, I used social network analysis to map the connections between different actors in order to show how transnational advocacy coalitions were organized and how the resulting network connections served as mobilizing structures. I conducted the social network analysis using UCInet software and original datasets I constructed for each case. Each dataset includes IWM advocates (foreign and national) working in the watershed, national government agencies actively working in the watershed, the main organizations in each local stakeholder group (landowners, water users, and local government), and any new linking and governance institutions created through the IWM reform process. The datasets measure whether or not formal ties exist between two organizations, as expressed by an agreement to collaborate on a project related to watershed management and to share material and/or informational resources. While interviews yielded a wealth of information on organizational ties, in each case I verified those ties using written documents (e.g., contracts, partnership arrangements, project reports) and partnerships listed on organization websites. I also coded two organizations as having formal ties when one organization was a member of another (e.g., a newly created linking institution), verified through membership lists and attendance at meetings.

Third, I used frame analysis to study different strategies used to create IWM as an issue and to motivate local politicians and social groups to support the reform process. I identified framing strategies through the content and structure of frames chosen by IWM advocates at particular times and comparing them to the preexisting master frame at the start of each campaign. Recognizing that neither frames nor framing strategies are static, I tracked changes in frame contents at different points in the reform process. Taking soundings during the ongoing negotiation and emergence of collective action frames is the only way to measure how frames change over time (Johnston 2002). I identified and categorized different watershed management frames by analyzing the text and symbolic images found in written documents (e.g., campaign posters, promotional pamphlets, training materials, program documents) as well as speeches, radio and TV ads, interviews, slogans, and songs. My analysis reveals five principal watershed management frames used by different actors at different times, detailed in chapter 6.

REFERENCES

Abers, Rebecca Neaera. 2000. *Inventing Local Democracy: Grassroots Politics in Brazil*. Boulder, CO: Westview Press.

Abers, Rebecca Neaera. 2007. "Organizing for Governance: Building Collaboration in Brazilian River Basins." *World Development* 35 (8): 1450–63.

Abers, Rebecca Neaera, and Margaret E. Keck. 2009. "Mobilizing the State: The Erratic Partner in Brazil's Participatory Water Policy." *Politics & Society* 37 (2): 289–314.

Abers, Rebecca Neaera, and Margaret E. Keck. 2013. *Practical Authority: Agency and Institutional Change in Brazilian Water Politics*. Oxford: Oxford University Press.

Acción Ecológica. 2006. "Declaración Ante los Servicios Ambientales: La Naturaleza Como Mercancía." Quito: Acción Ecológica. http://www.accionecologica.org/servicios-ambientes/documentos-de-organizaciones-sociales/1414-declaracion-ante-los-servicios-ambientales (Accessed March 22, 2016).

Acharya, Amitav. 2004. "How Ideas Spread: Whose Norms Matter? Norm Localization and Institutional Change in Asian Regionalism." *International Organization* 58 (2): 239–75.

Acharya, Amitav. 2009. *Whose Ideas Matter? Agency and Power in Asian Regionalism*. Ithaca, NY: Cornell University Press.

Acosta, Alberto. 2009. "Los grandes cambios requieren de esfuerzos audaces." In *Derechos de la Naturaleza. El futuro es ahora*, eds. A. Acosta and E. Martínez. Quito: Abya-Yala, 15–23.

Acosta, Alberto. 2010. "El Buen Vivir en el camino del post-desarrollo: Una lectura desde la Constitución de Montecristi." Policy Paper 9. Quito: Fundación Friedrich Ebert Stiftung.

Acosta, Alberto, and Esperanza Martínez, eds. 2009. *El Buen Vivir: Una vía para el desarrollo*. Quito: Abya-Yala.

Agrawal, Arun. 2002. "Common Resources and Institutional Sustainability." In *The Drama of the Commons*, eds. E. Ostrom, T. Dietz, N. Dolsak, P. C. Stern, S. Stonich, and E. U. Weber. Washington, DC: National Academy Press, 41–86.

Agresti, Alan, and Barbara F. Agresti. 1977. "Statistical Analysis of Qualitative Variation." In *Sociological Methodology*, ed. K. F. Schuessler. San Francisco: Jossey-Bass, 204–37.

Albán, Montserrat, and Sven Wunder. 2005. "Decentralized Payments for Environmental Services: Comparing the Cases of Pimampiro and PROFAFOR in Ecuador." Presented at the ZEF-CIFOR workshop on Payments for Environmental Services: Methods and Design in Developing and Developed Countries, Titisee, Germany.

Albó, Xavier. 2009. "Suma qamaña = convivir bien. ¿Cómo medirlo?" Alicante, Spain: Instituto de Estudios Internacionales de la Universidad de Alicante.

Altmann, Philipp. 2013. "Good Life as a Social Movement Proposal for Natural Resource Use: The Indigenous Movement in Ecuador." *Consilience: The Journal of Sustainable Development* 12 (1): 82–94.

Aminzade, Ronald. 1993. "Class Analysis, Politics, and French Labor History." In *Rethinking Labor History*, ed. L. Berlanstein. Urbana: University of Illinois Press, 90–113.

Andolina, Robert. 1994. "Second Indigenous Uprising Secures Concessions on Agrarian Reform." *Abya Yala News* 8 (3): 19–21.

Andolina, Robert. 1999. "Colonial Legacies and Plurinational Imaginaries: Indigenous Movement Politics in Ecuador and Bolivia." Ph.D. diss. Department of Political Science, University of Minnesota.

Andolina, Robert. 2003. "The Sovereign and Its Shadow: Constituent Assembly and Indigenous Movement in Ecuador." *Journal of Latin American Studies* 35 (4): 721–50.

Andolina, Robert, Nina Laurie, and Sarah A. Radcliffe. 2009. *Indigenous Development in the Andes: Culture, Power, and Transnationalism*. Durham, NC: Duke University Press.

Andonova, Liliana B., Michele M. Betsill, and Harriet Bulkeley. 2009. "Transnational Climate Governance." *Global Environmental Politics* 9 (2): 52–73.

Andonova, Liliana B., and Ronald B. Mitchell. 2010. "The Rescaling of Global Environmental Politics." *Annual Review of Environment and Resources* 35: 255–82.

Ansell, Chris. 2011. *Pragmatist Democracy*. Oxford: Oxford University Press.

Arévalo, José, ed. 2003. *Documentos de discussion: Foro de los Recursos Hídricos Segundo Encuentro Nacional*. Quito: CAMAREN.

Arias, Andrea, María Augusta Almeida, and Pool Segarra. 2005. "Mapeo Participativo con las comunidades de Llangahua, Tambaló, Castillo, Pucaucho y Estancia en la cuenca alta del río Ambato." Internal Report. Quito: Corporación ECOPAR, Gobierno Provincial de Tungurahua.

Arroyo, Aline, ed. 2005. *Documentos de discussion: Foro de los Recursos Hídricos Tercer Encuentro Nacional*. Quito: CAMAREN.

Atwood, Katherine, Graham Colditz, and Ichiro Kawachi. 1997. "From Public Health Science to Prevention Policy: Placing Science in Its Social and Political Contexts." *American Journal of Public Health* 87 (10): 1603–6.

Avant, Deborah D., Martha Finnemore, and Susan K. Sell. 2010. *Who Governs the Globe?* Cambridge: Cambridge University Press.

Avritzer, Leonardo. 2002. *Democracy and the Public Space in Latin America*. Princeton: Princeton University Press.

Avritzer, Leonardo. 2009. *Participatory Institutions in Democratic Brazil*. Baltimore: Johns Hopkins University Press.

Baiocchi, Gianpaolo. 2005. *Militants and Citizens: The Politics of Participatory Democracy in Porto Alegre*. Stanford: Stanford University Press.

Barrera, Augusto. 2007. "Agotamiento de la descentralización y oportunidades de cambio en el Ecuador." In *La descentralización en el Ecuador: opciones comparadas*, ed. F. Carrión. Quito: FLACSO Ecuador, 175–206.

Bebbington, Anthony, Galo Ramon, Hernan Carrasco, Victor Hugo Torres, Lourdes Peralvo, and Jorge Trujillo. 1992. *Actores de una década ganada: Tribus, comunidades y campesinos en la modernidad*. Quito: COMUNIDEC.

Becker, Marc. 2008. *Indians and Leftists in the Making of Ecuador's Modern Indigenous Movements*. Durham: Duke University Press.

Becker, Marc. 2011a. "Correa, Indigenous Movements, and the Writing of a New Constitution in Ecuador." *Latin American Perspectives* 38 (1): 47–62.

Becker, Marc. 2011b. *Pachakutik: Indigenous Movements and Electoral Politics in Ecuador*. New York: Rowman & Littlefield.

Berk, Gerald, and Dennis Galvan. 2009. "How People Experience and Change Institutions: A Field Guide to Creative Syncretism." *Theory and Society* 38: 543–80.

Berk, Gerald, and Dennis Galvan. 2013. "Processes of Creative Syncretism: Experiential Origins of Institutional Order and Change." In *Political Creativity: Reconfiguring Institutional Order and Change*, eds. G. Berk, D. Galvan, and V. Hattam. Philadelphia: University of Pennsylvania Press, 29–54.

Berman, Sheri. 2007. "How Democracies Emerge: Lessons from Europe." *Journal of Democracy* 18 (1): 28–41.

Betsill, Michele M., and Harriet Bulkeley. 2006. "Cities and the Multilevel Governance of Global Climate Change." *Global Governance* 12 (2): 141–59.

Biederbick, Christian. 1999. "Planificación Estratégica de la Cooperación Germano—Ecuatoriana en el Sector Verde." Informe Preliminar para la Misión Evaluadora, Proyecto de Manejo de Cuencas Hidrográficas (PROMACH). Ambato, Ecuador: GTZ.

Biermann, Frank, Philipp Pattberg, and Fariborz Zelli, eds. 2010. *Global Climate Governance Beyond 2012: Architecture, Agency and Adaptation.* Cambridge: Cambridge University Press.

Blankstein, Charles S., and Clarence Zuvekas Jr. 1973. "Agrarian Reform in Ecuador: An Evaluation of Past Efforts and the Development of a New Approach." *Economic Development and Cultural Change* 22 (1): 73–94.

Blaser, Arthur. 1992. "How to Advance Human Rights without Really Trying: An Analysis of Nongovernmental Tribunals." *Human Rights Quarterly* 14 (3): 339–70.

Bob, Clifford. 2002. "Merchants of Morality." *Foreign Policy* 129 (November): 36–45.

Bob, Clifford. 2005. *The Marketing of Rebellion: Insurgents, Media, and International Activism.* Cambridge: Cambridge University Press.

Boelens, Rutgerd, and Margreet Zwarteveen. 2005. "Prices and Politics in Andean Water Reforms." *Development and Change* 36 (4): 735–58.

Boelens, Rutgerd, Jaime Hoogesteger, and Michiel Baud. 2015. "Water Reform Governmentality in Ecuador: Neoliberalism, Centralization, and the Restraining of Polycentric Authority and Community Rule-making." *Geoforum* 64: 281–91.

Boutellier, Hans, and Ronald van Steden. 2011. "Governing Nodal Governance: The 'Anchoring' of Local Security Networks." In *International and Comparative Criminal Justice and Urban Governance,* eds. H. Boutellier and R. van Steden. Cambridge: Cambridge University Press, 461–82.

Bradford, Alina. 2015. "Deforestation: Facts, Causes & Effects." *Live Science.* www.livescience.com/27692-deforestation.html (Accessed March 26, 2016).

Brand, Ulrich. 2005. "Order and Regulation: Global Governance as a Hegemonic Discourse of International Politics?" *Review of International Political Economy* 12 (1): 155–76.

Brinkerhoff, Jennifer M., and Derick W. Brinkerhoff. 2010. "International Development Management: A Northern Perspective." *Public Administration and Development* 30 (2): 102–15.

Brundtland, Gro Harlem. 1987. *World Commission on Environment and Development: Our Common Future.* Oxford: Oxford University Press.

Brysk, Alison. 1996. "From Above and Below: Social Movements, the International System, and Human Rights in Argentina." *Comparative Political Studies* 26 (3): 259–85.

Brysk, Alison. 2000. *From Tribal Village to Global Village: Indian Rights and International Relations in Latin America.* Stanford: Stanford University Press.

Brysk, Alison. 2009. *Global Good Samaritans: Human Rights as Foreign Policy.* Oxford: Oxford University Press.

Bulkeley, Harriet, and Michele Merrill Betsill. 2003. *Cities and Climate Change: Urban Sustainability and Global Environmental Governance.* New York: Routledge.

Bulkeley, Harriet, and Michele M. Betsill. 2013. "Revisiting the Urban Politics of Climate Change." *Environmental Politics* 22 (1): 136–54.

Burau, Dominique. 2002. "El Manejo del Parque Nacional Cajas: La Experiencia del Ilustre Municipio de Cuenca." In *Las áreas protegidas y los páramos,* eds. D. Ortiz and P. Mena. Quito: Abya Yala, 38–49.

Burris, Scott. 2004. "Governance, Microgovernance and Health." *Temple Law Review* 77 (2): 335–62.

Burris, Scott, Peter Drahos, and Clifford Shearing. 2005. "Nodal Governance." *Australian Journal of Legal Philosophy* 30: 30–58.

Bustamante, Manuel. 2004. *Gestión Ambiental Concertada: Una Experiencia en Participación Ciudadana.* Loja, Ecuador: SNV; Proyecto Bosque Seco.

Cabrera Haro, Patricio. 2008. "Gestión Integrada de los Recursos Hídricos: Buena Gobernanza para el abastecimiento de la población y la protección del recurso." Paper presented at the Water and Sustainable Development International Expo, Zaragosa, Spain.

CAMAREN. 2002. *Foro de los Recursos Hídricos: Conclusiones, propuestas y acuerdos del Primer Encuentro Nacional.* Quito, Ecuador: CAMAREN.

Cameron, John. 2003. "The Social Origins of Municipal Democracy in Rural Ecuador: Agrarian Structures, Indigenous–Peasant Movements, and Non–Governmental Organizations." Ph.D. diss. Department of Political Science, York University, Toronto.

Carpenter, Charli. 2011. "Governing the Global Agenda: 'Gatekeepers' and 'Issue Adoption' in Transnational Advocacy Networks." In *Who Governs the Globe?* eds. D. D. Avant, M. Finnemore, and S. K. Sell. Cambridge: Cambridge University Press, 202–37.

Carrión, Fernando, ed. 2007. *La descentralización en el Ecuador: opciones comparadas.* Quito: FLACSO Ecuador.

Carrión, Fernando, and Manuel Dammert. 2007. "La descentralización en el Ecuador: un tema de Estado." In *La descentralización en el Ecuador: opciones comparadas,* ed. F. Carrión. Quito: FLACSO Ecuador, 9–18.

CEDERENA. 2002. "Pago por servicios ambientales: La experiencia de la Asociación Nueva América." Ibarra, Ecuador: CEDERENA, Interamerican Foundation, Municipio de Pimampiro, Asociación Nueva América, DFC-FAO.

CEDERENA. 2003. "Selección del municipio beneficiario." Ibarra, Ecuador: CEDERENA.

CELEC. 2012. "Declaración de Quito: Reunión de Ministros de Medio Ambiente de CELAC." Quito: Comunidad de Estados Latinoamericanos y Caribeños. http://alainet.org/active/52568&lang=es (Accessed February 15, 2016).

Célleri, Rolando. 2009. "Servicios ambientales para la conservación de los recursos hídricos: lecciones desde los Andes. Estado del conocimiento técnico científico sobre los servicios ambientales hidrológicos generados en los Andes." Lima: Consorcio para el Desarrollo Sostenible de la Ecorregión Andina.

Checkel, Jeffrey. 1999. "Norms, Institutions, and National Identity in Contemporary Europe." *International Studies Quarterly* 43 (1): 84–114.

Checkel, Jeffrey. 2001. "Why Comply? Social Learning and European Identity Change." *International Organization* 55 (3): 553–88.

Checkel, Jeffrey. 2005. "International Institutions and Socialization in Europe: Introduction and Framework." *International Organization* 59 (4): 801–26.

Cholango, Humberto. 2007. "Un Estado Plurinacional Significa Transformar el Estado." *Rikcharishun* 35 (May): 3–6.

Cholango, Humberto. 2010. "Sumak Kawsay y mundo indígena." In *Pueblos indígenas, derechos y desafíos: homenaje a Monseñor Leónidas Proaño,* eds. J. J. Tamayo Acosta and N. Arrobo Rodas. Valencia, España: ADG-N Libros, 91–98.

Chuji, Mónica. 2014. "Sumak Kawsay versus desarrollo." In *Antología del Pensamiento Indigenista Ecuatoriano sobre Sumak Kawsay,* eds. A. L. Hidalgo-Capitán, A. Guillén García, and N. Deleg Guazha. Cuenca, Ecuador: FIUCUHU, 229–36.

Clunan, Anne L. 2013. "Epistemic Community." *Encyclopedia Britannica Online.* www.britannica.com/topic/epistemic-community (Accessed March 26, 2016).

Comisión Ejecutiva Provincial. 2002. "Propuesta Para la Implementación del Pago por Servicio Ambiental Hídrico en la Provincia de Tungurahua y su Aplicación en una Zona Piloto." Ambato, Ecuador: Gobierno Provincial de Tungurahua.

Conca, Ken. 2006. *Governing Water: Contentious Transnational Politics and Global Institution Building.* Cambridge, MA: MIT Press.

Cooley, Alexander, and James Ron. 2002. "The NGO Scramble: Organizational Insecurity and the Political Economy of Transnational Action." *International Security* 27 (1): 5–39.

Cordero, Doris. 2008. "Esquemas de pagos por servicios ambientales para la conservación de cuencas hidrográficas en el Ecuador." *Investigación Agraria: Sistemas y Recursos Forestales 2008* 17 (1): 54–66.

Corfee-Morlot, Jan, Lamia Kamal-Chaoui, Michael G. Donovan, Ian Cochran, Alexis Robert, and Pierre-Jonathan Teasdale. 2009. "Cities, Climate Change and Multilevel Governance." OECD Environmental Working Papers N° 14. Paris: OECD.

Coronel, René, and Angel Jaramillo. 2005. "Valoración Económica del Servicio Ambiental Hídrico de la Microcuenca Hidrográfica 'El Limón'-Zamora Chinchipe," Master's thesis. Universidad Nacional de Loja, Ecuador.

Costanza, Robert, Ralph d'Arge, Rudolf de Groot, Stephen Farberk, Monica Grasso, Bruce Hannon, Karin Limburg, Shahid Naeem, Robert V. O'Neill, Jose Paruelo, Robert G. Raskin, Paul Suttonkk, and Marjan van den Belt. 1997. "The Value of the World's Ecosystem Services and Natural Capital." *Nature* 387: 253–60.

Costanza, Robert, and Carl Folke. 1997. "Valuing Ecosystem Services with Efficiency, Fairness, and Sustainability as Goals." In *Nature's Services: Societal Dependence on Natural Ecosystems*, ed. G. Daily. Washington, DC: Island Press, 49–68.

Cremers, Leontien, Marjolein Ooijevaar, and Rutgerd Boelens. 2005. "Institutional Reform in the Andean Irrigation Sector: Enabling Policies for Strengthening Local Rights and Water Management." *Natural Resources Forum* 29 (1): 37–50.

Crespo, Patricio. 2003. "Propuesta de guía técnica y metodológica para la realización de inventarios de agua." In *Foro de los Recursos Hídricos: Segundo Encuentro Nacional*, ed. J. Arévalo. Quito: CAMAREN, 83–95.

Crespo, Patricio. 2004. "Sistematización de la experiencia del 'Inventario de los recursos hídricos en la Provincia de Tungurahua.'" Ambato, Ecuador: GTZ-PROMACH.

Crook, Richard, and James Manor. 1998. *Democracy and Decentralization in South Asia and West Africa: Participation, Accountability, and Performance.* Cambridge: Cambridge University Press.

Cuenca, Jimmy. 2008. "Protección de la Cantidad y Calidad del Agua: La experiencia del municipio de Celica." Celica, Ecuador: CEDERENA; Municipio de Celica.

Dedeurwaerdere, Tom. 2005. "The Contribution of Network Governance to Sustainable Development." Paris: Iddri. http://www.iddri.org/Evenements/Seminaires-reguliers/s13_dedeurwaerdere.pdf (Accessed March 26, 2016).

Dewey, John. 1927. *The Public and Its Problems.* Chicago: Swallow Press.

Dewey, John. 2002 [1922]. *Human Nature and Conduct.* Amherst: Prometheus Books.

DiMaggio, Paul, and Walter Powell. 1983. "The Iron Cage Revisited: Institutional Isomorphism and Collective Rationality in Organizational Fields." *American Sociological Review* 48 (2): 147–60.

Dinar, Ariel, Karin E. Kemper, William Blomquist, Michele Diez, Gisele Sine, and William Fru. 2005. "Decentralization of River Basin Management: A Global Analysis." Policy Research Working Papers. Washington, DC: World Bank.

Donoso Harris, Guillermo. 2003. "Water Markets: Case Study of Chile's 1981 Water Code." Global Water Partnership South America. Santiago, Chile: Pontificia Universidad Católica de Chile. Faculty of Agriculture and Forestry. Department of Agricultural Economics.

Dourojeanni, Axel. 1994. "Politicas Públicas Para el Desarrollo Sustentable: La Gestión Integrada de Cuencas." Presentado en el Segundo Congreso Latinoamericano de Cuencas Hidrograficas en Merida. Santiago, Chile: CEPAL.

Dourojeanni, Axel. 2001. "Water Management at the River Basin Level: Challenges in Latin America." Recursos Naturales e Infraestructura, 29. Santiago, Chile: CEPAL.

Dourojeanni, Axel, and Andrei Jouravlev. 1999. "Gestión de cuencas y ríos vinculados con centros urbanos." ECLAC Studies and Research Papers. LC/R 1948. CEPAL. Recursos Naturales e Infraestructura.

Dourojeanni, Axel, Andrei Jouravlev, and Guillermo Chávez. 2002. "Gestión del agua a nivel de cuencas: teoría y práctica." ECLAC Series. LC/L.1777-P. CEPAL. Recursos Naturales e Infraestructura.

Drahos, Peter. 2004. "Intellectual Property and Pharmaceutical Markets: A Nodal Governance Approach." *Temple Law Review* 77 (3): 401–24.

DRI-Cotacachi. 2005. "Fortelaciendo las Potencialidades Locales de Desarrollo." Ibarra, Ecuador: Agencia Española de Cooperación Internacional; Proyecto DRI Cotacachi-Imbabura.

Duffett, John, ed. 1968. *Against the Crime of Silence: Proceedings of the Russell International War Crimes Tribunal.* New York: Simon and Schuster.

Echavarria, Marta, Joseph Vogel, Montserrat Albán, and Fernanda Meneses. 2004. *The Impacts of Payments for Watershed Services in Ecuador: Emerging Lessons from Pimampiro and Cuenca.* London: International Institute for Environment and Development (IIED).

EcoCiencia. 2009. "Memoria de la Mesa Redonda 'Agua Líquido Vital.'" El Chaco, Ecuador: EcoCiencia; Comité de Gestión Ambiental de El Chaco.

Ecuador Permanent Mission to the United Nations. 2008. "Statement by Her Excellency Ambassador Maria Fernanda Espinosa, Permanent Representative of Ecuador to the United Nations at the Sixty-Third Session of the United Nations General Assembly." New York: Republic of Ecuador.

Ecuadorian Permanent Mission to the United Nations. 2012. *Armonia con la Naturaleza. Diálogo Interactivo de la Asamblea General de Naciones Unidas.* www.uncsd2012.org//content/documents/771StatementEcuador.HwN.April2012.pdf (Accessed March 26, 2016).

Espinoza, Nelson, Javier Gatica, and James Walter Smyle. 1999. *El pago de servicios ambientales y el desarrollo sostenible en el medio rural.* San José, Costa Rica: Unidad Regional de Asistencia Técnica (RUTA).

Falconí, Fander, and Pabel Muñoz. 2007. "En busqueda de salidas a la crisis ética, política y de pensamiento." In *La descentralización en el Ecuador: opciones comparadas,* ed. F. Carrión. Quito: FLACSO Ecuador, 19–27.

Falkner, Robert, and Aarti Gupta. 2009. "The Limits of Regulatory Convergence: Globalization and GMO Politics in the South." *International Environmental Agreements: Politics, Law and Economics* 9: 113–33.

Falleti, Tulia Gabriela. 2006. "Theory-Guided Process-Tracing: Something Old, Something New." *Newsletter of the Organized Section in Comparative Politics of the APSA* 17 (1): 9–14.

FAO. 2006. *The New Generation of Watershed Management Programmes and Projects.* Rome: UN Food and Agriculture Organization.

Fatheurer, Thomas. 2011. *Buen Vivir: A Brief Introduction to Latin America's New Concepts for the Good Life and the Rights of Nature.* Berlin: Heinrich Böll Foundation.

Faust, Jörg, Nicolaus von der Goltz, and Michael Schloms. 2007. "Promoting Subsidiarity-Oriented Decentralization in Fragmented Polities—Some Lessons from Ecuador." In *From Project to Policy Reform: Experiences of German Development Cooperation,* ed. T. Altenburg. Bonn, Germany: German Development Institute, 31–56.

Finnemore, Martha. 1996. *National Interests in International Society.* Ithaca, NY: Cornell University Press.

Finnemore, Martha, and Kathryn Sikkink. 1998. "International Norms and Political Change." *International Organization* 52 (4): 887–917.

Flores, Edmundo, and Tim Merrill. 2013. *A Country Study: Ecuador.* The Library of Congress 1989 [cited June 20 2013]. http://lcweb2.loc.gov/frd/cs/ectoc.html (Accessed March 25, 2016).

Florini, Ann M., ed. 2000. *The Third Force: The Rise of Transnational Civil Society.* Washington, DC: Carnegie Endowment for International Peace.

Foro de Recursos Hídricos de Pastaza. 2008. "Primer Encuentro Amazónico del Agua." Puyo, Ecuador: Gobierno Provincial de Pastaza; Gobierno Municipal del Cantón Pastaza; Foro Nacional de Recursos Hídricos; Fundación Natura.

Foro Provincial de los Recursos Hídricos en Tungurahua. 2002. "Documento Final: Recopilación detallada de Talleres Provinciales, Entrevistas, Foro Provincial y Mesas de Trabajo." Ambato, Ecuador: CAMAREN.

Fox, Jonathan. 2009. "Coalitions and Networks." In *International Encyclopedia of Civil Society,* eds. H. K. Anheier, S. Toepler, and R. List. New York: Springer, 486–92.

Frank, Jonas. 2007. *Decentralization in Ecuador: Actors, Institutions, and Incentives.* Munich: Nomos.

Franklin, James C. 2009. "Contentious Challenges and Government Responses in Latin America." *Political Research Quarterly* 62 (4): 700–14.

Freudenberg, Nicholas. 2004. "Community Capacity for Environmental Health Promotion: Determinants and Implications for Practice." *Health Education Behavior* 31 (4): 472–90.

Freudenberg, Nicholas, Marc Rogers, Casandra Ritas, and Sister Mary Nerney. 2005. "Policy Analysis and Advocacy: An Approach to Community-Based Participatory Research." In *Methods in Community-Based Participatory Research for Health*, eds. B. Israel, E. Eng, A. Schulz, and E. Parker. San Francisco: Jossey-Bass, 349–70.

Fung, Archon, and Erik Olin Wright. 2003. "Thinking about Empowered Participatory Governance." In *Deepening Democracy: Institutional Innovations in Empowered Participatory Governance.* Vol 4 of *The Real Utopias Project*, eds. A. Fung and E. O. Wright. London: Verso, 3–42.

G77. 2014. "For a New World Order for Living Well." Declaration of the Summit of Heads of State and Government of the Group of 77. Santa Cruz, Bolivia. www.g77.org/doc/A-68-948(E).pdf (Accessed March 26, 2015).

Ganz, Marshall. 2000. "Resources and Resourcefulness: Strategic Capacity in the Unionization of California Agriculture, 1959–1966." *American Journal of Sociology* 105: 1003–62.

Ganz, Marshall. 2003. "Why David Sometimes Wins." In *Rethinking Social Movements*, eds. J. Goodwin and J. Jasper. Lanham, MD: Rowman and Littlefield, 177–98.

Garzón, Andrea. 2009. "Estado de la Acción sobre los Mecanismos de Financiamiento de la Protección y Recuperación de los Servicios Ambientales Hidrológicos." Informe Final de la Síntesis Regional Sobre Servicios Ambiental Hídricos en Los Andes. Lima, Peru: Consorcio para el Desarrollo Sostenible de la Ecorregión Andina.

Garzón, Andrea, and Carolina Mancheno. 2008. "Sistematización del Proyecto Instalación de un Fondo Ambiental para la Conservación y Recuperación de las Microcuencas Puyo y Pambay." Puyo, Ecuador: Fundación Natura; Municipio de Pastaza; CODEAMA.

Gauvin, Francois-Pierre, and Julia Abelson. 2006. *Primer on Public Involvement.* Toronto: Health Council of Canada.

George, Alexander L., and Andrew Bennett. 2005. *Case Studies and Theory Development in the Social Sciences.* Cambridge, MA: MIT Press.

Gerhards, Jürgen, and Dieter Rucht. 1992. "Mesomobilization: Organizing and Framing in Two Protest Campaigns in West Germany." *American Journal of Sociology* 98 (3): 555–96.

Gilovich, Thomas, Dale Griffin, and Daniel Kahneman, eds. 2002. *Heuristics and Biases: The Psychology of Intuitive Judgment.* Cambridge: Cambridge University Press.

Gleick, Peter H. 1998. *The World's Water 1998–99: The Biennial Report on Freshwater Resources.* Washington, DC: Island Press.

Global Water Partnership. 2000. *Towards Water Security: A Framework for Action.* Stockholm: Global Water Partnership.

Global Water Partnership. 2003. "La Gobernabilidad de La Gestión del Agua en el Ecuador." Quito: GWP-SAMTAC.

Global Water Partnership. 2010. "History of GWP." www.gwp.org/en/About-GWP/History/ (Accessed March 26, 2016).

Gobierno Provincial de Tungurahua. 2006. *El Camino Recorrido: Nuevo Modelo de Gestión.* Ambato, Ecuador: GPT.

Gobierno Provincial de Tungurahua. 2008. *Agenda Tungurahua 2008–2010.* Ambato, Ecuador: GPT.

Gobierno Provincial de Tungurahua. 2009. *El Nuevo Modelo de Gestión: una forma diferente de ser Gobierno Provincial de Tungurahua.* Ambato, Ecuador: GPT.

Goldman, Michael. 2009. "Water for All! The Phenomenal Rise of Transnational Knowledge and Policy Networks." In *Environmental Governance: Power and Knowledge in a Local-Global World*, eds. G. Kutting and R. D. Lipschutz. New York: Routledge, 145–69.

Goldman-Benner, Rebecca, Silvia Benitez, Timothy Boucher, Alejandro Calvache, Gretchen Daily, Peter Kareiva, Tim Kroeger, and Aurelio Ramos. 2012. "Water Funds and Payments for Ecosystem Services: Practice Learns from Theory and Theory Can Learn from Practice." *Oryx* 46 (1): 55–63.

Grindle, Merilee S. 2007. *Going Local: Decentralization, Democratization, and the Promise of Good Governance*. Princeton, NJ: Princeton University Press.

GTZ. 1999. "Marco Institucional y Organizativo." Internal Report. Quito, Ecuador: GTZ.

Gudynas, Eduardo. 2011. "Buen Vivir: Today's Tomorrow." *Development* 54 (4): 441–7.

Haas, Peter J. 1992. "Introduction: Epistemic Communities and International Policy Coordination." *International Organization* 46 (1): 1–35.

Hanneman, Robert A., and Mark Riddle. 2005. *Introduction to Social Network Methods*. Riverside: University of California, Riverside.

Haunss, Sebastian, and Lars Kohlmorgen. 2009. "Lobbying or Politics? Political Claims Making in IP Conflicts." In *Politics of Intellectual Property: Contestation Over the Ownership, Use, and Control of Knowledge and Information*, eds. S. Haunss and K. C. Shadlen. Cheltenham, UK: Edward Elgar Publishing, 107–28.

Heathcote, Isobel W. 2009. *Integrated Watershed Management: Principles and Practice*. 2nd ed. Hoboken, New Jersey: John Wiley & Sons.

Hein, Wolfgang. 2007. "Global Health Governance and WTO/TRIPS: Conflicts Between 'Global Market-Creation' and 'Global Social Rights.'" In *Global Health Governance and the Fight against HIV/AIDS*, eds. W. Hein, S. Bartsch, and L. Kohlmorgen. Basingstoke, UK: Palgrave Macmillan, 38–66.

Hein, Wolfgang, Scott Burris, and Clifford Shearing. 2009. "Conceptual Models for Global Governance." In *Making Sense of Global Health Governance: A Policy Perspective*, eds. K. Buse, W. Hein and N. Drager. Basingstoke, UK: Palgrave Macmillan, 72–98.

Hein, Wolfgang, and Lars Kohlmorgen. 2008. "Global Health Governance: Conflicts on Global Social Rights." *Global Social Policy* 8 (1): 80–108.

Hidalgo-Capitán, Antonio Luis, Alejandro Guillén García, and Nancy Deleg Guazha, eds. 2014. *Antología del Pensamiento Indigenista Ecuatoriano sobre Sumak Kawsay*. Cuenca, Ecuador: FIUCUHU.

Hill, Michael James. 2009. *The Public Policy Process*. 5th ed. Harlow, UK: Pearson Education.

Hirschman, Albert. 1984. *Getting Ahead Collectively: Grassroots Experiences in Latin America*. New York: Pergamon Press.

Hochstetler, Kathryn, and Margaret E. Keck. 2007. *Greening Brazil*. Durham, NC: Duke University Press.

Hoelscher, David, and Marc Quintyn. 2003. "Managing Systemic Banking Crises." IMF Occasional Paper 224. Washington, DC: International Monetary Fund.

Hoffmann, Matthew J. 2011. *Climate Governance at the Crossroads: Experimenting with a Global Response after Kyoto*. Oxford: Oxford University Press.

Honorable Consejo Provincial de Tungurahua. 2006. "Propuesta para la Formulación e Implementación del Plan Maestro de los Recursos Hídricos de Tungurahua." Ambato, Ecuador: HCPT.

Honorable Consejo Provincial de Tungurahua, CNRH, PROMACH, IEDECA, and CESA. 2004. "Inventario y Diagnóstico del Recurso Hídrico, Provincia del Tungurahua." Ambato, Ecuador: HCPT.

Hooghe, Lisbet, and Gary Marks. 2001. "Types of Multi-Level Governance." *European Integration Online Papers* 5 (11). http://eiop.or.at/eiop/texte/2001-011.htm (Accessed March 25, 2016).

Huang, Marjorie, and Shyam K. Upadhyaya. 2007. "Watershed-Based Payment for Environmental Services in Asia." Blacksburg, VA: Virginia Tech.

Hughes, Ross, and Fiona Flintan. 2001. *Integrating Conservation and Development Experience: A Review and Bibliography of the ICDP Literature*. London: International Institute for Environment and Development.

IEDECA. 2006a. "Consolidación de la Estratégica Participativa de Manejo Sostenible de la Cuenca Alta del Río Ambato." Ambato, Ecuador: Instituto de Ecología y Desarrollo de las Comunidades Andinas.

IEDECA. 2006b. "Proyecto Consolidación de la Estrategia Participativa de Manejo Sostenible de la Cuenca Alta del Río Ambato." Ambato, Ecuador: Instituto de Ecología y Desarrollo de las Comunidades Andinas.

International Conference on Water and the Environment. 1992. "The Dublin Statement on Water and Sustainable Development." Dublin: International Conference on Water and the Environment.

Isch López, Edgar. 2005. "El derecho al agua y el dilema de los servicios ambientales." In *Foro de los Recursos Hídricos: Tercer Encuentro Nacional*, ed. A. Arroyo. Quito: CAMAREN.

Isch López, Edgar, and Ingo Gentes, eds. 2006. *Agua y servicios ambientales: Visiones críticas desde los Andes*. Quito, Ecuador: Abya-Yala.

Israel, Barbara, Chris Coombe, Rebecca Cheezum, Amy Schulz, Robert McGranaghan, Richard Lichtenstein, Angela Reyes, Jaye Clement, and Akosua Burris. 2010. "Community-Based Participatory Research: A Capacity-Building Approach for Policy Advocacy Aimed at Eliminating Health Disparities." *American Journal of Public Health* 100 (11): 2094–102.

IUCN. 1980. *World Conservation Strategy: Living Resource Conservation for Sustainable Development*. Gland, Switzerland: International Union for Conservation of Nature.

IUCN. 2012. *Resolutions and Recommendations, World Conservation Congress*. Jeju, South Korea: International Union for Conservation of Nature.

Jacome, Luis. 2004. "The Late 1990s Financial Crisis in Ecuador: Institutional Weaknesses, Fiscal Rigidities, and Financial Dollarization at Work." Working Paper 04/12. Washington, DC: International Monetary Fund.

Jasper, James. 1997. *The Art of Moral Protest*. Chicago: University of Chicago Press.

Jasper, James. 2004. "A Strategic Approach to Collective Action: Looking for Agency in Social Movement Choices." *Mobilization: An International Journal* 9 (1):1–16.

Jasper, James. 2006. *Getting Your Way: Strategic Dilemmas in the Real World*. Chicago: The University of Chicago Press.

Jaspers, Frank G.W. 2003. "Institutional Arrangements for Integrated River Basin Management." *Water Policy* 5 (1): 77–90.

Jenkins-Smith, Hank C., and Paul A. Sabatier. 2003. "The Study of Public Policy Processes." In *The Nation's Health*, eds. P. R. Lee, C. L. Estes, and F. M. Rodríguez. London: Jones & Bartlett Learning, 135–44.

Joas, Hans. 1993. *Pragmatism and Social Theory*. Chicago: University of Chicago Press.

Joas, Hans. 1996. *The Creativity of Action*. Chicago: University of Chicago Press.

Johnston, Hank. 2002. "Verification and Proof in Frame and Discourse Analysis." In *Methods of Social Movements Research*, eds. B. Klandermans and S. Staggenborg. Minneapolis: University of Minnesota Press, 62–91.

Johnston, Hank, and John A. Noakes, eds. 2005. *Frames of Protest: Social Movements and the Framing Perspective*. Lanham, MD: Rowman & Littlefield Publishers.

Jones, T., B. Phillips, C. Williams, J. Pittock, and T. Davis, eds. 2003. *Conserving Rivers: Lessons from WWF's Work for Integrated River Basin Management*. Gland, Switzerland: World Wildlife Fund.

Kahneman, Daniel, Paul Slovic, and Amos Tversky, eds. 1982. *Judgment under Uncertainty: Heuristics and Biases*. Cambridge: Cambridge University Press.

Kaplan, Stephen. 2013. *Globalization and Austerity Politics in Latin America*. Cambridge: Cambridge University Press.

Kareiva, Peter, and John Wiens. 2005. "Ecosystem Services and Conservation: A Science Perspective." Arlington, VA: The Nature Conservancy.

Kates, Robert, Thomas M. Parris, and Anthony A. Leiserowitz. 2005. "What Is Sustainable Development? Goals, Indicators, Values, and Practice." *Environment: Science and Policy for Sustainable Development* 47 (3): 8–21.

Kauffman, Craig M. 2014. "Financing Watershed Conservation: Lessons from Ecuador's Evolving Water Trust Funds." *Agricultural Water Management* 145: 39–49.

Kauffman, Craig M. and Pamela L. Martin. 2016. "Testing Ecuador's Rights of Nature: Why Some Lawsuits Succeed and Others Fail." Presented at the International Studies Association Annual Convention, Atlanta, GA.

Kauffman, Craig M., and William C. Terry. 2016. "Pursuing Costly Reform: The Case of Ecuadorian Natural Resource Management." *Latin American Research Review* 51 (4). https://lasa.international.pitt.edu/eng/larr/article-search.asp (Accessed June 22, 2016).

Kaufmann, Daniel, Frannie Léautier, and Massimo Mastruzzi. 2004. "Governance and the City: An Empirical Exploration into Global Determinants of Urban Performance." Washington, DC: The World Bank.

Keck, Margaret E., and Kathryn Sikkink. 1998. *Activists Beyond Borders: Advocacy Networks in International Politics.* Ithaca, NY: Cornell University Press.

Khagram, Sanjeev, James V. Riker, and Kathryn Sikkink. 2002. *Transnational Social Movements, Networks, and Norms.* Minneapolis: University of Minnesota Press.

Kidder, Tracy. 2009. *Mountains beyond Mountains: The Quest of Dr. Paul Farmer, a Man Who Would Cure the World.* New York: Random House.

Kjaer, Anne Mette. 2004. *Governance.* Cambridge: Polity Press.

Kjellman, Kjell Erling. 2007. "The Power of Persuasion: Transnational Activism and Normative Processes." Oslo: International Peace Research Institute.

Klingler-Vidra, Robyn, and Philip Schleifer. 2014. "Convergence More or Less: Why Do Practices Vary as They Diffuse?" *International Studies Review* 16 (2): 264–74.

Krchnak, Karin M. 2007. "Watershed Valuation as a Tool for Biodiversity Conservation." Watershed Report. Arlington, VA: The Nature Conservancy.

Kriesi, Hanspeter. 2007. "Political Context and Opportunity." In *The Blackwell Companion to Social Movements*, eds. D. A. Snow, S. A. Soule, and H. Kriesi. Malden, MA: Blackwell Publishing, 67–90.

Lalander, Rickard. 2005. "Movimiento indígena, participación política y buen gobierno municipal en Ecuador: El Alcalde Mario Conejo de Otavalo." *Ecuador Debate* 66: 153–82.

Lalander, Rickard. 2014. "Rights of Nature and the Indigenous Peoples in Bolivia and Ecuador: a Straitjacket for Progressive Development Politics?" *Iberoamerican Journal of Development Studies* 3 (2): 148–73.

Leach, William, D., and Neil W. Pelkey. 2001. "Making Watershed Partnerships Work: A Review of the Empirical Literature." *Journal of Water Resources Planning and Management* 127 (6): 378–85.

Levi-Faur, David. 2005. "The Global Diffusion of Regulatory Capitalism." *Annals of the American Academy of Political and Social Science* 598 (March): 12–32.

Levy, Yoram, and Marcel Wissenburg. 2004. "Sustainable Development as a Policy Telos: A New Approach to Political Problem Solving." *Political Studies* 52 (4): 785–801.

López, Hernando. 2005. *Estado de concreción del proceso de descentralización en el Ecuador: línea base de la descentralización a julio de 2004.* Quito, Ecuador: Consejo Nacional de Modernización del Estado.

López, Víctor, ed. 2008. *Memoria de la Jornada "Descentralización, Gestión Ambiental y Conservación."* Quito: EcoCiencia.

López, Víctor, Janett Ulloa, and Cristina Herdoíza. 2007. *Gestión Democrática de los Recursos Naturales. Sistematización del proyecto "Conservación a través del fortalecimiento de capacidades de actores locales en la Biorreserva del Cóndor." El Chaco y Gonzalo Pizarro, Amazonía ecuatoriana.* Quito: EcoCiencia.

Lucero, Jose Antonio. 2008. *Struggles of Voice: The Politics of Indigenous Representation in the Andes.* Pittsburgh: University of Pittsburgh Press.

Lutz, Ellen, and Kathryn Sikkink. 2001. "The Justice Cascade: The Evolution and Impact of Foreign Human Rights Trials in Latin America." *Chicago Journal of International Law* 2 (1): 1–33.

MAE. 2000a. *Estrategia Ambiental para el Desarrollo Sostenible del Ecuador.* Quito: Ministerio de Ambiente del Ecuador.

MAE. 2000b. *Estrategia Para el Desarrollo Forestal Sustentable del Ecuador.* Quito: Ministerio de Ambiente del Ecuador.

MAE. 2003. "Proyecto 'Desarrollo del Sistema Descentralizado de Gestión Ambiental' (MAE/BID ATN/SF-8182-EC)." Quito: Ministerio de Ambiente del Ecuador.

Maldonado, Rafael, and Marina Kosmus. 2003. "El Pago por Servicios Ambientales (PSA): Una alternativa para disponer de agua en cantidad y calidad. Tungurahua, Ecuador." Presented at III Congreso Latinoamericano de Manejo de Cuencas Hidrográficas. Arequipa, Peru.

Martin, Pamela L. 2011. "Global Governance from the Amazon: Leaving Oil Underground in Yasuní National Park, Ecuador." *Global Environmental Politics* 11 (4): 22–42.

Marullo, Sam, Ron Pagnucco, and Jackie Smith. 1996. "Frame Changes and Social Movement Contraction: US Peace Movement Framing After the Cold War." *Sociological Inquiry* 66 (1): 1–28.

McAdam, Doug, John D. McCarthy, and Mayer N. Zald, eds. 1996. *Comparative Perspectives on Social Movements: Political Opportunities, Mobilizing Structures, and Cultural Framings.* New York: Cambridge University Press.

McAdam, Doug, Sidney Tarrow, and Charles Tilly. 1997. "Toward an Integrated Perspective on Social Movements and Revolution." In *Comparative Politics: Rationality Culture, and Structure,* eds. M. I. Lichbach and A. S. Zuckerman. Cambridge: Cambridge University Press, 142–73.

McCarthy, John D. 1996. "Constraints and Opportunities in Adopting, Adapting and Inventing." In *Comparative Perspectives on Social Movements, Political Opportunities, Mobilizing Structures, and Cultural Framings,* eds. D. McAdam, J. D. McCarthy, and M. N. Zald. Cambridge: Cambridge University Press, 141–51.

McNulty, Stephanie. 2011. *Voice and Vote: Decentralization and Participation in Post-Fujimori Peru.* Stanford: Stanford University Press.

Mercer, Jonathan. 2005. "Prospect Theory and Political Science." *Annual Review of Political Science* 8 (June): 1–21.

Mesa de Trabajo Provincial. 2001. "Foro de los Recursos Hídricos en la Provincia de Tungurahua: Primera Versión Borrador." Ambato, Ecuador: Foro de los Recursos Hídricos en la Provincia de Tungurahua.

Mesa de Trabajo Provincial. 2002. "Documento Final: Recopilación detallada de Talleres Provinciales, Entrevistas, Foro Provincial y Mesas de Trabajo." Ambato, Ecuador: Foro Provincial de los Recursos Hídricos en Tungurahua.

Metais, Sara, and Alfredo Cruz. 2003. "Gestión Integral en el Manejo y Conservación de la Cuenca del Río Ambato." In *Foro de Los Recursos Hídricos: Segundo Encuentro Nacional,* ed. J. Arévalo. Quito: CAMAREN, 44–61.

Meyer, John W., John Boli, George M. Thomas, and Francisco O. Ramirez. 1997. "World Society and the Nation-State." *American Journal of Sociology* 103 (1): 144–81.

Michel, James H. 1997. "Shaping the 21st Century: The Contribution of Development Co-operation." In *Sustainable Development: OECD Policy Approaches for the 21st Century,* ed. M. Yakowitz. Paris: OECD, 29–36.

Millennium Ecosystem Assessment. 2005a. *Ecosystems and Human Well-Being: Synthesis.* Washington, DC: Island Press.

Millennium Ecosystem Assessment. 2005b. *Ecosystems and Human Well-Being: Wetlands and Water, Synthesis.* Washington, DC: World Resources Institute.

Minkler, Meredith, Angela Glover Blackwell, Mildred Thompson, and Heather Tamir. 2003. "Community-Based Participatory Research: Implications for Public Health Funding." *American Journal of Public Health* 93 (8): 1210–3.

Minkler, Meredith, Victoria Breckwich Vásquez, and Shepard Peggy. 2006. "Promoting Environmental Health Policy through Community Based Participatory Research: A Case Study from Harlem, New York." *Journal of Urban Health* 83 (1): 101–10.

Molle, Francois. 2008. "Nirvana Concepts, Narratives and Policy Models: Insights from the Water Sector." *Water Alternatives* 1 (1): 131–56.

Moreno-Jaimes, Carlos. 2007. "Do Competitive Elections Produce Better-Quality Governments? Evidence from Mexican Municipalities, 1990–2000." *Latin American Research Review* 42 (2): 136–53.

Moreta, Carlos, Antonio Chachipanta, and Waldemar Wirsig. 2004. "Convenio de Cooperación Entre el Movimiento Indígena de Tungurahua MIT, el Movimiento Indígena de Tungurahua Con Sede en Atocha MITA, la Asociación de Indígenas Evangelicos de Tungurahua

AIET y el Proyecto de Manejo de Cuencas Hidrográricas PROMACH-GTZ." Ambato, Ecuador: GTZ-PROMACH.

Morrison, Jenny Knowles. 2010. "From Global Paradigms to Grounded Policies: Local Socio-Cognitive Constructions of International Development Policies and Implications for Development Management." *Public Administration and Development* 30 (2): 159–74.

Mosley, Layna. 2003. *Global Capital and National Governments.* Cambridge: Cambridge University Press.

Nadelman, Ethan. 1990. "Global Prohibition Regimes: The Evolution of Norms in International Society." *International Organization* 44 (4): 479–526.

Nelson, Anita, Andrea Babon, Mike Berry, and Nina Keath. 2008. "Engagement, but for What Kind of Marriage? Community Members and Local Planning Authorities." *Community Development Journal* 42 (1): 37–51.

Neuman, Lawrence W. 2007. *Basics of Social Research: Qualitative and Quantitative Approaches.* 2nd ed. Boston: Pearson Education.

Newig, Jens, Dirk Günther, and Claudia Pahl-Wostl. 2010. "Synapses in the Network: Learning in Governance Networks in the Context of Environmental Management." *Ecology and Society* 15(4). http://www.ecologyandsociety.org/vol15/iss4/art24/ (Accessed April 1, 2016).

O'Neill, Kathleen. 2009. *The Environment and International Relations.* Cambridge: Cambridge University Press.

Ojeda, Lautaro. 2004. "¿Por qué la descentralización no avanza?" *Ecuador Debate* 61: 95–116.

Okereke, Chukwumerije, Harriet Bulkeley, and Heike Schroeder. 2009. "Conceptualizing Climate Change Governance beyond the International Regime: A Review of Four Theoretical Approaches." *Global Environmental Politics* 9 (1): 58–78.

Olleta, Andrés. 2007. "The World Bank's Influence on Water Privatization in Argentina." IELRC Working Paper 2007-02. Geneva: International Environmental Law Research Centre.

Ortiz Crespo, Fernando. 1998. "¿Tres lustros menos para salvar la Tierra?" In *Diario Hoy: Especial 15 años (1982–1997).* Quito: Diario Hoy.

Ostrom, Elinor. 1990. *Governing the Commons: The Evolution of Institutions for Collective Action.* Cambridge: Cambridge University Press.

Ostrom, Elinor. 1999. "Institutional Rational Choice: An Assessment of the Institutional Analysis and Development Framework." In *Theories of the Policy Process,* ed. P. A. Sabatier. Boulder, CO: Westview Press, 35–71.

Ostrom, Elinor. 2002. "Common-Pool Resources and Institutions: Toward a Revised Theory." In *Handbook of Agricultural Economics,* eds. B. Gardner and G. Rausser. Amsterdam: Elsevier, 1315–39.

Oviedo, Atawallpa. 2014. "El Buen Vivir posmoderno y el Sumakawsay ancestral." In *Antología del Pensamiento Indigenista Ecuatoriano sobre Sumak Kawsay,* eds. A. L. Hidalgo-Capitán, A. Guillén García, and N. Deleg Guazha. Huelva & Cuenca: FIUCUHU, 267–97.

Pagiola, Stefano. 2006. "Payments for Environmental Services in Costa Rica." Washington, DC: The World Bank.

Pallares, Amalia Veronika. 1997. "From Peasant Struggles to Indian Resistance: Political Identity in Highland Ecuador 1964-1992." Ph.D. diss. University of Texas at Austin.

Payne, Rodger A. 2001. "Persuasion, Frames and Norm Construction." *European Journal of International Relations* 7 (1): 37–61.

Peña, Humberto, and Miguel Solanes. 2003. "La Gobernabilidad Efectiva del Agua en las Américas, un Tema Crítico." Presented at the 3rd World Water Forum. Kyoto, Japan.

Pérez De Mora, Susana. 2009. "Modelo de Gestión de la Mancomunidad Frente Sur Occidental (FSO) Provincia de Tungurahua." Ambato, Ecuador: GTZ-Gesoren.

Pérez-Foguet, Agustí, M. Morales, and A. Saz-Carranza. 2005. *Introducción a la Cooperación al Desarrollo para las ingenierías. Una propuesta para el estudio.* Barcelona: UPC-Ingeniería Sin Fronteras.

Petersen, Dana, Meredith Minkler, Victoria Breckwich Vásquez, Michelle Kegler, Lorraine Malcoe, and Sally Whitecrow. 2007. "Using Community-Based Participatory Research to

Shape Policy and Prevent Lead Exposure among Native American Children." *Progress in Community Health Partnerships* 1 (3): 249–56.

Poats, Susan. 2007. "Report on the Latin American Regional Workshop on Compensation for Environmental Services and Poverty Alleviation in Latin America." Nairobi: World Agroforestry Centre.

Poeschel-Renz, Ursula. 2001. *No quisimos soltar el agua: Formas de resistencia indígena y continuidad étnica en una comunidad ecuatoriana, 1960–1965.* Quito: Abya-Yala.

Poole, Deborah. 2010. "El Buen Vivir: Peruvian Indigenous Leader Mario Palacios." *NACLA Report on the Americas*, September/October. https://nacla.org/news/el-buen-vivir-peruvian-indigenous-leader-mario-palacios (Accessed February 14, 2016).

Porras, Ina, Maryanne Grieg-Gran, and Nanete Neves. 2008. *All that Glitters: A Review of Payments for Watershed Services in Developing Countries.* London: IIED.

Postero, Nancy Grey, and Leon Zamosc, eds. 2004. *The Struggle for Indigenous Rights in Latin America.* Portland, OR: Sussex Academic Press.

Price, Richard. 2003. "Transnational Civil Society and Advocacy in World Politics." *World Politics* 55 (4): 579–606.

Price, Richard, and Nina Tannenwald. 1996. "Norms and Deterrence: the Nuclear and Chemical Weapons Taboos." In *The Culture of National Security: Norms and Identity in World Politics*, ed. P. J. Katzenstein. New York: Columbia University Press, 114–52.

PRODERENA. 2007. "Ficha de Acción POA-2 N° 04: Proyectos de Subvención." Ibarra, Ecuador: PRODERENA; Gobierno Provincial de Imbabura.

PROFAFOR. 2001. "Contrato de Forestación, Comunidad de Zuleta." Solicitud No: For-391. Quito: PROFAFOR.

PROFAFOR. 2005a. "Cuarto Informe de Avance: Valoración de servicios ambientales hidrológicos." Quito: PROFAFOR.

PROFAFOR. 2005b. "Primer Informe de Avance: Diagnóstico Ambiental Rápido de la Microcuenca del río Tahuando." Quito: PROFAFOR.

Proyecto Bosque Seco. 1999a. "2nd Informe Semestral: Julio a Diciembre 1998." Celica, Ecuador: SNV.

Proyecto Bosque Seco. 1999b. "3er Informe Semestral: Enero a Junio 1999." Loja, Ecuador: SNV.

Rahaman, Muhammad Mizanur, and Olli Varis. 2005. "Integrated Water Resources Management: Evolution, Prospects and Future Challenges." *Sustainability: Science, Practice, & Policy* 1 (1): 15–21.

Ravnborg, Helle Munk, Mette Gervin Damsgaard, and Kim Raben. 2007. "Payments for Ecosystem Services: Issues and Pro-Poor Opportunities for Development Assistance." Copenhagen: Danish Institute for International Studies.

REDLACH. 2002. "Informe Sobre la Situación del Manejo de Cuencas Hidrográficas en el Ecuador." Tercer Congreso Latinoamericano de Manejo de Cuencas en Zonas de Montaña de la REDLACH-FAO. Ambato, Ecuador: UN Food and Agriculture Organization.

Rein, Martin, and Donald Schön. 1993. "Reframing Policy Discourse." In *The Argumentative Turn in Policy Analysis and Planning*, eds. F. Fischer and J. Forester. Durham, NC: Duke University Press, 145–66.

Republic of Ecuador. 2008. "Constitution of the Ecuadorian Republic." Political Database of the Americas. http://pdba.georgetown.edu/Constitutions/Ecuador/english08 (Accessed February 14, 2016).

Rieckmann, Marco, Maik Adomßent, Werner Härdtle, and Patricia Aguirre. 2011. "Sustainable Development and Conservation of Biodiversity Hotspots in Latin America: The Case of Ecuador." In *Biodiversity Hotspots: Distribution and Protection of Conservation Priority Areas*, eds. F. Zachos and J. C. Habel. Berlin: Springer, 435–52.

Risse, Thomas, Stephen C. Ropp, and Kathryn Sikkink, eds. 1999. *The Power of Human Rights: International Norms and Domestic Change.* Cambridge: Cambridge University Press.

Rojas, Oscar. 2012. "Informe de Gestión, Febrero 2012." Ambato, Ecuador: Fideicomiso Fondo de Páramos Tungurahua y Lucha Contra la Pobreza.

Ryan, Charlotte. 1991. *Prime Time Activism: Media Strategies for Grassroots Organizing.* Boston: South End.

Sabatier, Paul A. 1986. "Top-Down and Bottom-Up Approaches to Implementation Research: A Critical Analysis and Suggested Synthesis." *Journal of Public Policy* 6 (1):21–48.

Sabatier, Paul A., ed. 2007. *Theories of the Policy Process.* Boulder, CO: Westview Press.

Sabatier, Paul A., Will Focht, Mark Lubell, Zev Trachtenberg, Arnold Vedlitz, and Marty Matlock, eds. 2005. *Swimming Upstream: Collaborative Approaches to Watershed Management.* Cambridge, MA: MIT Press.

Salazar, Ana, José Astudillo, Dután Hugo, Iván Gonzáles, Paciente Vásquez, and Enrique Orellana. 2004. *Gestión de redes: una estrategia para el desarrollo sustentable y la construcción del poder local.* Cuenca, Ecuador: UN Food and Agriculture Organization.

Salazar, Gabriel, and Hugh Rudnick. 2008. "Hydro Power Plants in Ecuador: A Technical and Economical Analysis." Presented at Power and Energy Society General Meeting, "Conversion and Delivery of Electrical Energy in the 21st Century," Pittsburgh, PA. http://ieeexplore. ieee.org/xpl/login.jsp?tp=&arnumber=4596897&url=http%3A%2F%2Fieeexplore.ieee. org%2Fxpls%2Fabs_all.jsp%3Farnumber%3D4596897 (Accessed April 1, 2016).

Schickler, Eric. 2001. *Disjointed Pluralism: Institutional Innovation and the Development of the U.S. Congress.* Princeton: Princeton University Press.

Seawright, Jason, and John Gerring. 2008. "Case Selection Techniques in Case Study Research: A Menu of Qualitative and Quantitative Options." *Political Research Quarterly* 61 (2): 294–308.

Selee, Andrew, and Joseph S. Tulchin. 2004. "Decentralization and Democratic Governance: Lessons and Challenges." In *Decentralization, Democratic Governance, and Civil Society in Comparative Perspective*, eds. P. Oxhorn, J. S. Tulchin, and A. Selee. Washington, DC: Woodrow Wilson Center for International Scholars, 295–320.

Sell, Susan K. 2003. *Private Power, Public Law: The Globalization of Intellectual Property Rights.* Cambridge: Cambridge University Press.

Shearing, Clifford, and Jennifer Wood. 2003. "Nodal Governance, Democracy, and the New 'Denizens.'" *Journal of Law and Society* 30 (3): 400–19.

Sikkink, Kathryn. 2011. *The Justice Cascade: How Human Rights Prosecutions Are Changing World Politics.* New York: W. W. Norton & Company.

Simbaña, Floresmilo. 2011. "El Sumak Kawsay como proyecto político." *R, Revista para un Debate Político Socialista* 37 (7): 21–26.

Sintomer, Yves, Carsten Herzberg, Giovanni Allegretti, and Anja Röcke. 2010. *Learning from the South: Participatory Budgeting Worldwide—an Invitation to Global Cooperation.* Bonn, Germany: GIZ.

Smith, Mark, Dolf de Groot, Daniele Perrot-Maître, and Ger Bergkamp. 2006. *Pay: Establishing Payments for Watershed Services.* Gland, Switzerland: IUCN.

Snow, David A. 2007. "Framing Processes, Ideology, and Discursive Fields." In *The Blackwell Companion to Social Movements*, eds. D. A. Snow, S. A. Soule, and H. Kriesi. Malden, MA: Blackwell Publishing, 380–412.

Snow, David A., and Robert D. Benford. 1988. "Ideology, Frame Resonance, and Participant Mobilization." *International Social Movement Research* 1 (1):197–217.

Snow, David A., and Robert D. Benford. 1992. "Master Frames and Cycles of Protest." In *Frontiers in Social Movement Theory*, eds. A. Morris and C. M. Mueller. New Haven, CT: Yale University, 133–55.

Snow, David A., E. Burke Rochford, Steven K. Worden, and Robert D. Benford. 1986. "Frame Alignment Processes, Micromobilization, and Movement Participation." *American Sociological Review* 51 (4): 464–81.

Solanes, Miguel, and Axel Dourojeanni. 1995. "Mercados de Derechos de Agua." *Debate Agrario* 21 (1): 15–36.

Solingen, Etel. 2012. "Of Dominoes and Firewalls: The Domestic, Regional, and Global Politics of International Diffusion." *International Studies Quarterly* 56 (4): 631–44.

Steinberg, Paul F. 2001. *Environmental Leadership in Developing Countries*. Cambridge, MA: MIT Press.

Swidler, Ann. 1986. "Culture in Action: Symbols and Strategies." *American Sociological Review* 51 (2): 273–86.

Tarrow, Sidney. 1996. "States and Opportunities: The Political Structuring of Social Movements." In *Comparative Perspectives on Social Movements. Political Opportunities, Mobilizing Structures, and Cultural Framings*, eds. D. McAdam, J. D. McCarthy, and M. N. Zald. Cambridge: Cambridge University Press, 41–61.

Tarrow, Sidney. 2005. *The New Transnational Activism*. Cambridge: Cambridge University Press.

Téllez, Jorge. 2008. "Aproximación a los Proyectos de Desarrollo Forestal Desde el Diálogo Entre Los Sistemas de Conocimiento y los Intereses Involucrados." Ph.D. diss. Escuela Técnica Superior de Ingenieros Agrónomos y de Montes, Universidad de Córdoba, España.

Terán, Juan Fernando. 2005. *La sequedad del ajuste: Implicaciones de la gobernanza global del agua para la seguridad humana en Ecuador*. Quito: Universidad Andina Simón Bolívar.

Third World Water Forum. 2003. "Summary Forum Statement." Kyoto, Japan. http://www.world-watercouncil.org/forum/kyoto-2003/ (Accessed April 1, 2016).

Thomson, Bob. 2011. "Pachakuti: Indigenous Perspectives, Buen Vivir, Sumaq Kawsay and Degrowth." *Development* 54 (4): 448–54.

Troya, Roberto, and Randy Curtis. 1998. "Water: Together We Can Care for It!" Case Study of a Watershed Conservation Fund for Quito, Ecuador. Arlington, VA: The Nature Conservancy.

Tsai, Lily. 2002. "Cadres, Temple and Lineage Institutions, and Governance in Rural China." *The China Journal* 48 (July): 1–27.

Tsai, Lily. 2007. *Accountability Without Democracy: Solidary Groups and Public Goods Provision in Rural China*. Cambridge: Cambridge University Press.

Turton, Anthony, Hanlie J. Hattingh, Marius Claassen, Dirk J. Roux, and Peter J. Ashton. 2007a. "Towards a Model for Ecosystem Governance: An Integrated Water Resource Management Example." In *Governance as a Trialogue*, eds. A. Turton, H. J. Hattingh, G. A. Maree, D. J. Roux, M. Claassen, and W. F. Strydom. New York: Springer, 2–28.

Turton, Anthony, Hanlie J. Hattingh, Gillian A. Maree, Dirk J. Roux, Marius Claassen, and Wilma F. Strydom, eds. 2007b. *Governance as a Trialogue*. New York: Springer.

Tversky, Amos, and Daniel Kahneman. 1981. "The Framing of Decisions and the Psychology of Choice." *Science* 211 (4481): 453–8.

Ulfelder, William. 1998. "The Community Park Ranger Program in the Cayambe-Coca Ecological Reserve." *International Journal of Wilderness* 4 (2): 39–42.

UN High Commissioner on Human Rights. 2010. "Putting Human Rights into Practice through Development: The Equadorian Experience." www.ohchr.org/EN/NewsEvents/Pages/PuttingHRintopracticethroughdevelopmenttheEcuadorianexperience.aspx (Accessed February 13, 2016).

UNEP. 2012. "The UN-Water Status Report on the Application of Integrated Approaches to Water Resources Management." Nairobi, Kenya: United Nations Environment Programme.

UNEP. 2013. "Recommended Conceptual Framework of the Intergovernmental Science-Policy Platform on Biodiversity and Ecosystem Services." Presented at Plenary of the Intergovernmental Science-Policy Platform on Biodiversity and Ecosystem Services Second Session, Anatolya, Turkey, December 9–14.

United Nations. 2002. "Report of the World Summit on Sustainable Development." A/Conf. 199/20. New York: United Nations. www.unmillenniumproject.org/documents/131302_wssd_report_reissued.pdf (Accessed April 1, 2016).

United Nations. 2012. *The Future We Want*. Rio de Janeiro: United Nations. http://www.un.org/disabilities/documents/rio20_outcome_document_complete.pdf (Accessed April 1, 2016).

United Nations. 2013a. "Harmony with Nature." Report of the Secretary-General. A/68/325. New York: UN General Assembly.

United Nations. 2013b. "Marking International Mother Earth Day, General Assembly President Urges Rapid Action on Sustainable Development to Rescue Planet from Humankind's Excesses." www.un.org/press/en/2013/ga11362.doc.htm (Accessed April 1, 2016).

United Nations Economic Commission for Europe. 2007. *Recommendations on Payments for Ecosystem Services in Integrated Water Resources Management.* Geneva: UNECE.

Vallejo, Santiago. 2008. "¿La Gestión del Agua Como Bien Público Contribuye a la Conservación Ambiental?" Ph.D. diss. Programa de Estudios Ambientales, Facultad Latinoamericana de Ciencias Sociales Sede Ecuador.

Van Cott, Donna Lee. 2008. *Radical Democracy in the Andes.* Cambridge: Cambridge University Press.

Viterna, Jocelyn. 2013. *Women in War: The Micro-Processes of Mobilization in El Salvador.* Oxford: Oxford University Press.

Wade, Robert. 1988. *Village Republics: Economic Conditions for Collective Action in South India.* San Francisco: ICS Press.

Wallerstein, Nina B., and Bonnie Duran. 2003. *The Conceptual, Historical and Practical Roots of Community Based Participatory Research and Related Participatory Traditions.* San Francsico: Jossey-Bass.

Wampler, Brian. 2010. "The Diffusion of Brazil's Participatory Budgeting: Should 'Best Practices' be Promoted?" International Budget Partnership. http://www.internationalbudget.org/themes/PB/AdoptingParticipatoryDemocracy.pdf (Accessed April 1, 2016).

Weiss, Thomas G., and Rorden Wilkinson. 2014. "Rethinking Global Governance? Complexity, Authority, Power, Change." *International Studies Quarterly* 58 (1): 207–15.

Weyland, Kurt. 2005. "Theories of Policy Diffusion: Lessons from Latin American Pension Reform." *World Politics* 57 (2): 262–95.

Williams, Russell Alan. 2013. "Climate Change Adaptation and Multilevel Governance: Challenges to Policy Capacity in Canadian Finance." In *Making Multilevel Public Management Work: Stories of Success and Failure from Europe and North America,* eds. D. Cepiku, D. K. Jesuit, and I. Roberge. Boca Raton, FL: CRC Press, 119–40.

Winters, Paul, Patricio Espinosa, and Charles C. Crissman. 1998. "Resource Management in the Ecuadorian Andes: An Evaluation of CARE's PROMUSTA Program." Social Science Department Working Paper No. 1998-2. Lima: International Potato Center.

Wood, Jennifer, Clifford Shearing, and Jan Froestad. 2011. "Restorative Justice and Nodal Governance." *International Journal of Comparative and Applied Criminal Justice* 35 (1): 1–18.

World Bank. 1993. "Water Resources Management." Washington, DC: The World Bank. www-wds.worldbank.org/external/default/WDSContentServer/WDSP/IB/2000/02/23/000178830_98101911251888/Rendered/PDF/multi_page.pdf (Accessed April 2, 2016).

World Bank. 2007. *A Decade of Measuring the Quality of Governance.* Washington, DC: The World Bank.

Wunder, Sven. 2005. "Payments for Environmental Services: Some Nuts and Bolts." Occasional Paper No. 42. Bogor, Indonesia: Center for International Forestry Research.

Wunder, Sven. 2008. "Necessary Conditions for Ecosystem Service Payments." Presented at the conference Economics and Conservation in the Tropics, San Francisco, CA. www.rff.org/files/sharepoint/Documents/08_Tropics_Conference/Tropics_Conference_Papers/Tropics_Conference_Wunder_PES_markets.pdf (Accessed April 1, 2016).

Yaguache, Robert, Diana Domínguez, Ramiro Carrión, Patricio Coro, Esteban Zarría, and Luis Yaguache. 2004. "Pago por servicios ambientales, El Chaco-Napo-Ecuador." El Chaco, Ecuador: CEDERENA.

Yaguache, Robert, Diana Domínguez, Ramiro Carrión, and Esteban Zarría. 2005. *La Experiencia del Cantón El Chaco en la Protección de sus Fuentes de Agua.* El Chaco, Ecuador: Ministerio del Ambiente del Ecuador; Gobierno Municipal de El Chaco.

Yashar, Deborah J. 2005. *Contesting Citizenship in Latin America: The Rise of Indigenous Movements and the Postliberal Challenge.* Princeton: Princeton University Press.

Yeo, Yukyung, and Martin Painter. 2011. "Diffusion, Transmutation, and Regulatory Regime in Socialist Market Economies: Telecoms Reform in China and Vietnam." *Pacific Review* 24 (4): 375–95.

Zapata, Alex. 2005. "Desarrollo de un modelo alternativo de gestión pública del riego." In *Foro de los Recursos Hídricos Tercer Encuentro Nacional*, ed. A. Arroyo. Quito, Ecuador: CAMAREN, 85–114.

Zapata, Alex. 2009. "Construcción de políticas del agua en el Ecuador." *Boletín ICCI-ARY Rimay* 11 (128), http://icci.nativeweb.org/boletin/128/zapata.html (Accessed April 2, 2016).

Zarria, Esteban. 2009. "Implementación del programa 'Servicios Ambientales del cantón El Chaco' para la Conservación de las microcuencas reguladoras de agua de consumo humano." El Chaco: Gobierno Municipal de El Chaco.

Zimmerer, Karl S. 2011. "'Conservation Booms' With Agricultural Growth: Sustainability and Shifting Environmental Governance in Latin America, 1985–2008." *Latin American Research Review* 43 (Special Issue): 82–114.

INDEX